MATHEMATICS
DICTIONARY
and
HANDBOOK

Eugene D. Nichols, Ph.D.

Sharon L. Schwartz, M.S.

NICHOLS
SCHWARTZ
PUBLISHING

About the Authors

Eugene D. Nichols
Distinguished Professor Emeritus
of Mathematics Education
Florida State University
*Author of elementary, high school,
and college mathematics textbooks*

Sharon L. Schwartz
Mathematics Teacher
*Author and editor of elementary and
secondary mathematics textbooks*

Art and Design

Joan Gazdik Gillner

Nichols Schwartz Publishing
P.O. Box 254
Honesdale, PA 18431-0254

Printed in the United States of America

ISBN 1-882269-09-8
Library of Congress Catalog Card Number 98-60974

CONTENTS

READ ME FIRST

The Nichols Schwartz Mathematics Dictionary and Handbook is a book about the language of mathematics. It can be the most useful book you own, since you will need to think mathematically, to communicate with others in mathematical terms, and to understand the meaning of mathematical terms for every new mathematical concept and skill you learn. This book can also answer questions about how to perform operations needed in everyday life, from addition, fractions, and percents to working with the often troublesome number zero. It also contains entries of terms that you may not encounter regularly but ones that you might be curious about, from abacus to calculus to magic squares to Zeno's paradox.

The Nichols Schwartz Mathematics Dictionary and Handbook has been written to be easy to understand. Terms are explained in simple and clear language. Effective use is made of pictures and diagrams, since pictures can often explain a concept more clearly than a word definition alone.

More than one thousand terms are defined and illustrated in this book along with more than one hundred handbook items. The handbook items are written to help you understand concepts and perform mathematical operations, such as place value, rounding off decimals and whole numbers, mathematical properties, scientific notation, evaluating algebraic expressions, operations with different kinds of fractions, making graphs, using strategies for mental computations and estimation, classifying geometric figures, simplifying complex algebraic inequalities and systems of equations and inequalities, using trigonometric ratios in finding distances to inaccessible objects, and much more.

The terms included in this book are those most often encountered in grades five through nine. Terms from elementary algebra, geometry, probability, and trigonometry are included. The book is designed to be an aid to students, teachers, and parents.

The Nichols Schwartz Mathematics Dictionary and Handbook offers much more than the ordinary mathematics dictionary.

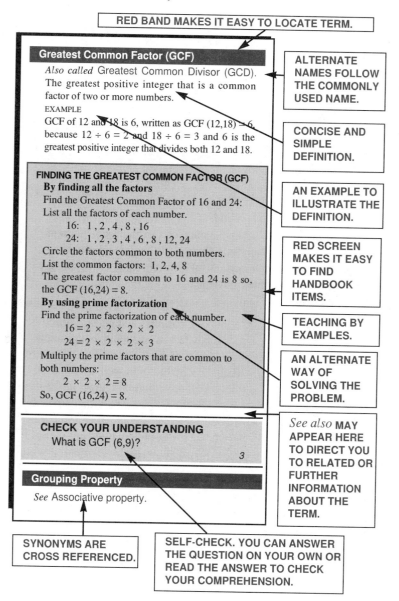

RED BAND MAKES IT EASY TO LOCATE TERM.

Greatest Common Factor (GCF)

Also called Greatest Common Divisor (GCD). The greatest positive integer that is a common factor of two or more numbers.

EXAMPLE

GCF of 12 and 18 is 6, written as GCF (12,18) = 6, because 12 ÷ 6 = 2 and 18 ÷ 6 = 3 and 6 is the greatest positive integer that divides both 12 and 18.

ALTERNATE NAMES FOLLOW THE COMMONLY USED NAME.

CONCISE AND SIMPLE DEFINITION.

FINDING THE GREATEST COMMON FACTOR (GCF)
By finding all the factors
Find the Greatest Common Factor of 16 and 24:
List all the factors of each number.
  16: 1 , 2 , 4 , 8 , 16
  24: 1 , 2 , 3 , 4 , 6 , 8 , 12, 24
Circle the factors common to both numbers.
List the common factors: 1, 2, 4, 8
The greatest factor common to 16 and 24 is 8 so, the GCF (16,24) = 8.

By using prime factorization
Find the prime factorization of each number.
  16 = 2 × 2 × 2 × 2
  24 = 2 × 2 × 2 × 3
Multiply the prime factors that are common to both numbers:
  2 × 2 × 2 = 8
So, GCF (16,24) = 8.

AN EXAMPLE TO ILLUSTRATE THE DEFINITION.

RED SCREEN MAKES IT EASY TO FIND HANDBOOK ITEMS.

TEACHING BY EXAMPLES.

AN ALTERNATE WAY OF SOLVING THE PROBLEM.

CHECK YOUR UNDERSTANDING
What is GCF (6,9)?

3

See also MAY APPEAR HERE TO DIRECT YOU TO RELATED OR FURTHER INFORMATION ABOUT THE TERM.

Grouping Property

See Associative property.

SYNONYMS ARE CROSS REFERENCED.

SELF-CHECK. YOU CAN ANSWER THE QUESTION ON YOUR OWN OR READ THE ANSWER TO CHECK YOUR COMPREHENSION.

LOOKING UP WORDS

All entries are arranged in alphabetical order. A red thumb tab helps you to quickly locate the letter that corresponds to the first letter of the term you are looking for. The alphabetical arrangement is word by word, rather than letter by letter. For example, Line of reflection, Line of symmetry, and Line segment come before Linear equation.

Some terms have more than one meaning. For example, the term *base* has three different meanings in mathematics. The entry word in the red band is Base. Base of a geometric figure, base of a numeration system, and the base of a power are defined and illustrated under the subheads: **Of a geometric figure, Of a numeration system,** and **Of a power.**

If you do not understand the meaning of a mathematical term used in a definition, look for the definition of that term under its own entry. Terms that are important for understanding the meaning of the entry word are printed in red.

FINDING HANDBOOK TOPICS

There are more than 100 handbook concepts and skills. To find a handbook topic, look under the key term of the topic. For example, if you want to learn how to add fractions, look under the F's for Fraction. Following the definition of the term, you will find the headings ADDING AND SUBTRACTING FRACTIONS AND MIXED NUMBERS WITH LIKE DENOMINATORS and ADDING AND SUBRACTING FRACTIONS AND MIXED NUMBERS WITH UNLIKE DENOMINATORS. There you will find examples worked out to show how to add fractions.

TABLES, FORMULAS, AND SYMBOLS

In the back of the *Mathematics Dictionary and Handbook* are the following: Table of Percent, Decimal and Fraction Equivalents; Laws of Exponents (Properties of Powers); Other Properties and Laws; Quadrillions, etc; Time; Tables of Measures; Converting Measures; Table of Roots and Powers; Trigonometric Ratios; Formulas; Coordinate Geometry Formulas; and Symbols.

Abacus   *plural* abaci

A device designed for recording numbers and calculating.

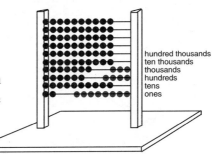

hundred thousands
ten thousands
thousands
hundreds
tens
ones

In some countries, such as China and Japan, the abacus is still used for computing. In the United States it is used mostly as a device for teaching and demonstrating the concept of place value.

An abacus showing the number 3,408.

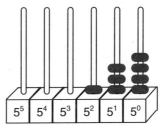

5^5 5^4 5^3 5^2 5^1 5^0

An abacus can be used to count in other bases.

$$134_{\text{base five}} = (1 \times 5^2) + (3 \times 5^1) + (4 \times 5^0) = 44$$

See also Place value *and* Base of a numeration system.

ADDING WITH A RUSSIAN ABACUS

On a Russian abacus, addition is performed by moving the beads to the left. Subtraction is performed by moving the beads back. When ten beads are on the left on a column, they are pushed back and 1 bead from the upper column is pushed to the left. To borrow for subtraction in a column when no beads are left, a bead from the upper column is moved back and ten beads are moved to the left.

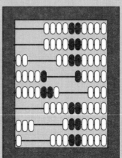

2 5 7 0 3 1
A Russian abacus showing the number 257,031.

CHINESE AND JAPANESE ABACI

On a Chinese and Japanese abacus each lower bead represents 1 unit. Each upper bead represents 5 units. A bead is pushed toward the crossbar to represent a number.

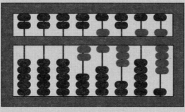

2 6 3 5 9
A Chinese abacus showing the number 26,359.

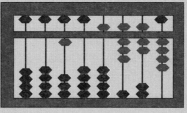

1 0 5 8 7 4
A Japanese abacus showing the number 105,874.

ADDING WITH A JAPANESE ABACUS

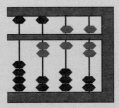

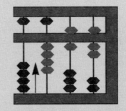

1. To add 241 to 267, first register 267.

2. The Japanese customarily add from left to right. Move up two hundreds beads to add the 2 hundreds of 241.

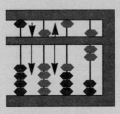

3. Next 4 tens need to be added, but there are not enough ten beads. 100 cannot be added and 60 subtracted because all the hundred beads are used up. So add 500, subtract 4 hundreds and 6 tens to add 40.

4. Then add 1 one. The result is 508.

Abscissa   *plural* abscissas or abscissae

Another name for the *x*-coordinate that indicates the horizontal distance of a point from the origin along the *x*-axis in a coordinate system. The abscissa is the first number in an ordered pair that gives the coordinates of a point.

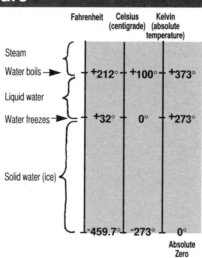

Ordered pair A (5,⁻2)

abscissa ordinate

CHECK YOUR UNDERSTANDING
What is the abscissa of point B whose coordinates are (⁻4,3)?

⁻4

Absolute temperature

Also called Kelvin (°K). A scale for measuring temperature in which 0°K is the absolute limit of possible coldness. At 0°K the particles of matter, whose motion constitute heat, are at rest. 0°K is called absolute zero.
0°K = ⁻273.15°Celsius or ⁻459.7°Fahrenheit.

	Fahrenheit	Celsius (centigrade)	Kelvin (absolute temperature)
Steam			
Water boils →	⁺212°	⁺100°	⁺373°
Liquid water			
Water freezes →	⁺32°	0°	⁺273°
Solid water (ice)			
	⁻459.7°	⁻273°	0°

Absolute Zero

CHECK YOUR UNDERSTANDING
What temperature on the Kelvin scale corresponds to 0°C or 32°F?

273.15

Absolute value (I I)

The absolute value of a number is its distance from zero on a number line.

The absolute value of ⁻3 is 3.   The absolute value of 5 is 5.

$$|{-3}| = 3$$ $$|5| = 5$$

The absolute value of 0 is 0. $|0| = 0$

CHECK YOUR UNDERSTANDING

What is the absolute value of ⁻7? of 12?

7; 12

Absolute zero

See Absolute temperature.

Abundant number

Also called Redundant number. A number for which the sum of its proper factors is greater than the number. For example, 12 is an abundant number. Its proper factors are 1, 2, 3, 4, and 6.

$$1 + 2 + 3 + 4 + 6 = 16 \text{ and } 16 > 12.$$

See also Amicable numbers, Perfect number, *and* Deficient number.

CHECK YOUR UNDERSTANDING

Is 15 an abundant number?

no; its proper factors are 1, 3, and 5; 1 + 3 + 5 = 9 and 9 < 15

Acceleration

The rate at which speed changes per unit of time. For example, the speed of a car on a straight road increases from 30 miles per hour to 40 miles per hour in 5 seconds. The average acceleration is

$$\frac{10 \text{ mph}}{5s} = \frac{52,800 \text{ ft/h}}{5s} = \frac{52,800 \text{ ft/s}}{60 \times 60 \times 5s} = 2.93 \text{ ft/s}^2$$

Read: 2.93 feet per second per second

CHECK YOUR UNDERSTANDING

The speed of an airplane moving in a straight line increases from 2 mi/min to 8 mi/min in 2 min. What is the average acceleration in feet per second per second?

$$\frac{6 \text{ mi/min}}{2 \text{ min}} = \frac{31,680 \text{ ft/min}}{2 \text{ min}} = \frac{31,680 \text{ ft/s}}{60 \times 120 \text{ s}} = 4.4 \text{ ft/s}^2$$

Accuracy of an approximate number

An indication of how close an approximate number is to the true value. For example, the approximate number 3.14 for π is accurate to 2 decimal places. This indicates that the true value of π is between 3.135 and 3.145.

CHECK YOUR UNDERSTANDING

A measurement is given to be 4.346 kilometers. Between what two numbers is the true value?

4.3455 and 4.3465

Acute angle

An angle that measures less than 90°. $\angle$ COB measures less than 90°, so it is an acute angle.

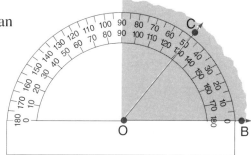

Acute triangle

A triangle in which each of the three angles is acute (less than 90°).
See also Acute angle.

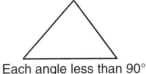

Each angle less than 90°

Addend

A number to be added in an addition expression. In 3 + 4 + 6, 3, 4, and 6 are the addends.

Addition

A shortcut to counting. A mathematical operation that tells how many things there are when two sets are put together. The plus sign (+) tells you to add. You can add 7 + 5 by counting five numbers past 7, "8", "9", "10", "11", "12". To add without counting, you simply need to know the basic addition fact: 7 + 5 = 12. The numbers to be added are called the addends. The result is called the sum.

ADDING FROM RIGHT TO LEFT

STEP 1 Add ones. Rename 19 ones as 9 ones and 1 ten.	**STEP 2** Add tens. Rename 10 as 0 tens and 1 hundred.	**STEP 3** Add hundreds.
356 235 +618	1 356 235 +618 9	11 356 235 +618 09	11 356 235 +618 1209

Rename is also called regroup or carry.

ADDING FROM LEFT TO RIGHT

Also called scratch method.

Add the ten thousands.	Add the thousands (17). Write 7, add the 1 to the 4, scratch out the 4 and write 5.	Add the hundreds (25). Write 5, add the 2 to 7, scratch out the 7 and write 9.	Add the tens (20). Write 0, add the 2 to 5, scratch out the 5 and write 7.	Add the ones (12). Write 2, add the 1 to 0, scratch out the 0, and write 1.
36542 7821 987 +14362 4	36542 7821 987 +14362 47 5	36542 7821 987 +14362 475 59	36542 7821 987 +14362 4750 597	36542 7821 987 +14362 47502 5971

The answer is 59,712.

See also Basic facts.

HOW TO CHECK ADDITION

By adding up   By subtracting back on a calculator

| 1518 |

874 ↑	874	0 ⟩ it checks
246	246	−874 ⟩
374	374	−246 ⟩
+ 24	+ 24	−374 ⟩
1518	1518	−24 ⟩
		enter	1518	⟩

See also Casting out nines.

PROPERTIES OF ADDITION

Associative *Also called* Grouping property. Changing the grouping of the numbers does not change the result of addition. $(a + b) + c = a + (b + c)$.

Closure For all real numbers x and y, there is a unique (exactly one) real number z, such that $x + y = z$.

Commutative *Also called* Order property. Changing the order of numbers does not change the sum. $a + b = b + a$.

Identity *Also called* Zero property. Zero plus any number is that number. $a + 0 = 0 + a = a$.

Inverse *Also called* Additive inverse property. The sum of a number and its opposite (additive inverse) is equal to 0 (the additive identity or identity for addition). $a + (-a) = 0$.

Zero property The sum of zero and any number is equal to that number. $n + 0 = 0 + n = n$.

Addition property of equations

Also called Addition property of equality. Adding the same number to each side of an equation results in an equivalent equation (an equation with the same solution). For all real numbers x, y, and n, if $x = y$, then $x + n = y + n$.

EXAMPLES
$$9 = 5 + 4 \qquad x = 6$$
$$9 + 2 = 5 + 4 + 2 \qquad x + 8 = 6 + 8$$
$$11 = 11 \qquad x + 8 = 14$$

CHECK YOUR UNDERSTANDING
Is the statement, if $7 = 3 + 4$, then $7 + 3 = 3 + 4$, an example of the addition property of equations?

no

Addition property of inequality

Adding the same number to each side of an inequality does not change the order of the inequality. For all numbers x, y, and n, if $x > y$, then $x + n > y + n$ and if $x < y$, then $x + n < y + n$.

EXAMPLES
$$6 > 2 \qquad 2 < 4$$
$$6 + 3 > 2 + 3 \qquad 2 + 3 < 4 + 3$$
$$9 > 5 \qquad 5 < 7$$

CHECK YOUR UNDERSTANDING
Is the statement, if $12 > 9$, then $12 + 4 > 9 + 3$ an example of the addition property of inequality?

no

Addition table

See Basic facts.

Additive identity

See Identity for addition.

Additive inverse of a number

See Opposite of a number.

Additive inverse property

See Inverse property of addition.

Adjacent angles

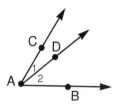

Two angles that have the same vertex and a common side and have no common interior points. Angles 1 and 2 are adjacent angles.

CHECK YOUR UNDERSTANDING
What is the common side of angles 1 and 2?

side AD

Adjacent sides

Two sides of a polygon that share a common vertex. Sides *c* and *d* are adjacent sides.

CHECK YOUR UNDERSTANDING
Are the sides labeled *a* and *c* in this polygon adjacent?

no, the two sides have no common vertex

Algebra

Algebra is the generalization of the ideas of arithmetic. It is a branch of mathematics where unknown numbers can be represented by letters and their values found to solve problems.

EXAMPLE $x + 4 = 9$

$$x + 4 - 4 = 9 - 4$$

Subtract 4 from each side of the equation.

$$x = 5$$

The value of the unknown, or variable x, is 5.

CHECK YOUR UNDERSTANDING
What number for x makes this equation true? $x + 7 = 10$

3

Algebraic expression

See Expression.

Algorithm

A systematic scheme for carrying out computations, usually consisting of a set of rules or steps. The long division algorithm is an example.

	STEPS OR RULES
65R1	Divide.
3)196	Multiply.
−18	Subtract.
16	Bring down. Repeat if necessary.
−15	
1	

CHECK YOUR UNDERSTANDING
What is the first step in the addition algorithm?

add the ones

Alternate exterior angles

A pair of angles formed on the outside of two lines that are cut by a third line (a transversal). If two parallel lines are cut by a transversal, then alternate exterior angles are congruent (their measures are equal).

A

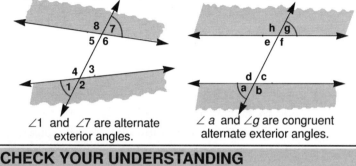

∠1 and ∠7 are alternate exterior angles.

∠a and ∠g are congruent alternate exterior angles.

CHECK YOUR UNDERSTANDING

Are the two angles labeled 8 and 2 in the figure above alternate exterior angles?

yes

Alternate interior angles

A pair of angles formed between two lines that are cut by a third line (a transversal). If two parallel lines are cut by a transversal, then alternate interior angles are congruent (their measures are equal).

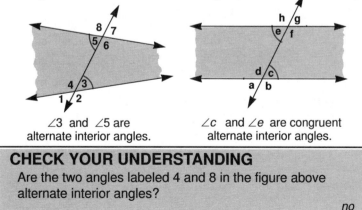

∠3 and ∠5 are alternate interior angles.

∠c and ∠e are congruent alternate interior angles.

CHECK YOUR UNDERSTANDING

Are the two angles labeled 4 and 8 in the figure above alternate interior angles?

no

Altitude

A line segment (or its length) showing the height of a figure. An altitude of a triangle is a segment from a vertex of the triangle perpendicular to the opposite side of the triangle.

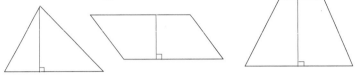

triangle   parallelogram   trapezoid

The altitude of a parallelogram, trapezoid, prism, or cylinder is any segment perpendicular to both bases. The altitude of a cone or pyramid is a segment from the vertex perpendicular to the base.

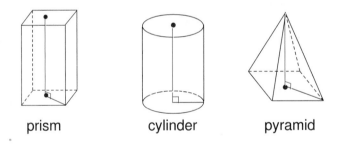

prism   cylinder   pyramid

THREE CASES OF ALTITUDES IN TRIANGLES

There are three different cases for the three altitudes that can be drawn for any triangle:

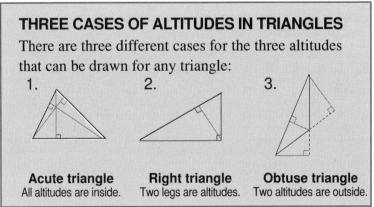

1.   2.   3.

Acute triangle
All altitudes are inside.

Right triangle
Two legs are altitudes.

Obtuse triangle
Two altitudes are outside.

14

Amicable numbers

Two numbers are amicable numbers if the sum of the proper divisors (divisors other than the number itself) of one number is equal to the other number.

EXAMPLE 1210 and 1184 are amicable numbers.

The sum of the proper divisors of 1210 equals 1184.

$1 + 2 + 5 + 10 + 11 + 22 + 55 + 110 + 121 + 242 + 605 = 1184$

The sum of the proper divisors of 1184 equals 1210.

$1 + 2 + 4 + 8 + 16 + 32 + 37 + 74 + 148 + 296 + 592 = 1210$

Another example of two amicable numbers is 2924 and 2620.

See also Abundant, Deficient, Perfect, *and* Redundant numbers.

CHECK YOUR UNDERSTANDING

The proper divisors of 220 are 1,2,4,5,10,11,20,22,44, 55,110. The proper divisiors of 284 are 1, 2, 4, 71, 142. Are 220 and 284 amicable numbers?

yes

Analytic geometry

See Coordinate geometry.

Angle ($\angle$)

A geometric figure made up of two rays or two line segments that have the same endpoint. The endpoint is called the vertex.

An angle can be named in three ways. When using three letters to name an angle, the letter for the vertex is always in the middle.

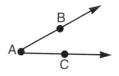

$\angle$ BAC or $\angle$ CAB or $\angle$ A

15

CLASSIFICATION OF ANGLES

Angles are classified according to their size.

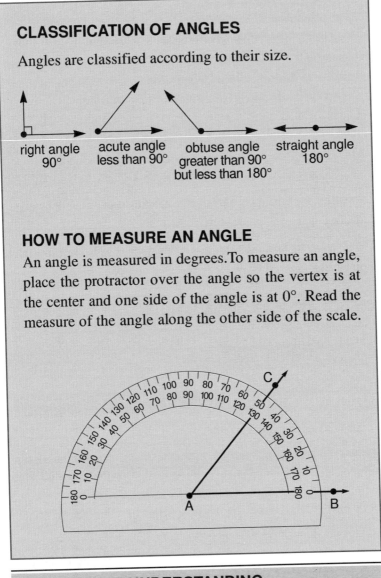

right angle
90°

acute angle
less than 90°

obtuse angle
greater than 90°
but less than 180°

straight angle
180°

HOW TO MEASURE AN ANGLE

An angle is measured in degrees. To measure an angle, place the protractor over the angle so the vertex is at the center and one side of the angle is at 0°. Read the measure of the angle along the other side of the scale.

CHECK YOUR UNDERSTANDING

In what three ways can the angle shown above be named?

∠A, ∠CAB, ∠BAC

Angle of depression

An angle between the horizontal and a line of sight toward a point on the ground below. Angle c is an angle of depression. The horizontal is $\overline{CD}$. The line of sight toward point E below is $\overline{CE}$.

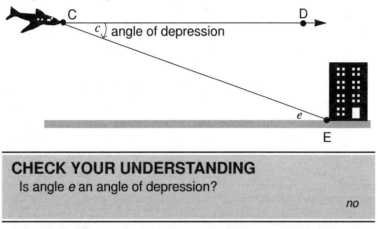

CHECK YOUR UNDERSTANDING
Is angle e an angle of depression?

no

Angle of elevation

An angle between the horizontal and a line of sight toward a point above the ground. Angle a is an angle of elevation. The horizontal is $\overline{AB}$. The line of sight toward point C above is $\overline{AC}$.

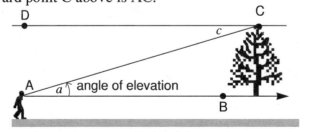

CHECK YOUR UNDERSTANDING
Is angle c an angle of elevation?

no

Angle of incidence

An angle which an incident ray of light makes with the normal at the point of incidence.

See also
Angle of reflection.

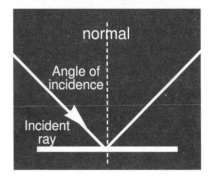

CHECK YOUR UNDERSTANDING
What is the approximate measure of the angle of incidence above?

45°

Angle of inclination

In a coordinate system, an angle formed by the x-axis and a line rotated from the x-axis in a counterclockwise direction. The measure of an angle of inclination can be between 0° and 180°. The angle of inclination for line ℓ shown in the picture below is 135°.

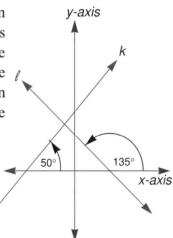

CHECK YOUR UNDERSTANDING
What is the measure of the angle of inclination for line k?

50°

Angle of reflection

An angle which a reflected ray of light makes with the normal at the point of reflection. The angle of reflection is always equal to the angle of incidence. That is, a ray of light bounces off a surface at the same angle at which it hits the surface.

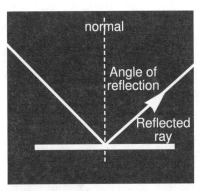

See also Angle of incidence.

Antecedent

The proposition p in the conditional "If p, then q."

EXAMPLE

If **a number is an even number,**

then it is divisible by 2.

antecedent

Apex
plural apexes or apices

The highest point of a geometric figure relative to some base line or plane.

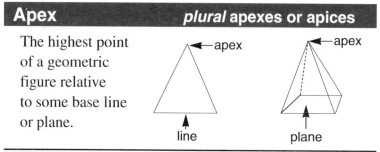

CHECK YOUR UNDERSTANDING
What is another name for the apex of a cone?

vertex

Apothem

A perpendicular line segment (or its length) from the center of a regular polygon to a side of the polygon. It is also a radius of a circle inscribed in the polygon. In the picture, line segment AB is an apothem.

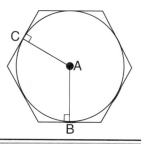

CHECK YOUR UNDERSTANDING
What is another apothem shown in the polygon above?

line segment AC

Approximate number

A number that is close to the true number.

Every reported measurement is approximate:

  0.0078 mm   5 ft   7 mi $3\frac{1}{2}$ in.

Results of computations with irrational numbers are often approximate numbers. An approximation of $\sqrt{2} \times \sqrt{3}$ to two decimal places is 1.41×1.73. The product, 2.4393, is also given as an approximate number to two decimal places, 2.44.

See also accuracy of an approximate number.

A part of a circle or curve between two points.

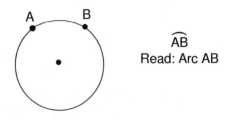

$\overset{\frown}{AB}$
Read: Arc AB

If an arc of a circle is shorter than one-half of the circle, it is called a minor arc. If it is longer than one-half of the circle, it is called a major arc. If it is equal to one-half of the circle, it is called a semicircle.

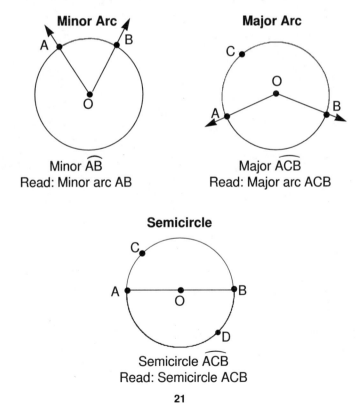

Minor Arc

Minor $\overset{\frown}{AB}$
Read: Minor arc AB

Major Arc

Major $\overset{\frown}{ACB}$
Read: Major arc ACB

Semicircle

Semicircle $\overset{\frown}{ACB}$
Read: Semicircle ACB

DEGREE MEASURE OF AN ARC

The degree measure of a minor arc is equal to the degree measure of its central angle.

The degree measure of a major arc is equal to 360 minus the degree measure of its central angle.

The degree measure of a semicircle is 180.

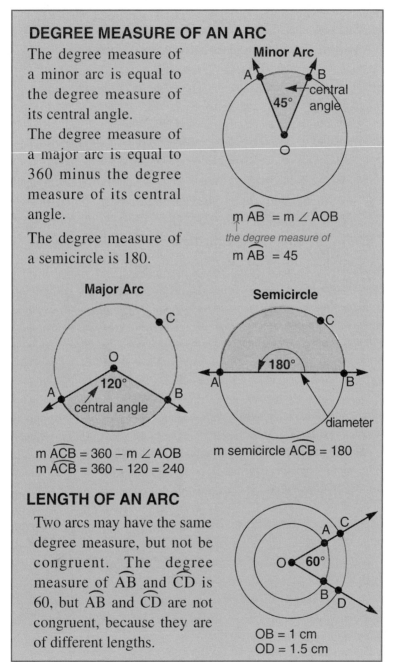

Minor Arc

$$m \overarc{AB} = m \angle AOB$$

the degree measure of

$$m \overarc{AB} = 45$$

Major Arc

$$m \overarc{ACB} = 360 - m \angle AOB$$
$$m \overarc{ACB} = 360 - 120 = 240$$

Semicircle

m semicircle $\overarc{ACB}$ = 180

LENGTH OF AN ARC

Two arcs may have the same degree measure, but not be congruent. The degree measure of $\overarc{AB}$ and $\overarc{CD}$ is 60, but $\overarc{AB}$ and $\overarc{CD}$ are not congruent, because they are of different lengths.

OB = 1 cm
OD = 1.5 cm

FINDING THE LENGTH OF AN ARC

When you find the length of an arc, you are really finding part of the circumference of the circle. The length of an arc is $\frac{m}{360} \times 2\pi r$, where m is the degree measure of the central angle.

The central angle, $\angle$ COD on page 22, intercepts $\frac{60}{360}$ or $\frac{1}{6}$ of each circle, so the lengths of arcs AB and CD are $\frac{1}{6}$ of the circumference of their respective circles.

Length of arc AB

$L = \frac{1}{6} \times 2\pi r$

$\approx \frac{1}{6} \times 2 \times 3.14 \times 1$

≈ 1.05 cm

is approximately equal to

Length of arc CD

$L = \frac{1}{6} \times 2\pi r$

$\approx \frac{1}{6} \times 2 \times 3.14 \times 1.5$

≈ 1.57 cm

Two arcs are congruent if they have the same length and are parts of the same circle or congruent circles.

CHECK YOUR UNDERSTANDING
Which is longer, $\overset{\frown}{AB}$ or $\overset{\frown}{CD}$?

$\overset{\frown}{CD}$

Are (a)

A metric unit for measuring area. One are (a) is equal to 100 square meters (m^2). It is equivalent to 119.60 square yards (yd^2).

$$1 \text{ a} = 100 \text{ m}^2 = 119.6 \text{ yd}^2$$

CHECK YOUR UNDERSTANDING
How many square meters are there in 5 ares?

500

Area

The number of square units in a region.

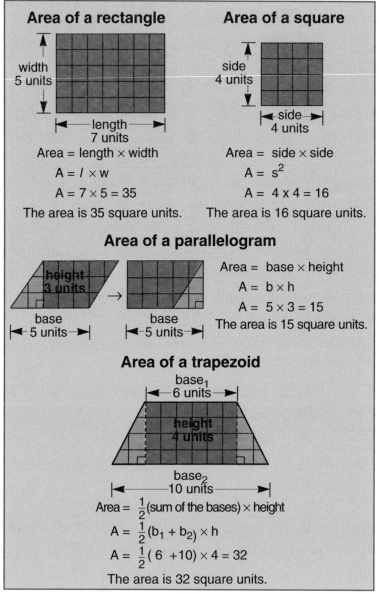

Area of a rectangle

width
5 units

length
7 units

Area = length × width

A = l × w

A = 7 × 5 = 35

The area is 35 square units.

Area of a square

side
4 units

side
4 units

Area = side × side

A = s^2

A = 4 x 4 = 16

The area is 16 square units.

Area of a parallelogram

height
3 units

base
5 units

→

base
5 units

Area = base × height

A = b × h

A = 5 × 3 = 15

The area is 15 square units.

Area of a trapezoid

base$_1$
6 units

height
4 units

base$_2$
10 units

Area = $\frac{1}{2}$(sum of the bases) × height

A = $\frac{1}{2}$(b$_1$ + b$_2$) × h

A = $\frac{1}{2}$(6 +10) × 4 = 32

The area is 32 square units.

Area of a triangle

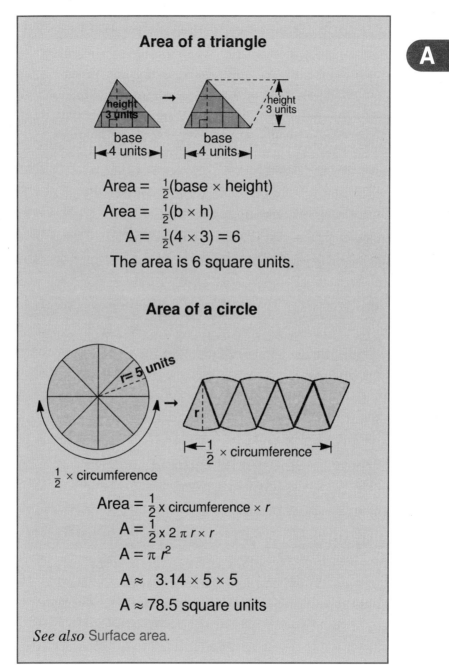

Area = $\frac{1}{2}$(base × height)

Area = $\frac{1}{2}$(b × h)

A = $\frac{1}{2}$(4 × 3) = 6

The area is 6 square units.

Area of a circle

Area = $\frac{1}{2}$ × circumference × r

A = $\frac{1}{2}$ × 2 π r × r

A = π r²

A ≈ 3.14 × 5 × 5

A ≈ 78.5 square units

See also Surface area.

Arithmetic

A branch of mathematics where problems are solved by calculating with numbers, using any one or a combination of the operations of addition, subtraction, multiplication, and division. It is sometimes called "the art of calculation" or "the science of numbers." There are two main types of problems in arithmetic. One type is solved by counting, grouping, and regrouping objects. The other type is solved by measuring or comparing quantities.

Arithmetic mean

Also called Average. It is the sum of given numbers divided by the number of numbers used in computing the sum.

EXAMPLE The arithmetic mean of 3, 7, 17, and 33 is:

$$\frac{\text{Sum of the numbers} \rightarrow 3 + 7 + 17 + 33}{\text{Number of numbers} \rightarrow 4} = \frac{60}{4} = 15$$

Arithmetic progression

Also called Arithmetic sequence. A sequence of numbers in which the difference of two consecutive numbers is the same. The difference of the two consecutive numbers is called the common difference.

EXAMPLE $\underset{3\ \ \ 3\ \ \ 3\ \ \ 3}{3, 6, 9, 12, 15, \ldots}$

The common difference is 3. The three dots at the end indicate that the progression continues without end.

In general, a, $a + d$, $a + 2d$, $a + 3d$, . . . is an arithmetic progression, where a is the first term and d is the common difference.

CHECK YOUR UNDERSTANDING

Is the sequence 2, 6, 10, 14, 18, . . . an arithmetic progression? If yes, what is the common difference?

yes; 4

Arithmetic series

The indicated sum of the terms of an arithmetic progression.

EXAMPLE Arithmetic progression: 1, 3, 5, 7, 9.
Arithmetic series: $1 + 3 + 5 + 7 + 9$.

CHECK YOUR UNDERSTANDING

What is the arithmetic series for the arithmetic progression 2, 5, 8, 11?

2 + 5 + 8 + 11

Ascending order of a polynomial

A polynomial in which the terms are arranged from the smallest to the largest powers of the variable. The following polynomial is in ascending order.

$$3x + 4x^2 - 7x^4 + 2x^5$$

See also Descending order of a polynomial.

CHECK YOUR UNDERSTANDING

Is the following polynomial in ascending order?

$$2y - 4y^4 - 6y^2 + 3y^7$$

no

Associative property

Also called Grouping property. Changing the grouping of the numbers does not change the result of an operation (∗).

$$(a * b) * c = a * (b * c)$$

Addition The operation of addition has the associative property.

$$(3 + 4) + 5 \overset{?}{=} 3 + (4 + 5)$$
$$7 + 5 \overset{?}{=} 3 + 9$$
$$12 = 12$$

Multiplication The operation of multiplication has the associative property.

$$(2 \times 3) \times 4 \overset{?}{=} 2 \times (3 \times 4)$$
$$6 \times 4 \overset{?}{=} 2 \times 12$$
$$24 = 24$$

Subtraction The operation of subtraction does not have the associative property.

$$(5 - 3) - 2 \overset{?}{=} 5 - (3 - 2)$$
$$2 - 2 \overset{?}{=} 5 - 1$$
$$0 \neq 4$$

Division The operation of division does not have the associative property.

$$(12 \div 6) \div 2 \overset{?}{=} 12 \div (6 \div 2)$$
$$2 \div 2 \overset{?}{=} 12 \div 3$$
$$1 \neq 4$$

CHECK YOUR UNDERSTANDING
Is the following statement an example of the associative property?

$$(4 + 6) + 8 = (6 + 4) + 8$$

no; it is an example of the commutative property.

Assumption

See Axiom.

Average

See Arithmetic mean.

Axiom

Also called Assumption, Hypothesis, Postulate, *or* Premise. A statement accepted to be true without proof. It is customary to use hypothesis or postulate in geometry, axiom in algebra, and premise in logic.

Axis
plural **axes**

A reference line on a graph. On a coordinate graph, the horizontal line along which the x-coordinates are measured is called the x-axis. The vertical line along which the y-coordinates are measured is called the y-axis. The point where the axes meet is called the origin.

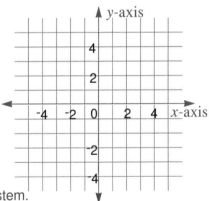

See also Coordinate system.

Axis of symmetry

See Line of symmetry.

Babylonian numeration system

A system of recording numbers developed by the Babylonians about 2000 B.C. It consists of wedge-shaped (cuneiform) symbols, which were pressed into clay tablets with a stylus. It is essentially a system in base sixty. However, numbers less than 60 are represented by grouping symbols, using base 10.

The basic symbols used are the following:

Y   1

<   10

⟩   subtractive symbol

For example,

⟪ YYY means $(4 \times 10) + 6$ or 46

The following example illustrates the use of the subtractive symbol:

⟪⟪ ⟩YY means $50 - 2$ or 48

CHECK YOUR UNDERSTANDING

In the Babylonian system, what number is represented by these symbols? ⟪ YYY

23

31

Bar graph

A graph in which information is shown by means of rectangular bars or objects. Bar graphs make it easy to compare data by looking at the length or height of the bars or objects.

Average Length of Snakes

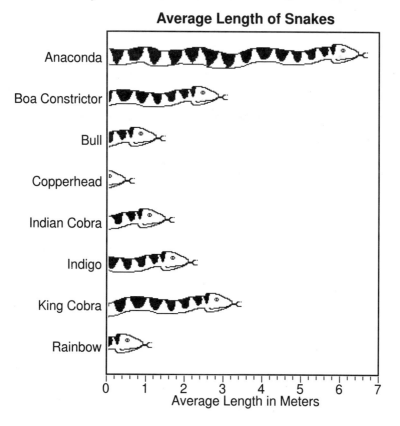

To find how long the Anaconda snake is, look for the snake labeled Anaconda. Look in a straight line from the end of the snake's tongue to the scale. Each mark represents 0.2 meter. The scale shows the Anaconda snake has an average length of about 6.8 meters.

HOW TO MAKE A BAR GRAPH

1. Decide whether the number of bars you will need to represent the data will fit better horizontally or vertically on the paper.

FAVORITE MOVIE THEMES

Movie Theme	Number of People
Comedy	30
Musical	20
Adventure	10
Science fiction	25
Drama	10
Other	5

2. Decide on a scale. The smallest number in the data about Favorite Movie Themes is 5; the largest is 30. For these data, a scale with each mark representing 5 units is appropriate.

3. Draw a rectangle that fills the entire space, but leave room for labels on the left and bottom.

6. Give the graph a title.

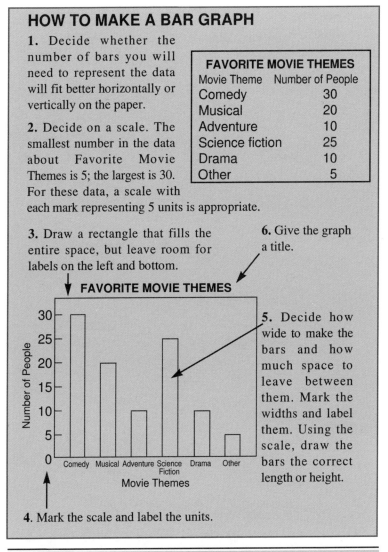

5. Decide how wide to make the bars and how much space to leave between them. Mark the widths and label them. Using the scale, draw the bars the correct length or height.

4. Mark the scale and label the units.

CHECK YOUR UNDERSTANDING

In the bar graph above, what was the most favorite movie theme?

comedy

Of a geometric figure A bottom side or face of a geometric figure.

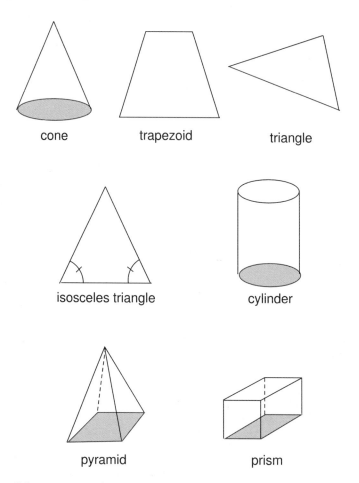

cone   trapezoid   triangle

isosceles triangle   cylinder

pyramid   prism

Of a numeration system The number that is raised to various powers to generate the place values of the numeration system. In the base-ten numeration system the base is ten. The first place is 10^0 or 1, the second is 10^1 or 10, the third is 10^2 or 100, and so on.

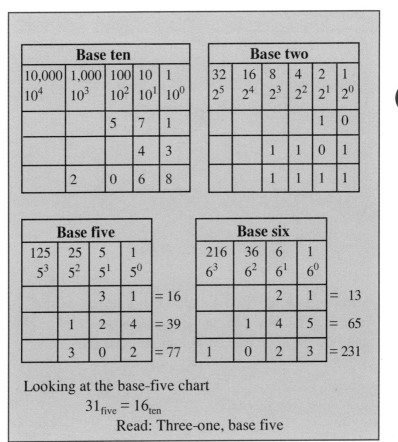

Base ten				
10,000 10^4	1,000 10^3	100 10^2	10 10^1	1 10^0
		5	7	1
			4	3
	2	0	6	8

Base two					
32 2^5	16 2^4	8 2^3	4 2^2	2 2^1	1 2^0
				1	0
		1	1	0	1
		1	1	1	1

Base five				
125 5^3	25 5^2	5 5^1	1 5^0	
		3	1	= 16
	1	2	4	= 39
	3	0	2	= 77

Base six				
216 6^3	36 6^2	6 6^1	1 6^0	
		2	1	= 13
	1	4	5	= 65
1	0	2	3	= 231

Looking at the base-five chart

$$31_{\text{five}} = 16_{\text{ten}}$$

Read: Three-one, base five

Of a power The number which is to be raised to a given power. In 4^3 the base is 4.

4^3 ← exponent $4^3 = 4 \times 4 \times 4 = 64$

↑
base

CHECK YOUR UNDERSTANDING

What is the shape of the base of a cylinder? What number is named by 1101_{two}? What is the base in 6^5?

a circle; thirteen; 6

Base angles

Of an isosceles triangle The two angles in an isosceles triangle that have the base as a side. In the picture below, angles A and C are base angles of the isosceles triangle ABC. $\overline{AC}$ is the base.

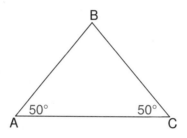

Of a trapezoid The two angles in a trapezoid that have the base as a side. In the picture below, angles A and B of the trapezoid are base angles. $\overline{AB}$ is the base.

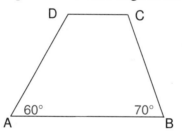

CHECK YOUR UNDERSTANDING
What is the measure of each of the base angles of triangle ABC? What are the measures of the base angles of the trapezoid above?

50°; 60° and 70°

Basic counting principle

See Fundamental counting principle.

Basic Facts

All addition or multiplication pairs of numbers 0 through 9. For example, $7 + 5 = 12$ and $9 \times 3 = 27$ are basic facts.

B

ADDITION TABLE OF BASIC FACTS

The black arrows show how to locate $3 + 4 = 7$.

+	0	1	2	3	4	5	6	7	8	9
0	0	1	2	3	4	5	6	7	8	9
1	1	2	3	4	5	6	7	8	9	10
2	2	3	4	5	6	7	8	9	10	11
3	3	4	5	6	7	8	9	10	11	12
4	4	5	6	7	8	9	10	11	12	13
5	5	6	7	8	9	10	11	12	13	14
6	6	7	8	9	10	11	12	13	14	15
7	7	8	9	10	11	12	13	14	15	16
8	8	9	10	11	12	13	14	15	16	17
9	9	10	11	12	13	14	15	16	17	18

The red arrows show how to locate the subtraction fact $13 - 6 = 7$.

Look for 13 in the row across from 6. Then look up to the top of the chart to 7.

MULTIPLICATION TABLE OF BASIC FACTS

The black arrows show how to locate $4 \times 2 = 8$ and $2 \times 4 = 8$.

×	0	1	2	3	4	5	6	7	8	9
0	0	0	0	0	0	0	0	0	0	0
1	0	1	2	3	4	5	6	7	8	9
2	0	2	4	6	8	10	12	14	16	18
3	0	3	6	9	12	15	18	21	24	27
4	0	4	8	12	16	20	24	28	32	36
5	0	5	10	15	20	25	30	35	40	45
6	0	6	12	18	24	30	36	42	48	54
7	0	7	14	21	28	35	42	49	56	63
8	0	8	16	24	32	40	48	56	64	72
9	0	9	18	27	36	45	54	63	72	81

The red arrows show how to locate the division fact $48 \div 6 = 8$. Look for 48 in the row across from 6. Then look up to the top of the chart to 8.

CHECK YOUR UNDERSTANDING

Is $23 \times 9 = 207$ a basic fact? Is $7 + 4 = 11$ a basic fact?

no; yes

Bearing

The measure of the clockwise angle from North to an object. Bearings are always written using three digits.

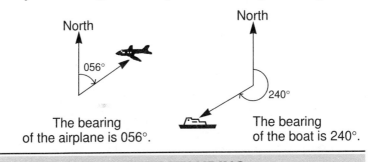

The bearing of the airplane is 056°.

The bearing of the boat is 240°.

B

CHECK YOUR UNDERSTANDING

What is the bearing of an airplane that is 90° from North?

090°

Biconditional

A statement of the form *p if and only if q*. For example,

A $\underbrace{\text{triangle is a right triangle}}_{p}$ *if and only if* $\underbrace{\text{it has one right angle}}_{q}$.

A biconditional is true only when both of the statements p and q are either true or false. All cases of a biconditional statement are summarized in the truth table below.

p	q	p if and only if q
T	T	T
F	T	F
T	F	F
F	F	T

CHECK YOUR UNDERSTANDING

Is the statement below a biconditional?

If an angle measures 90°, then it is a right angle.

no

Billion

The number 1,000,000,000. It is one thousand million. Using exponential notation, it can be written as 10^9.

Binary numeration system

A system for naming numbers using the base two. The value of each place is a power of 2. Each place has a value 2 times greater than the value of the place to its right. The only digits needed for the binary system are 0 and 1. The following shows how the values of the digits in the binary system are found.

16 2^4	8 2^3	4 2^2	2 2^1	1 2^0	
1	1	1	1	1_{two}	$= 16 + 8 + 4 + 2 + 1 = 31_{ten}$
1	0	1	1	0_{two}	$= 16 + 4 + 2 = 22_{ten}$
	1	0	0	1_{two}	$= 8 + 1 = 9_{ten}$

To find what number in base ten is named by 11111 in base two, add the values of the five digits: $16 + 8 + 4 + 2 + 1 = 31$.

$$11111_{two} = 31_{ten}$$
Read: one-one-one-one-one, base two.

Binary operation

An operation performed on two numbers to produce one number for an answer. Addition is an example of a binary operation. It combines two numbers to produce one number, called the sum.

CHECK YOUR UNDERSTANDING
Is subtraction a binary operation?

yes

Binomial

An expression made up of two terms.

EXAMPLES $2x + 4y$ $az^2 + 6bz$ $5k - 3n$

CHECK YOUR UNDERSTANDING
Is 3x a binomial?

no; it has only one term

Bisect

To divide a line segment, an angle, or an arc into two congruent parts. For example, to bisect an angle of 90°, divide it into two angles of 45° each.

See also Constructions.

CHECK YOUR UNDERSTANDING
A line segment 7 inches long is divided into two line segments, one 3 inches long, the other 4 inches long. Is this segment bisected?

no

Bisector

A point, segment, ray, or line that divides a line segment, an angle, or an arc into two congruent parts.

EXAMPLES

Point M is a bisector
of segment AB.

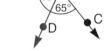

$\overline{AM} \cong \overline{MB}$

$AM = MB$

$\overline{GI}$ is the bisector of $\overline{EF}$.

$\overline{EH} \cong \overline{HF}$

$EH = HF$

Ray AD is a bisector
of angle BAC.

$\angle BAD \cong \angle CAD$

$m \angle BAD = m \angle CAD$

Line ℓ is the bisector of
arc AB.

$\overset{\frown}{AM} \cong \overset{\frown}{MB}$

$m \overset{\frown}{AM} = m \overset{\frown}{MB}$

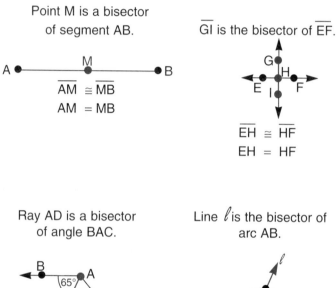

Borrow

Also called regroup *or* rename. The term is sometimes used in subtraction when a regrouping is necessary in order to have a larger or equal number from which to subtract.

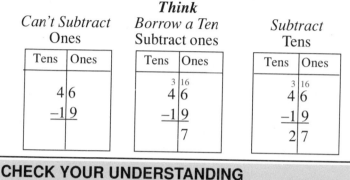

Think

Can't Subtract Ones		Borrow a Ten Subtract ones		Subtract Tens	
Tens	Ones	Tens	Ones	Tens	Ones
4	6	³4	¹⁶6	³4	¹⁶6
−1	9	−1	9	−1	9
			7	2	7

CHECK YOUR UNDERSTANDING

In performing the following subtraction from which place will the borrowing be done?

        2354
    −   614

thousands

Box and whisker plot

A graphic way of showing a summary of data using the median, quartiles, and extremes of the data. A box and whisker plot makes it easy to see where the data are spread out and where they are concentrated. The longer the box the more the data are spread out.

On the next page you can find how to construct a box and whisker plot to summarize these data.

Bowling scores of 11 teenagers

110	118	100	94	105
121	91	101	107	125

107

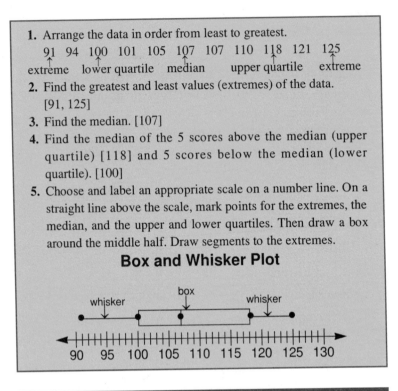

1. Arrange the data in order from least to greatest.

   91 94 100 101 105 107 107 110 118 121 125

   extreme   lower quartile   median   upper quartile   extreme

2. Find the greatest and least values (extremes) of the data. [91, 125]

3. Find the median. [107]

4. Find the median of the 5 scores above the median (upper quartile) [118] and 5 scores below the median (lower quartile). [100]

5. Choose and label an appropriate scale on a number line. On a straight line above the scale, mark points for the extremes, the median, and the upper and lower quartiles. Then draw a box around the middle half. Draw segments to the extremes.

Box and Whisker Plot

box

whisker   whisker

90   95   100   105   110   115   120   125   130

Brackets

See Grouping symbols.

Bushel

A unit of capacity or volume in the U.S. customary system of measurement. A bushel is equal to 4 pecks or 32 quarts of dry measure. It has a volume of about 2,150 cubic inches or $1\frac{1}{4}$ cubic feet.

CHECK YOUR UNDERSTANDING

About how many bushels of apples will fit in a box with a volume of $2\frac{1}{2}$ cubic feet?

two

C

Calculus

A branch of mathematics developed by Gottfried Wilhelm Leibnitz and Isaac Newton during the 17th century as a way of measuring motion. Using the techniques of calculus, a moving object can be traced as a path of points through space. By stopping the action, like a frame from a motion picture, the speed and acceleration of the object at a specific instant can be calculated.

CHECK YOUR UNDERSTANDING
Why was calculus invented?

to measure motion

Calendar

A system for dividing time into periods. One year is divided into 12 months. September, April, June, and November have 30 days. The other months except February (January, March, May, July, August, October, December) have 31 days each. February has 28 days, except in leap years, when it has 29 days.

A year is a leap year if it is divisible by 4, except for century years, such as 2100, which must be divisible by 400. February 29 is called a leap day. A leap year has 366 days; other years have 365 days each.

CHECK YOUR UNDERSTANDING
Will the year 2400 be a leap year?

yes

Cancellation

In fractions To divide out common factors from the numerator and denominator of a fractional expression before multiplying.

$$\frac{\cancel{2}^{1}}{3} \times \frac{1}{\cancel{4}_{2}} = \frac{1}{6} \qquad \text{Divide out 2.}$$

$$\frac{\cancel{5}^{1}}{\cancel{6}_{2}} \times \frac{\cancel{9}^{3}}{\cancel{20}_{4}} = \frac{3}{8} \qquad \begin{array}{l}\text{Divide out 5.}\\ \text{Divide out 3.}\end{array}$$

In equations To subtract or divide out common factors or terms from both sides of an equation or inequality.

$$\begin{array}{rcl} 2x+5 &=& x+9 \\ -x &=& -x \\ \hline x+5 &=& 9 \end{array} \qquad \begin{array}{rcl} 4x^2y &=& 8x \\ \div 4x &=& \div 4x \\ \hline xy &=& 2 \end{array}$$

CHECK YOUR UNDERSTANDING
What common factor can be divided out from the numerator and the denominator of this fractional expression: $\frac{3}{5} \times \frac{10}{11}$?

5

Capacity

The volume of a container given in units of liquid measure.

CHECK YOUR UNDERSTANDING
What is the approximate capacity of a soda can?

12 fl oz or 354 mL

Cardinal number

A whole number that answers the question "How many?" We say that this set has 4 elements or has the cardinal number 4.

$$\left\{ \text{🍎 🍊 🍌 🍐} \right\}$$

CHECK YOUR UNDERSTANDING
What is the cardinal number of this set: {a, b, c, d, e, f}?

6

Carry

Also called Regroup *or* Rename. The term is sometimes used in addition when the sum is ten or greater and it is necessary to carry a number of tens to the next place. In adding 7 and 6, for example, we say, "Write 3 and carry 1."

$$\begin{array}{r} \overset{1}{}37 \\ +\ 26 \\ \hline 3 \end{array}$$

Another way to describe this process: Add 7 and 6→13. Regroup or rename 13 as 1 ten and 3 ones.

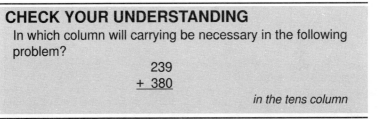

CHECK YOUR UNDERSTANDING
In which column will carrying be necessary in the following problem?

$$\begin{array}{r} 239 \\ +\ 380 \\ \hline \end{array}$$

in the tens column

Cartesian coordinate system

See Coordinate system.

Casting out nines

A process used for checking the answers to addition, subtraction, multiplication, and division of whole numbers. To check an answer, find the nines excess of each number and the nines excess of the answer. If the answer for the operation performed on nines excesses of the numbers is the same as the nines excess of the answer to the problem, then the answer is probably correct.

See the next page for examples of how to cast out nines to check an answer.

47

HOW TO CAST OUT NINES

To get the nines excess of a number, keep adding the digits of a number until you arrive at a single digit.

$478 \rightarrow 4+7+8 = 19 \rightarrow 1+9 = 10 \rightarrow 1+0 = 1$ (nines excess)

One type of error that casting out nines will not detect is an interchanging of the order of digits in an answer, since this will not change the nines excess of the answer.

Here is an example of checking a sum by casting out nines.

$$478 \rightarrow 4+7+8 = 19 \rightarrow 1+9 = 10 \rightarrow 1+0 = 1 \qquad \mathbf{1}$$
$$2{,}475 \rightarrow 2+4+7+5 = 18 \rightarrow 1+8 = 9 \qquad \mathbf{9}$$
$$\underline{+7{,}896} \rightarrow 7+8+9+6 = 30 \rightarrow 3+0 = 3 \qquad \underline{\mathbf{+3}}$$
$$10{,}489 \rightarrow 1+0+4+8+9 = 22 \rightarrow 2+2 = \mathbf{4} \qquad 13$$
$$\qquad\qquad\qquad\qquad\qquad 1+3 = \mathbf{4}$$

The nines excess of the answer and the sum of the nine excesses of the three addends is 4. The answer is probably correct.

Here is an example of checking a product by casting out nines.

$$364 \rightarrow 3+6+4 = 13 \rightarrow 1+3 = 4 \qquad \mathbf{4}$$
$$\times \underline{\ 786} \rightarrow 7+8+6 = 21 \rightarrow 2+1 = 3 \qquad \underline{\times \mathbf{3}}$$
$$2184 \qquad\qquad\qquad\qquad\qquad 12$$
$$2912 \qquad\qquad\qquad\qquad 1+2 = \mathbf{3}$$
$$\underline{+2548\ \ }$$
$$28{,}6104 \rightarrow 2+8+6+1+0+4 = 21 \rightarrow 2+1 = \mathbf{3}$$

The nines excess of the product and the product of the nine excesses of the factors is 3. The answer is probably correct.

Here is an example of checking a difference by casting out nines.   Add 9 so you can subtract 7.

$$256 \rightarrow 2 + 5 + 6 \rightarrow 13 \rightarrow 1 + 3 = 4 \rightarrow 4 + \overset{\downarrow}{9} = \mathbf{13}$$
$$\underline{-169} \rightarrow 1 + 6 + 9 \rightarrow 16 \rightarrow 1 + 6 = 7 \rightarrow 7 \qquad \underline{-7}$$
$$87 \rightarrow 8 + 7 = 15 \rightarrow 1 + 5 = 6 \qquad\qquad \mathbf{6}$$

The nines excess of the difference and the difference of the nines excesses of the subtrahend and the minuend is 6. The answer is probably correct.

Here is an example of checking a quotient using casting out nines.

40R8   Multiply the nines excess of the quotient (4)
12)488 by the nines excess of the divisor (3),then
        add the remainder. $4 \times 3 + 8 = 20 \rightarrow 2 + 0 = 2$

The nines excess of the dividend $(4 + 8 + 8 = 20 \rightarrow 2 + 0 = 2)$ is also 2. The answer is probably correct.

CHECK YOUR UNDERSTANDING
What is the nines excess of 8743?

4; 8 + 7 + 4 + 3 = 22 →2 + 2 = 4

Celsius (ºC)

Also called centigrade. A scale for measuring temperature. In this scale, 0°C is assigned to the freezing point of water and 100°C is assigned to the boiling point of water. There are 100 degrees between the freezing and boiling points of water on the Celsius scale. There are 180° between the freezing and boiling points of water on the Fahrenheit scale.

See the next page for how to convert temperature readings.

HOW TO CONVERT TEMPERATURE READINGS

The following formulas can be used to convert temperature readings.

Celsius to Fahrenheit	**Fahrenheit to Celsius**
$F = \frac{9}{5} C + 32$	$C = \frac{5}{9} (F - 32)$

What is 35°C in °F ?

$F = \frac{9}{5} C + 32$

$= (\frac{9}{5} \times 35) + 32$

$= 63 + 32$ or 95°F

What is 50°F in °C?

$C = \frac{5}{9} (F - 32)$

$= \frac{5}{9} (50 - 32)$

$= \frac{5}{9} \times 18$ or 10°C.

CHECK YOUR UNDERSTANDING

In the Celsius scale, between what two numbers are the temperatures of the freezing and boiling points of water?

0 and 100

Center of a circle

A point such that every point on the circle is the same distance from it.

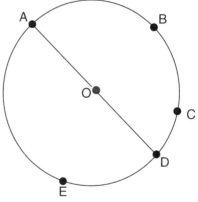

CHECK YOUR UNDERSTANDING

The distance from the center of the circle, O, to point A on the circle shown above is 12 mm. How long is segment AD?

24 mm

Center of a regular polygon

The center of the polygon's inscribed and circumscribed circles.

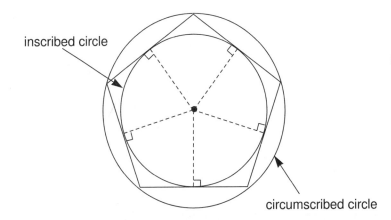

inscribed circle

circumscribed circle

CHECK YOUR UNDERSTANDING

Is the center of a regular polygon the same distance from every point on the polygon?

no

Center of a sphere

A point such that every point on the sphere is the same distance from it.

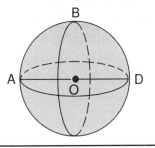

CHECK YOUR UNDERSTANDING

The distance from the center of the sphere, O, to point D on the sphere is 15 mm. How long is segment AD?

30 mm

Centi-

The prefix centi means "one hundredth".

Centigram (cg) means "one hundredth of a gram" (g).

$$1 \text{ cg} = \frac{1}{100}\text{g or } 0.01\text{g}$$

A centigram is a unit of mass in the metric system.
The mass of ten small seeds is about 1 cg.

Centiliter (cL) means "one hundredth of a liter" (L).

$$1 \text{ cL} = \frac{1}{100}\text{L or } 0.01\text{L}$$

A centiliter is a unit of capacity in the metric system.
Two teaspoons hold about 1 cL of water.

Centimeter (cm) means "one hundredth of a meter" (m).

$$1 \text{ cm} = \frac{1}{100}\text{m or } 0.01 \text{ m}$$

A centimeter is a unit of length in the metric system.
This line has a length of 1 cm. _____

CHECK YOUR UNDERSTANDING
What would centidollar mean if it were a word?

$\frac{1}{100}$ of a dollar or 1¢

Centigrade

See Celsius.

Central angle

An angle whose vertex
is the center of a circle.
Angle AOB is a central angle.

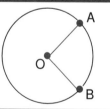

CHECK YOUR UNDERSTANDING
How can you tell that an angle within a circle is a central angle?

its vertex is the center of the circle

Centroid

A point at which a geometric figure balances. The centroid of a triangle is the point of intersection of the three medians of the triangle. If you would cut a triangle out of cardboard and place the centroid of the triangle on a pinhead, the triangle would balance. C is the centroid of triangle DEF. Its medians are $\overline{FG}$, $\overline{DH}$, and $\overline{EI}$.

C

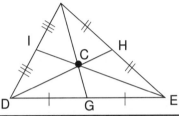

CHECK YOUR UNDERSTANDING
What is the centroid of a circle?

its center

Chord

Any line segment that connects two points on a circle. In the picture, $\overline{AC}$, $\overline{AB}$, $\overline{DE}$, and $\overline{FG}$ are chords. The longest chord in a circle is a diameter. The diameter is a chord that passes through the center of the circle.

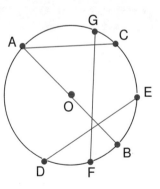

CHECK YOUR UNDERSTANDING
What is the longest chord in the picture above?

$\overline{AB}$

Circle

A set of all points in a plane that are the same distance, the radius, from a given point, the center. Each point on circle O to the right is 2 cm from the center. A circle is named by its center. Thus, we say circle O (⊙ O).

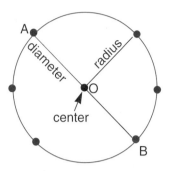

A segment connecting two points on the circle and passing through the center is a diameter. $\overline{AB}$ is a diameter of circle O.

See also Arc, Area, Chord, Circumference of a circle, Concentric circles, Sector of a circle, Segment of a circle, Semicircle.

CHECK YOUR UNDERSTANDING
What is the length of a diameter in circle O?

4 cm

Circle graph

Also called Pie graph. A graph in which data are represented by parts of a circle. Below is a circle graph of preferences of 100 students for TV shows. According to this graph, the most favorite shows are comedy. One-half of the circle is shaded red. One-half of the students surveyed, or 50 students, prefer comedy shows.

Favorite TV Shows

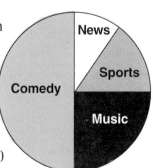

HOW TO MAKE A CIRCLE GRAPH

FAVORITE RECORDS				
Record	A	B	C	D
Number of votes	10	20	4	6

1. Make a chart like the one shown below for the data.
2. Find the fractional part of the total number of votes for each record. For example, record A represents $\frac{10}{40}$ or $\frac{1}{4}$ of all the votes.
3. Multiply the fractional part by the number of degrees in a circle, 360°. For example, $\frac{1}{4} \times 360° = 90°$. The central angle for the part on the circle graph representing the votes for Record A is 90°.

Record	Number	Fractional part of circle	Measure of central angle
A	10	$\frac{10}{40}$ or $\frac{1}{4}$	$\frac{1}{4} \times 360° = 90°$.
B	20	$\frac{20}{40}$ or $\frac{1}{2}$	$\frac{1}{2} \times 360° = 180°$.
C	4	$\frac{4}{40}$ or $\frac{1}{10}$	$\frac{1}{10} \times 360° = 36°$.
D	6	$\frac{6}{40}$ or $\frac{3}{20}$	$\frac{3}{20} \times 360° = 54°$.
Total	40	$\frac{40}{40}$ or 1	360°

4. Draw a circle. Make central angles of the measures shown in the chart. Label the parts.

FAVORITE RECORDS

5. Give the circle graph a title.

CHECK YOUR UNDERSTANDING
According to the circle graph on page 54, what is the second most favorite kind of TV shows? How many students preferred it?

music; 25

55

Circumference of a circle

The distance around a circle.

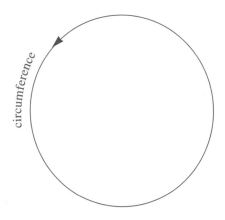

The circumference of a circle can be computed using the formula $C = 2\pi r$ or $C = \pi d$, where r is the radius and d is the diameter.

EXAMPLES

Find the circumference of a circle:

with a radius of 4 in.

$C = 2\pi r$

$\approx 2 \times 3.14 \times 4$

≈ 25.12 in.

is approximately equal to

with a diameter of 5 in.

$C = \pi d$

$\approx 3.14 \times 5$

≈ 15.7 in.

CHECK YOUR UNDERSTANDING

Using 3.14 for π, what is the approximate circumference of a circle with the radius of 2 in.?

12.56 in.

Circumscribed

A circle is circumscribed about a polygon if every vertex of the polygon lies on the circle. The center of the circle is the point of intersection of the perpendicular bisectors of the sides of the polygon. The polygon is said to be inscribed in the circle.

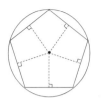

C

A polygon is circumscribed about a circle if every side of the polygon is tangent to the circle. The circle is said to be inscribed in the polygon.

CHECK YOUR UNDERSTANDING

In the picture above, what figure is circumscribed about the circle?

pentagon

Clock arithmetic

Also called Arithmetic modulo 12. Adding by going around a clock. Only the numbers 1 through 12 are used for the sum. When you add 1 to 12 using the clock, the sum is 1.

12 + 1 = 1 modulo 12.

OTHER EXAMPLES
7 + 8 = 3 modulo 12
9 + 10 = 7 modulo 12
25 + 4 = 5 modulo 12

Go around the clock twice for 24 then go 1 more space for 25, 1 + 4 = 5.

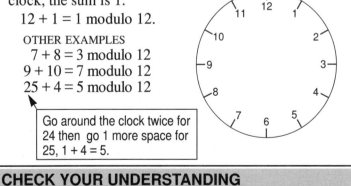

CHECK YOUR UNDERSTANDING

What is 11 + 3 modulo 12 equal to?

2

Closed curve

A curve with no endpoints. A closed curve is called a simple closed curve if it does not cross itself. The set of points inside a closed curve is called the interior of the curve. The set of points outside the closed curve is called the exterior of the curve. The curve itself is called the boundary.

Closed curve

Simple closed curve

CHECK YOUR UNDERSTANDING
Does a simple closed curve cross itself?

no

Closure property

A set of numbers is said to be closed, or to have closure property, under a given operation, such as addition, subtraction, multiplication, or division, if the result of this operation on any numbers in the set is also in that set.

The set of whole numbers is closed under addition, because the sum of any two whole numbers is a whole number: $3 + 5 = 8$.

The set of whole numbers is not closed under subtraction, because the difference of two whole numbers is not always a whole number: $3 - 5 = {}^-2$.

CHECK YOUR UNDERSTANDING
Is the set of whole numbers closed under multiplication; that is, is the product of two whole numbers always a whole number?

yes

Coefficient

In algebra, the numerical factor of a term. It is also customary to consider other parts of terms as coefficients.

$$5y \qquad\qquad 5ay^2$$

numerical coefficient coefficient of y^2

C

Collinear planes

Planes that contain the same line.

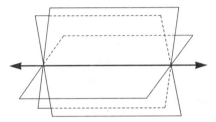

Collinear points

Points that lie on the same line. Any two points are collinear since a line can contain any two points. However, three points are not necessarily collinear.

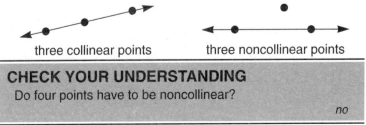

three collinear points   three noncollinear points

Combination

Any subset of things taken out of a given set. The order of the members of the subset is not important.

EXAMPLE

All arrangements of two letters taken out of the set {x,y,z} are:

{x,y} {x,z} {y,x} {y,z} {z,x} {z,y}

same combination of letters

So there are 3 possible combinations of two letters taken out of a set of three letters:

{x,y}, {x,z}, and {y,z}.

This formula in factorial notation can be used to find the number of combinations where n is the total number of things in the set and t is the number of things taken out of the set at a time.

$$C = \frac{n!}{(n-t)!\,t!}$$

How many combinations of three students can be formed from a group of 15 students?

$$n = 15 \quad t = 3$$

$$C = \frac{15!}{(15-3)!\,3!} = 455$$

There are 455 combinations of three students that can be formed from a group of 15 students.

See also Permutation.

CHECK YOUR UNDERSTANDING

How many combinations are there of two letters taken out of this set {u,v,w,x,y,z}?

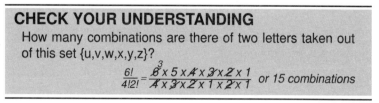

$$\frac{6!}{4!2!} = \frac{\overset{3}{\cancel{6}} \times 5 \times \cancel{4} \times \cancel{3} \times \cancel{2} \times 1}{\cancel{4} \times \cancel{3} \times \cancel{2} \times 1 \times \cancel{2} \times 1} \text{ or } 15 \text{ combinations}$$

Combining like terms

A method of performing the given operations on the coefficients of terms that are exactly alike except for their coefficients.

EXAMPLES

Think: $1-2=^-1$

$1y^2 - 2y^2 = -y^2$
↑ ↑
coefficients

Think: $7-5=2$

$7x^2y - 5x^2y = 2x^2y$
↑ ↑
coefficients

Think: $2+3=5$

$2ab + 3ab = 5ab$
↑ ↑
coefficients

C

CHECK YOUR UNDERSTANDING
Simplify by combining like terms: $7ax^2 - 4ax^2$

$3ax^2$

Commensurable

Also called Commensurate.

Line segments Two line segments are commensurable if each contains a common measure a whole number of times. For example, a line segment that measures $\frac{1}{6}$ yard is commensurable with a line segment that measures $\frac{1}{4}$ yard since they each contain a common measure of $\frac{1}{12}$ yard a whole number of times.

Numbers Two numbers are commensurable if their ratio is a whole number or a fraction. For example, $\frac{2}{3}$ and $\frac{3}{4}$ are commensurable since their ratio is $\frac{2}{3} \div \frac{3}{4}$ or $\frac{2}{3} \times \frac{4}{3} = \frac{8}{9}$.

See also incommensurable.

CHECK YOUR UNDERSTANDING
Are segments of 2 in. and 3 in. commensurable?

yes; 2 in. and 3 in. are whole-number multiples of 1 in.,
$\frac{1}{2}$ *in.,* $\frac{1}{3}$ *in., and other fractions of an inch*

Commission

The amount of money paid to a salesperson based on the total amount of sales. Ordinarily, commission is established as a rate of commission, that is, a percent of sales. For example, if a salesperson receives a commission of 20%, then the amount of commission for $1,000 in sales is $1,000 × 0.20, or $200.

Commission = total sales × commission rate

CHECK YOUR UNDERSTANDING
What will be the amount of commission at the commission rate of 30% on sales totaling $200?

$60

Common binomial factor

If two polynomials have the same factor in common, then this factor is called a common binomial factor.

EXAMPLE Two polynomials: $x^2 - 5x + 4$ and $x^2 + x - 2$
Factors: $(x - 1)(x - 4)$ and $(x - 1)(x + 2)$
The common binomial factor is $(x - 1)$.

CHECK YOUR UNDERSTANDING
What is the common binomial factor of $x^2 - 4$ and $x^2 + x - 2$?

x + 2

Common denominator

Any common multiple of the denominators of two or more fractions.

EXAMPLE $\dfrac{\text{numerator}}{\text{denominator}} \rightarrow \dfrac{1}{2}, \dfrac{2}{5}, \dfrac{3}{4}$

common denominators: $\dfrac{?}{20}, \dfrac{?}{40}, \dfrac{?}{60}, \dfrac{?}{80}, \dfrac{?}{100} \ldots$ ◄— 2, 5 and 4 divide into these numbers without a remainder.

The smallest or least common denominator (LCD) is 20.

CHECK YOUR UNDERSTANDING
What is the least common denominator for $\frac{1}{2}$ and $\frac{5}{6}$?

6

Common difference

The difference of a term and the preceding term in an arithmetic progression. For example, in the arithmetic progression 0, 2, 4, 6, 8, 10, . . . , the common difference is 2 $(2 - 0 = 2, 4 - 2 = 2, 6 - 4 = 2, 8 - 6 = 2, 10 - 8 = 2)$. To obtain the next term of an arithmetic progression, add the common difference to the preceding term.

CHECK YOUR UNDERSTANDING
What is the common difference in the following arithmetic progression: 0, 3, 6, 9, 12, 15, . . .?

3

Common factor

Also called Common divisor.

In arithmetic A number that is a factor of two or more numbers. For example, 10 is a common factor of 70 and 100. It is also the greatest common factor (GCF), since it is the largest number that divides both 70 and 100.

In algebra A polynomial that is a factor of two or more polynomials. That is, each of the polynomials is divisible by the common factor. For example, $x - 1$ is a common factor of $x^2 + x - 2$ and $x^2 - 6x + 5$, since each polynomial is divisible by $x - 1$.

HOW TO FIND COMMON FACTORS
Find the common factors of 18 and 24:
1. List the factors of 18: 1, 2, 3, 6, 9, 18
2. List the factors of 24: 1, 2, 3, 4, 6, 8, 12, 24.
3. Circle the factors common to both numbers. (1, 2, 3, 6)
   The common factors of 18 and 24 are: 1, 2, 3, 6.
   The greatest number that appears in this list is 6.
   So 6 is the greatest common factor (GCF) of 18 and 24.

CHECK YOUR UNDERSTANDING
What are the common factors of 20 and 30?

1,2,5,10

Common multiple

In arithmetic A number that is a multiple of two or more numbers. For example, 20 is a common multiple of 4 and 10 since 20 is a multiple of both 4 and 10. Every multiple of 20 is also a common multiple of 4 and 10. Thus, the set of common multiples of 4 and 10 is infinite: 20, 40, 60, 80, 100, ...

The least common multiple (LCM) of 4 and 10 is 20, because it is the smallest multiple of both 4 and 10.

In algebra A polynomial that is a multiple of two or more polynomials. For example, $x^2 + x - 2$ is a common multiple of $x - 1$ and $x + 2$ since $x^2 + x - 2 = (x + 2)(x - 1)$. Another common multiple of $x + 2$ and $x - 1$ is $x^3 + 2x^2 - x - 2$ since $x^3 + 2x^2 - x - 2 = (x - 1)(x + 2)(x + 1)$. The least common multiple (LCM) of $x - 1$ and $x + 2$ is $x^2 + x - 2$.

HOW TO FIND COMMON MULTIPLES

Finding the common multiples of 6 and 15:
1. List the first 5 multiples of 6: 6, 12, 18, 24, 30, . . .
2. List the first 5 multiples of 15: 15, 30, 45, 60, 75 . . .
3. Circle any numbers that appear in both lists. If there are no numbers common to both, find the next several multiples for each. There will always be one common multiple for the two numbers, the product of the two numbers.

A common multiple of 6 and 15 is 30. Other common multiples are 60, 90, 120, 150, 180, and so on. 30 is the *least common multiple (LCM)* of 6 and 15.

CHECK YOUR UNDERSTANDING

What is the least common multiple of 6 and 8?

24

Common ratio

The quotient of a term and the preceding term in a geometric progression. For example, in the geometric progression 1, 2, 4, 8, 16, 32, . . . , the common ratio is $2 (2 \div 1 = 2, 4 \div 2 = 2, 8 \div 4 = 2, 16 \div 8 = 2, 32 \div 16 = 2)$. To obtain the next term of a geometric progression, the preceding term is multiplied by the common ratio.

C

CHECK YOUR UNDERSTANDING
What is the common ratio in the following geometric progression: 1, 3, 9, 27, 81, . . .?

3

Common tangent

A line that is tangent to two or more curves. Of particular interest in geometry is a common tangent to two circles. For an external tangent the circles are on the same side of the tangent line. For an internal tangent the circles are on opposite sides of the tangent line.

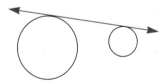   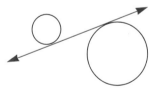

external tangent   internal tangent

CHECK YOUR UNDERSTANDING
Could the two circles at the left above have another external tangent?

yes

Commutative property

Also called Order property. The property of an operation such that changing the order of numbers does not change the result of an operation ($*$):

$$a * b = b * a.$$

Addition The operation of addition has the *commutative property*:

$$5 + 9 \overset{?}{=} 9 + 5$$
$$14 = 14$$

Multiplication The operation of multiplication has the *commutative property*:

$$3 \times 7 \overset{?}{=} 7 \times 3$$
$$21 = 21$$

Subtraction The operation of subtraction **does not** have the *commutative property*:

$$9 - 6 \overset{?}{=} 6 - 9$$
$$3 \neq {}^-3$$

Division The operation of division **does not** have the *commutative property*:

$$8 \div 2 \overset{?}{=} 2 \div 8$$
$$4 \neq \frac{1}{4}$$

CHECK YOUR UNDERSTANDING

In which statement is the commutative property of addition shown?

   a. (2 + 5) + 7 = 2 + (5 + 7)   b. (2 + 5) + 7 = (5 + 2) + 7

statement b

Compass   plural compasses

An instrument used for drawing circles or arcs or for transferring the distance between two points from one place to another.

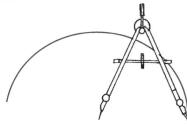

C

Compatible numbers

Two numbers that form a basic division fact. For example, 8 and 56 are compatible numbers: $56 \div 8 = 7$.

Compatible numbers can be used to estimate quotients.

EXAMPLES

Estimate: $478 \div 6$ ◄——— Change the dividend to a compatible number with 6.

Think: $480 \div 6 = 80$

Estimate: $29,874 \div 62$ ◄——— Round the divisor to the leftmost place. Change the dividend so you will have a number compatible with 6.

Think: $30,000 \div 60 = 500$

67

Compensation

Adding an amount to one addend and subtracting the same amount from the other addend to add mentally.

EXAMPLE   Add: 397 + 28

Think: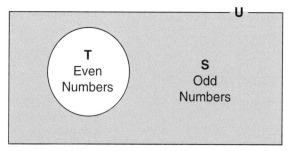

400 + 25 = 425

CHECK YOUR UNDERSTANDING
What number will you add and subtract using compensation to add 589 and 65 mentally?

11

Complement of a set

Set S is a complement of set T in the universal set U if it contains all the elements that are in the universal set U but not in set T.

EXAMPLE

If the universal set U = {all whole numbers}
and T = {all even numbers}
then the complement of T in U is S and S ={all odd numbers}.

U

T
Even
Numbers

S
Odd
Numbers

CHECK YOUR UNDERSTANDING
If the universal set U is the set of all whole numbers and set P is the set of all prime numbers, then what is the complement of set P?

the composite numbers and 1

68

Complementary angles

Two angles are complementary if the sum of their measures is 90°. Angle a is a complement of angle b, and angle b is a complement of angle a.

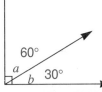

CHECK YOUR UNDERSTANDING
If angle C measures 50°, then what is the measure of the complement of angle C?

40°

Complete factorization

See Prime factorization.

Complex fraction

A fraction in which the numerator or denominator or both are fractions. For example, $\dfrac{2}{\frac{3}{5}}$ and $\dfrac{\frac{3}{5}}{\frac{1}{2}}$ are complex fractions.

HOW TO SIMPLIFY COMPLEX FRACTIONS
To simplify complex fractions, think of the fraction bar as a division sign. Write the fractions in a division sentence. Then divide by multiplying, using the reciprocal of the divisor.

EXAMPLES $\dfrac{2}{\frac{3}{5}} = 2 \div \dfrac{3}{5} = 2 \times \dfrac{5}{3} = \dfrac{10}{3}$

$\dfrac{\frac{3}{5}}{\frac{1}{2}} = \dfrac{3}{5} \div \dfrac{1}{2} = \dfrac{3}{5} \times \dfrac{2}{1} = \dfrac{6}{5}$

CHECK YOUR UNDERSTANDING
Is $\dfrac{5}{\frac{1}{2}}$ a complex fraction?

yes

Complex number

A number that can be written in the form $a + bi$, where a and b are real numbers and $i = \sqrt{-1}$. The form $a + bi$ is called the standard form of a complex number. If $a = 0$, then $a + bi$ becomes bi, and it is called an imaginary number or pure imaginary number.

EXAMPLES OF COMPLEX NUMBERS

$$3 + \sqrt{-6} \qquad 4 + 7i \qquad \sqrt{2} - 3i \qquad 2 - \sqrt{3}i \qquad 6i$$

CHECK YOUR UNDERSTANDING
Is $3 + 7i$ a complex number?

yes

Composite number

A number that has more than two factors. For example, 8 is a composite number, since it has four factors: 1, 2, 4, and 8.

CHECK YOUR UNDERSTANDING
Is 5 a composite number?

no

Compound interest

Interest paid on earned interest. Interest is computed on the principal for the first compounding period and then added to the principal. For the second compounding period the interest is computed on the principal plus the interest earned during the first compounding period, and so on.

EXAMPLE

Principal: $100.00
Annual interest rate: 10% compounded quarterly.
Interest for the first quarter: 2.5% (10% ÷ 4) of $100 = $2.50.
Interest for the second quarter: ($100 +$2.50) × 2.5% = $2.56.

principal + interest earned the first quarter

The interest for the third quarter is computed on $102.50 + $2.56 and so on.

USING A TABLE
TO FIND COMPOUND INTEREST

A compound interest table shows the amount $1.00 will earn for a number of interest rates and interest periods. To use the table, you need to know the number of interest periods and the interest rate per period.

C

Compound Interest Table			
Amount of $1.00			
Total Interest Periods	Interest Rate Per Period		
	1.25%	**1.375%**	**1.5%**	**2.75%**
1	1.01250	1.01375	1.01500	1.02749
2	1.02515	1.02768	1.03022	1.05575
3	1.03797	1.04182	1.04567	1.08478
4	1.05094	1.05614	1.06136	1.11462
5	1.06408	1.07066	1.07728	1.14527
6	1.07738	1.08539	1.09344	1.17676
7	1.09085	1.10031	1.10984	1.20912
8	1.10448	1.11544	1.12649	1.24237

Suppose you deposit $500 at an interest rate of 5.5% compounded quarterly. How much interest would you earn in two years?

1. Interest rate per period: compounding is quarterly, so divide the annual interest rate by 4.

$$5.5\% \div 4 = \mathbf{1.375\%}$$

2. Number of interest periods: quarterly for 2 years $\rightarrow 4 \times 2 = \mathbf{8}$

3. Look across the column from **8** and down from the interest rate of **1.375%**. The value from the table is **1.11544**. Multiply this value by the amount you deposited:

$$1.11544 \times \$500 = \$557.72.$$

4. Subtract the amount of the deposit: $557.72 − $500 = $57.72.

The amount of interest earned is $57.72.

USING THE COMPOUND INTEREST FORMULA

This formula can be used to find the amount of money accumulated after a given number of compounding periods: $f = P(1 + i)^n$ where f = amount of money at the end of n compounding periods, P = the original amount of money, i = interest rate for the compounding period expressed as a decimal, and n = the number of compounding periods.

Suppose the sum of $10,000 is invested, earning interest compounded annually at the rate of 6%. What will be the amount accumulated at the end of 3 years?

$f = P(1 + i)^n \qquad P = 10,000; \ i = 0.06; \ n = 3$
$f = 10,000 \times (1 + 0.06)^3 = 10,000 \times (1.06)^3$
$\quad = 10,000 \times 1.191016 = \$11,910.16$

At the end of 3 years there will be $11,910.16. The interest earned is $1,910.16.

CHECK YOUR UNDERSTANDING

You deposit $200. What amount of money will be on deposit at the end of 3 years, if the annual interest is 5.5% compounded semiannually?

Using the formula or the table: $235.35

Concave polygon

A polygon in whose interior there exists at least one pair of points that when connected by a segment some points of the segment will be in the exterior of the polygon.

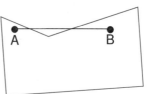

Polygons that are not concave are convex.

CHECK YOUR UNDERSTANDING

The word *concave* suggests that a polygon is "caved in". Is this consistent with the way a concave polygon looks?

yes

Concentric circles

Two or more circles that have the same center.

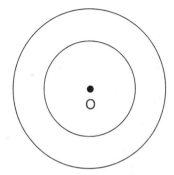

Concentric circles

C

CHECK YOUR UNDERSTANDING
Can four circles be concentric?

yes

Condition

A requirement, property, assumption, or truth. For example, three congruent sides is a condition for a triangle to be equilateral. A numeral ending in 0 or 5 is a condition for the number to be divisible by 5. It is a sufficient condition that a numeral end in 0 or 5 for the number to be divisible by 5. It is also a necessary condition that a numeral end in 0 or 5 for the number to be divisible by 5.

CHECK YOUR UNDERSTANDING
For a number to be an even number, is it a sufficient condition that the number be divisible by 2?

yes

Conditional

Also called Implication *or* If then statement.
A statement of the form *if p then q*. The following is an example of a conditional:

> *If* a triangle has three sides of the same length,
>   *then* it is an equilateral triangle.

The part following *if* is called an antecedent; and the part following *then,* a consequent. A conditional is false only when the antecedent (p) is true and the consequent (q) is false.

CHECK YOUR UNDERSTANDING
Is this statement a conditional? 5 added to 6 is 11

no, because it is not of the form if p then q

Cone

A three-dimensional geometric shape (solid) that has a circular base and a surface from the boundary of the base to the vertex. A cone is a right cone if its axis is perpendicular to the base; otherwise it is an oblique cone.

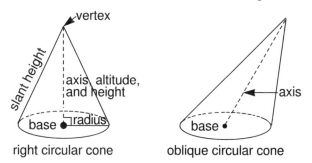

right circular cone   oblique circular cone

See also Lateral area, Surface area, *and* Volume.

CHECK YOUR UNDERSTANDING
Can a right cone be formed by rotating a right triangle about one leg?

yes

Congruent (≅)

Two geometric figures that are the same shape and size. Two angles are congruent if they have the same measure. Two line segments are congruent if they are the same length.

Triangles ABC and DEF are congruent. Their corresponding sides are of the same length and their corresponding angles are of the same measure:

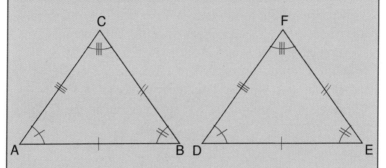

$$\triangle ABC \cong \triangle DEF$$
↑ is congruent to

$$\overline{AB} \cong \overline{DE} \qquad \overline{BC} \cong \overline{EF} \qquad \overline{AC} \cong \overline{DF}$$
$$\angle A \cong \angle D \qquad \angle B \cong \angle E \qquad \angle C \cong \angle F$$

It is common practice to mark corresponding parts with the same marks to indicate their congruence, as is done in the picture above.

CHECK YOUR UNDERSTANDING

What angle in triangle DEF is congruent to angle C in triangle ABC?

angle F

Conjecture

A statement that has not been proved to be true nor shown to be false.

CHECK YOUR UNDERSTANDING

Statement: Any even number greater than 2 can be shown as a sum of two prime numbers, for example 12 = 5 + 7. As of now, this has not been proved. Is this a conjecture?

yes

Conjunction

A statement of the form *p and q*. Two simple statements are connected with *and*. An example of a conjunction is:

I am in the 9th grade **and** I am on the basketball team.

To tell if a conjunction is true or false, the truth value of each of the two simple statements needs to be known. All cases of a conjunction are summarized in the truth table below.

p	q	p and q
T	T	T
T	F	F
F	T	F
F	F	F

CHECK YOUR UNDERSTANDING

What is the truth value of a conjunction when one simple statement is true and one is false?

false

Consecutive

Immediately following each other in some order. For example, 5 and 6 are consecutive whole numbers; 5 and 7 are not. 2 and 4 are consecutive even numbers.

CHECK YOUR UNDERSTANDING

Are 9 and 11 consecutive odd numbers ?

yes

76

Consistent system of equations

Also called Simultaneous equations. Two or more equations that have at least one common solution.

Consistent System of Equations	Common Solution
$x + y = 9$	(x,y)
$x - y = 1$	$(5,4)$

C

If a system of two or more equations does not have a common solution, then the system is *inconsistent.*

Inconsistent System of Equations   No Common Solution

$$x + y = 5$$
$$2x + 2y = 6$$

See also System of equations.

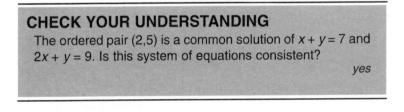

CHECK YOUR UNDERSTANDING

The ordered pair (2,5) is a common solution of $x + y = 7$ and $2x + y = 9$. Is this system of equations consistent?

yes

Constant

A symbol representing a value that doesn't change.

EXAMPLES 6 π $^-\sqrt{2}$

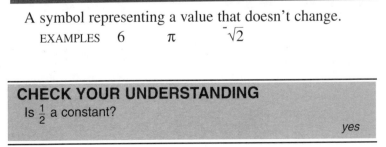

CHECK YOUR UNDERSTANDING

Is $\frac{1}{2}$ a constant?

yes

Constant function

A function whose equation is of the form $y = c$; that is, every value of y is the same number. For example, $y = 2$ is a constant function. The y-coordinate is always 2. The graph of a constant function is a horizontal line.

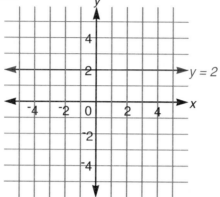

Vertical lines **do not** represent functions. For example, $x = 4$ is a relation that is not a function.

CHECK YOUR UNDERSTANDING
In the graph above, if $x = {}^-4$, then what is y equal to?

2

Constant of variation

See Direct variation.

Construction

A geometric construction made only with a compass and a straightedge. The straightedge is used to draw line segments. The compass is used to transfer equal distances and draw arcs and circles.

CONSTRUCTING CONGRUENT LINE SEGMENTS

To construct a segment congruent to segment MN:
Draw a line. Open the compass to length MN and transfer the distance to the line. Mark the distance PQ. Segment PQ is the same length as segment MN.

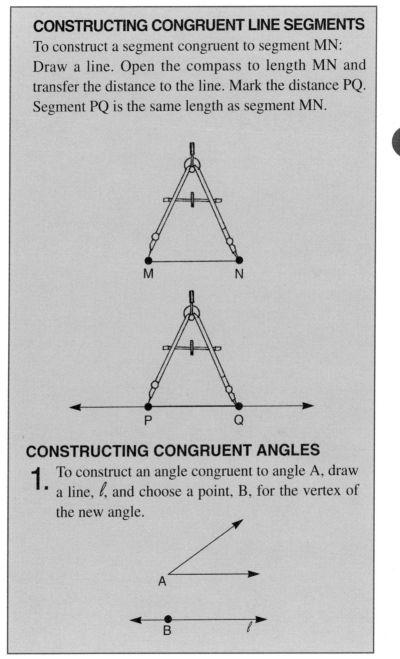

CONSTRUCTING CONGRUENT ANGLES

1. To construct an angle congruent to angle A, draw a line, ℓ, and choose a point, B, for the vertex of the new angle.

2. Open the compass, place the point of the compass on the vertex of ∠ A, and make an arc that crosses both sides. Then, without changing the size of the compass opening, place the point of the compass on point B, and make an arc like the first one.

3. Next, place the point of the compass where the arc crosses one side of ∠ A. Adjust the compass so the pencil point touches where the arc crosses the other side. Without changing the compass opening, mark this distance on the arc for ∠ B.

4. Draw a line from vertex B through the intersection of the arcs to form the other side of ∠ B.

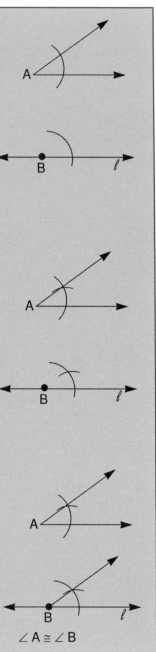

∠ A ≅ ∠ B

CONSTRUCTING ANGLE BISECTORS
To construct the bisector of angle ACB:

1. Draw an arc with the center at C. Label the points where the arc intersects the sides of the angle M and N.

2. With the center at M, draw an arc. Using the same compass opening, draw an arc with center at N. Label the point where the two arcs intersect X.

3. Draw $\overline{CX}$.
$\overline{CX}$ bisects angle C.

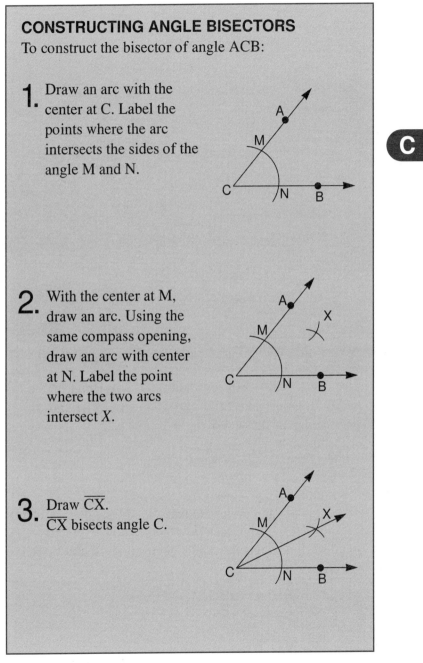

CONSTRUCTING PERPENDICULAR LINES AND SEGMENT BISECTORS.

To construct perpendicular lines, draw a straight angle (an angle of 180°) and bisect it into two angles of 90°. Extend the bisector through point D to form four right angles.

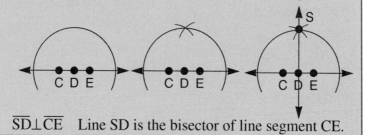

$\overline{SD} \perp \overline{CE}$ Line SD is the bisector of line segment CE.

CHECK YOUR UNDERSTANDING

Under the "rules of construction", is it permissible to measure off 1 inch with a ruler in constructing a segment 1 inch long?

no

Contrapositive

The contrapositive of a conditional is a denial of the part following *if* and the part following *then* and an interchange of the two parts.

Conditional, *if p then q*:
If a triangle has all three sides of the same length, then it is an equilateral triangle.

Contrapositive, *if not q then not p*:
If it is not an equilateral triangle, then it does not have all three sides of the same length.

A conditional and its contrapositive have the same truth value.

CHECK YOUR UNDERSTANDING

Is the second statement a contrapositive of the first statement? If $2x = 4$, then $x = 2$.   If $x \neq 2$, then $2x \neq 4$.

yes

Converse

The converse of a conditional is obtained by interchanging the parts following *if* and *then*. A converse of a conditional, *if p then q*, is *if q then p*.

Conditional, *if p then q*: **Converse,** *if q then p*:
If $x = 5$, then $2x = 10$. If $2x = 10$, then $x = 5$.

Convex polygon

A polygon is convex if the segment connecting any two points in the interior of the polygon is in the interior of the polygon.

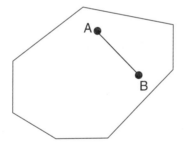

Polygons that are not convex are concave.

Coordinate geometry

Geometry based on the coordinate system.

See also Coordinate Geometry Formulas *on page 457.*

Coordinate system

Also called Rectangular coordinate system. A method of locating points in the plane or in space by means of numbers. A point in a plane can be located by its distances from both a horizontal and a vertical line called the axes. The horizontal line is called the *x*-axis. The vertical line is called the *y*-axis. The pairs of numbers are called ordered pairs. The first number, called the *x*-coordinate, designates the distance along the horizontal axis. The second number, called the *y*-coordinate, designates the distance along the vertical axis. The point at which the two axes intersect has the coordinates (0,0) and is called the origin.

The axes separate the coordinate plane into four quadrants.

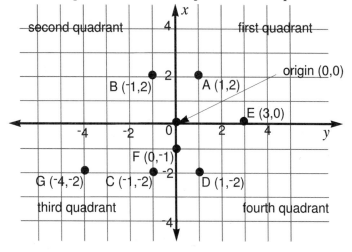

Signs of the coordinates of all points in each quadrant:

<table>
<tr><td>first quadrant</td><td>second quadrant</td></tr>
<tr><td>(+,+)</td><td>(−,+)</td></tr>
<tr><td>third quadrant</td><td>fourth quadrant</td></tr>
<tr><td>(−,−)</td><td>(+,−)</td></tr>
</table>

Every point on the *x*-axis has 0 for its second coordinate.
Every point on the *y*-axis has 0 for its first coordinate.

Coordinates

An ordered pair of numbers that locates a point in the coordinate plane with reference to the *x*- and *y*-axes. In general, coordinates are written:

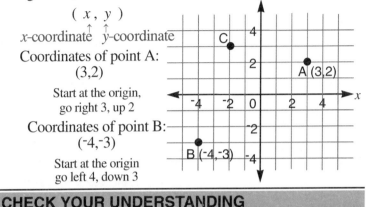

(*x*, *y*)

x-coordinate *y*-coordinate

Coordinates of point A:
(3,2)

Start at the origin,
go right 3, up 2

Coordinates of point B:
(-4,-3)

Start at the origin
go left 4, down 3

CHECK YOUR UNDERSTANDING

What are the coordinates of Point C above?

(-2,3)

Coplanar

Lying in the same plane.

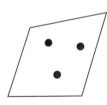
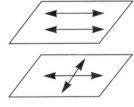
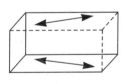

Coplanar points
Given any three points there is a plane that contains them.

Coplanar lines
Two lines are coplanar if they are parallel or they intersect.

Noncoplanar lines or skew lines
There is no plane that can contain them.

CHECK YOUR UNDERSTANDING

Are two lines that meet at right angles (perpendicular lines) coplanar?

yes

Correspondence

Also called Mapping *or* Transformation. Matching of members in one set with members in another set.

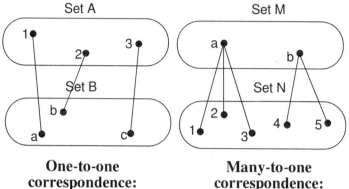

One-to-one correspondence:	Many-to-one correspondence:
Each member of set A is matched with exactly one member of set B and vice versa.	One member of set M is matched with more than one member of set N.

Sets that are in one-to-one correspondence are equivalent sets. Two finite equivalent sets have the same number of members. Two infinite sets are equivalent if there is a pattern that proves a one-to-one correspondence. For example, the set of all counting numbers, C, is equivalent to the set of all even numbers, E:

$$
\begin{array}{ccccccc}
C & 1 & 2 & 3 & 4 & 5 & 6\ldots \\
  & | & | & | & | & | & | \\
E & 2 & 4 & 6 & 8 & 10 & 12\ldots
\end{array}
$$

In general, n in set C is matched with $2n$ in set E. This pattern continues without end.

CHECK YOUR UNDERSTANDING
Are the sets {3, 5, 7} and {a, b, c} equivalent?

yes

86

Corresponding parts

See Congruent.

Corresponding points

See Reflection.

Cosine

See Trigonometric ratios.

C

Cotangent

See Trigonometric ratios.

Counterexample

An example that shows a general statement to be false.

EXAMPLE Statement: All numbers are even.

Counterexample: 3 is a number and it is not even.

It is sufficient to produce one counterexample to prove the statement false.

CHECK YOUR UNDERSTANDING

Does the following counterexample prove the statement false? Statement: Each number is divisible by 3. Counterexample: 10 is a number and it is not divisible by 3.

yes

Counting numbers

Also called natural numbers. Numbers used to answer "how many?". The counting numbers are 1, 2, 3, 4, 5, 6, ... The set of counting numbers is infinite (unending). There is no largest counting number.

CHECK YOUR UNDERSTANDING

What is the smallest counting number?

1

Cross-multiplication

Cross-multiplication is used to tell whether fractions are equal and proportions are true.

Fractions   Proportions

$$\frac{2}{3} \stackrel{?}{\bowtie} \frac{8}{12} \qquad \frac{5}{7} \stackrel{?}{\bowtie} \frac{2.5}{3.5}$$

$$2 \times 12 \stackrel{?}{=} 3 \times 8 \qquad 5 \times 3.5 \stackrel{?}{=} 7 \times 2.5$$

$$24 = 24 \qquad\qquad 17.5 = 17.5$$

The cross products are equal.   The cross products are equal.

$$\text{So, } \frac{2}{3} = \frac{8}{12} \qquad \text{The proportion } \frac{5}{7} = \frac{2.5}{3.5} \text{ is true.}$$

Cross-multiplication is also used to solve proportions.

$$\frac{3}{5} = \frac{x}{12}$$

$$3 \times 12 = 5 \times x$$

$$36 = 5x$$

$$\frac{36}{5} = x$$

$$7.2 = x$$

CHECK YOUR UNDERSTANDING
Use cross-multiplication to tell if the proportion $\frac{2}{5} = \frac{10}{20}$ is true or false.

false, 40 ≠ 50

Cube

A rectangular solid in which every face is a square and every edge is of the same length.

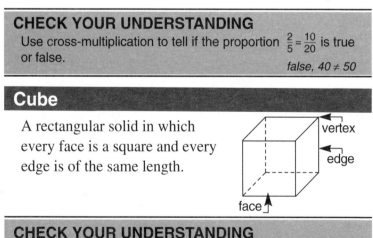

CHECK YOUR UNDERSTANDING
How many faces, edges, and vertices does a cube have?

6 faces, 12 edges, 8 vertices

Cubed

Raised to the third power.

EXAMPLE

$$7^3 \;=\; 7 \;\times\; 7 \;\times\; 7 \;=\; 343$$

↑   ↑
7 cubed or 7 to the third power   cube of 7

CHECK YOUR UNDERSTANDING   **C**

How would you write 10 cubed?

10^3 or 10 to the third power

Cube root ($\sqrt[3]{}$)

The cube root of a number, n, is a number whose cube is that number. For example, the cube root of 8 is 2 because $2^3 = 8$. In general, $\sqrt[3]{n} = a$ if $a^3 = n$.

OTHER EXAMPLES

$$\sqrt[3]{64} = 4 \qquad \sqrt[3]{125} = 5 \qquad \sqrt[3]{216} = 6$$

Think: $4^3 = 64$.   Think: $5^3 = 125$.   Think: $6^3 = 216$.

CHECK YOUR UNDERSTANDING

What is $\sqrt[3]{27}$ equal to?

3

Cubic centimeter (cm³)

A cubic centimeter is a unit for measuring volume. It is the volume of a cube with each edge 1 centimeter long. It holds 1 milliliter of liquid.

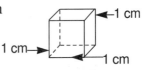

CHECK YOUR UNDERSTANDING

How many cubic centimeters are there in a cube with each edge 2 cm long?

8

Cubic decimeter (dm³)

One cubic decimeter, denoted by dm^3, is a unit for measuring volume. It is the volume of a cube with each edge 1 dm long. Since 1 dm = 10 cm, there are $10 \times 10 \times 10$ or 1,000 cm^3 in one cubic decimeter.

$1 dm^3 = 1,000 \, cm^3$ $1,000 \, cm^3 = 1,000 \, mL$ $1,000 \, ml = 1 \, L$

A container with a volume of one cubic decimeter holds 1 liter.

CHECK YOUR UNDERSTANDING
What fraction of 1 dm^3 is 1 cm^3?

one-thousandth or 0.001

Cubic equation

An equation in which the highest degree of a term is 3. For example, $x + 3 + 3x^2 - 4x^3 = 0$ is a cubic equation. We also say that the equation is of the third degree.

CHECK YOUR UNDERSTANDING
Is $x^2 + x - 3 = 0$ a cubic equation?

no

Cubic meter (m³)

A cubic meter is a unit for measuring volume. It is the volume of a cube with each edge 1m long. Since 1 m = 100 cm, there are $100 \times 100 \times 100$ or 1,000,000 cm^3 in one cubic meter.

$$1 \, m^3 = 1,000,000 \, cm^3$$

A container with a volume of one cubic meter holds 1,000 liters of liquid.

CHECK YOUR UNDERSTANDING
How many liters will a container with a volume of 2 m^3 hold?

2,000

Cup

Liquid measure of capacity. There are 2 cups in 1 pint.

CHECK YOUR UNDERSTANDING

What fraction of 1 pint is 1 cup?

$\frac{1}{2}$

Customary system of measurement

C

A system of measurement used in the United States. The basic units of length, capacity, and weight are shown below.

Length	Capacity (Liquid)
12 inches (in.) = 1 foot (ft)	8 ounces (oz) = 1 cup (c)
3 feet = 1 yard	2 cups = 1 pint
1,760 yards = 1 mile (mi)	2 pints = 1 quart
5,280 ft = 1 mile	

Weight

16 ounces (oz) =1 pound (lb)

2,000 pounds =1 ton (t)

Sometimes you need to convert from one unit to another when adding, subtracting, multiplying, and dividing with customary units.

6 ft 8 in.

+ 9 in.

6 ft 17 in. = 7 ft 5 in.

4 gal 1 qt = 3 gal 5 qt

– 1 gal 3 qt = – 1 gal 3 qt

2 gal 2 qt

8 lb 4 oz

× 5

40 lb 20 oz = 41 lb 4 oz

550 lb

4)1t 200 lb = 4)2200 lb

CHECK YOUR UNDERSTANDING

What fraction of 1 yard is 1 foot?

$\frac{1}{3}$

Cylinder

A solid figure (three-dimensional geometric shape or space figure) with two congruent parallel bases usually in the shape of a circle and the cylindrical surface connecting the two bases. A cylinder is a right circular cylinder if its axis is perpendicular to the base.

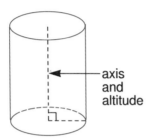

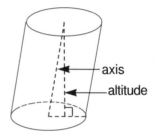

right circular cylinder   oblique circular cylinder

See also Lateral area, Surface area, *and* Volume.

CHECK YOUR UNDERSTANDING

Can a cylinder be formed by rotating a rectangle on one of its sides?

yes

Deca-

See Deka-.

Decagon

A polygon with ten sides.

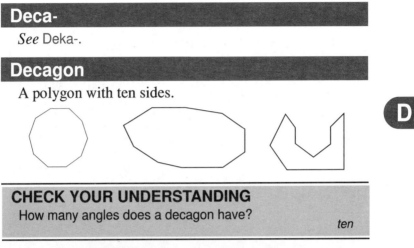

CHECK YOUR UNDERSTANDING

How many angles does a decagon have?

ten

Deci-

The prefix deci- means "one tenth".

Decigram (dm) means "one tenth of a gram" (g).

$$1 \text{ dm} = \tfrac{1}{10} \text{ g or } 0.1 \text{ g.}$$

A decigram is a unit of mass in the metric system.

Deciliter (dL) means "one tenth of a liter" (L).

$$1 \text{ dL} = \tfrac{1}{10} \text{ L} = 0.1 \text{ L.}$$

A deciliter is a unit of capacity in the metric system.

Decimeter (dm) means "one tenth of a meter" (m).

$$1 \text{ dm} = \tfrac{1}{10} \text{ m} = 0.1 \text{ m.}$$

A decimeter is a unit of length in the metric system.

CHECK YOUR UNDERSTANDING

What would *decidollar* mean if it were a word?

$\tfrac{1}{10}$ *of a dollar or 10¢*

Decimal

A number with a decimal point in it, such as 5.36, 0.04, or 0.3

DECIMAL PLACE VALUE

The value of digits in a decimal is based on the number ten. The chart shows the values of the digits to the right of the decimal point. The decimal point is read as *and*.

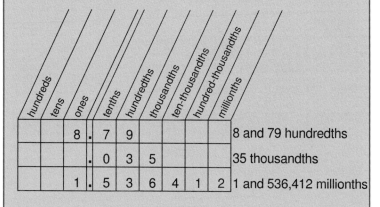

hundreds	tens	ones	.	tenths	hundredths	thousandths	ten-thousandths	hundred-thousandths	millionths	
		8	.	7	9					8 and 79 hundredths
			.	0	3	5				35 thousandths
		1	.	5	3	6	4	1	2	1 and 536,412 millionths

Another way to read 8.79 is eight *point* seven, nine.

Word form: six thousand forty-two ten-thousandths.
Standard form: 0.6042.
Expanded form: 0.6 + 0.00 + 0.004 + 0.0002 or
  (6 × 0.1) + (0 × 0.01) + (4 × 0.001) + (2 × 0.0001)
Equivalent decimals: Writing extra zeros after the last digit in a decimal does not change the value. The decimals 0.5, 0.50, and 0.500 are equivalent decimals.

COMPARING AND ORDERING DECIMALS
Compare 0.5832 and 0.584.

Line up the decimal points.	Start at the left and compare the digits in each place.	5 = 5, 8 = 8, 4 > 3, so 0.584 > 0.5832.
0.5832 0.584	0.5832 0.584	$0.584 > 0.5832$ is greater than

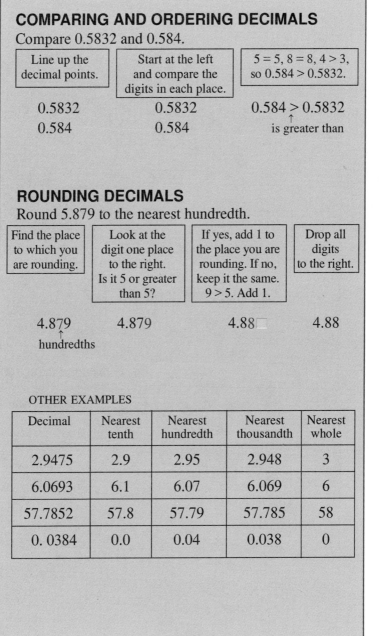

ROUNDING DECIMALS
Round 5.879 to the nearest hundredth.

Find the place to which you are rounding.	Look at the digit one place to the right. Is it 5 or greater than 5?	If yes, add 1 to the place you are rounding. If no, keep it the same. 9 > 5. Add 1.	Drop all digits to the right.
4.879 hundredths	4.879	4.88☐	4.88

OTHER EXAMPLES

Decimal	Nearest tenth	Nearest hundredth	Nearest thousandth	Nearest whole
2.9475	2.9	2.95	2.948	3
6.0693	6.1	6.07	6.069	6
57.7852	57.8	57.79	57.785	58
0.0384	0.0	0.04	0.038	0

D

ADDING DECIMALS

Add: 23.42 + 57.8 + 61.93.

STEP 1	STEP 2	STEP 3
Line up the decimal places. Annex zeros when necessary.	Add the same as whole numbers.	Place the decimal point in the answer in line with those above.

$$
\begin{array}{r}
23.42 \\
57.80 \\
+\,61.93 \\
\end{array}
\qquad
\begin{array}{r}
23.42 \\
57.80 \\
+\,61.93 \\
\hline
143\ 15
\end{array}
\qquad
\begin{array}{r}
23.42 \\
57.80 \\
+\,61.93 \\
\hline
143.15
\end{array}
$$

SUBTRACTING DECIMALS

Subtract: 65.2 − 32.46

STEP 1	STEP 2	STEP 3
Line up the decimal places. Annex zeros when necessary.	Subtract the same as whole numbers.	Place the decimal point in the answer in line with those above.

$$
\begin{array}{r}
65.20 \\
-\,32.46 \\
\end{array}
\qquad
\begin{array}{r}
65.20 \\
-\,32.46 \\
\hline
32\ 74
\end{array}
\qquad
\begin{array}{r}
65.20 \\
-\,32.46 \\
\hline
32.74
\end{array}
$$

MULTIPLYING DECIMALS

Multiply: 6.3×0.8

Multiply as with whole numbers. The number of decimal places in the product is the sum of decimal places in the factors.

$6.3 \rightarrow 1$ decimal place
$\times\ \underline{0.8} \rightarrow 1$ decimal place
$5.04 \rightarrow 2$ decimal places

OTHER EXAMPLES

$5.27 \rightarrow 2$ decimal places
$\times\ \underline{2.6} \rightarrow 1$ decimal place
$3\ 162$
$\underline{10\ 54}$
$13.702 \rightarrow 3$ decimal places

$0.75 \longrightarrow 2$ decimal places
$\times\ \underline{0.0009} \longrightarrow 4$ decimal places
$0.0\underset{\uparrow}{0}0675 \rightarrow 6$ decimal places

Annex zeros in the product to place the decimal point when necessary.

DIVIDING DECIMALS BY WHOLE NUMBERS

Divide: $37.2 \div 8$

Place the decimal point. Divide the whole number part.	Divide as with whole numbers. Annex zeros when necessary to complete the division.

$$\begin{array}{r} 4. \\ 8\overline{)37.2} \\ \underline{-32} \\ 5 \end{array}$$

$$\begin{array}{r} 4.65 \\ 8\overline{)37.20} \\ \underline{-32} \\ 5\,2 \\ \underline{-4\,8} \\ 40 \\ \underline{-40} \\ 0 \end{array}$$

Check: $\begin{array}{r} 4.65 \\ \times\ \underline{8} \\ 37.20 \end{array}$

DIVIDING DECIMALS BY DECIMALS

Divide: $6.4\overline{)362.88}$

| Multiply the divisor by a power of ten to make it a whole number. | Multiply the dividend by the same power of ten. | Divide. | Check. |

$$.64\overline{)36.288} \qquad 64\overline{)3628.8}$$

$$\begin{array}{r} 56.7 \\ 64\overline{)3628.8} \\ -\underline{320} \\ 428 \\ -\underline{384} \\ 448 \\ -\underline{448} \\ 0 \end{array}$$

$$\begin{array}{r} 56.7 \\ \times\,.64 \\ \hline 2268 \\ \underline{3402} \\ 36.288 \end{array}$$

DECIMALS TO FRACTIONS

A terminating decimal can be written as a fraction with a denominator that is a power of 10.

$$0.87 = 87 \text{ hundredths} = \frac{87}{100}$$

$$0.8 = 8 \text{ tenths} = \frac{8}{10} \text{ or } \frac{4}{5} \leftarrow \text{lowest terms}$$

$$0.087 = 87 \text{ thousandths} = \frac{87}{1000}$$

$$6.8 = 6 \text{ and } 8 \text{ tenths} = 6\frac{8}{10} = 6\frac{4}{5}$$

DECIMALS TO PERCENTS

To write 0.9 as a percent, first change 0.9 to a fraction with a denominator of 100.

$$0.9 = 0.90 = \frac{90}{100} = 90\%, \text{ so } 0.9 = 90\%$$

A shortcut for writing a decimal as a percent is to move the decimal point 2 places to the right.

$$0.85 \longrightarrow 0.85 \longrightarrow 85\%$$

REPEATING DECIMAL AS A FRACTION

Every repeating decimal can be written as a fraction. To write a repeating decimal as a fraction, use the following:

$$0.\overline{1} = \frac{1}{9}, \ 0.\overline{01} = \frac{1}{99}, \ 0.\overline{001} = \frac{1}{999}, \text{ and so on.}$$

Write $0.\overline{7}$ as a fraction.

$$0.\overline{7} = 7 \times 0.\overline{1} = 7 \times \frac{1}{9} = \frac{7}{9}$$

Write $0.\overline{36}$ as a fraction in lowest terms (simplest form).

$$0.\overline{36} = 36 \times 0.\overline{01} = 36 \times \frac{1}{99} = 36 \times \frac{1}{99} = \frac{36}{99} = \frac{4}{11}$$

D

See also Power of ten – **SHORT CUTS FOR MULTIPLYING DECIMALS BY POWERS OF TEN.**

CHECK YOUR UNDERSTANDING
What is the name of the place two places to the right of the decimal point?

one hundredth

Decimal numeration system

A system for writing names for numbers based on the number ten. It is a positional system; that is, each place has its value that is a power of ten. The value of each place is shown below, using exponents.

$34,598.267 = (3 \times 10^4) + (4 \times 10^3) + (5 \times 10^2) + (9 \times 10^1) + (8 \times 10^0) + (2 \times 10^{-1}) + (6 \times 10^{-2}) + (7 \times 10^{-3})$

See also Decimal place value *for the names of some of the places in this system.*

CHECK YOUR UNDERSTANDING

What is the value of the first place just to the right of the decimal point in a numeral in base ten?

one tenth

Decimal point

A dot in a decimal used to separate the whole number from the decimal part, like in 34.6. The decimal point is read "point" or "and". The decimal 34.6 is read thirty-four *point* six or thirty-four *and* six tenths.

CHECK YOUR UNDERSTANDING

How would you write the standard numeral for sixteen and five hundredths?

16.05

Decomposition method of subtraction

See Subtraction.

Deduction

Also called Deductive thinking *or* deductive reasoning. A method of reasoning in which the beginning point is an assumption and the conclusion is reached by a sequence of logical steps. For example,

Assumption: $2x + 3 = 13$

Deduce to the conclusion: $x = 5$

$2x + 3 = 13$	Assumption
$2x + 3 - 3 = 13 - 3$	Property of subtraction for equations
$2x + 0 = 10$	Arithmetic facts $(3 - 3 = 0, 13 - 3 = 10)$
$2x = 10$	Property of zero for addition
$\dfrac{2x}{2} = \dfrac{10}{2}$	Division property of equations
$1 \cdot x = 5$	Arithmetic facts $(2 \div 2 = 1, 10 \div 2 = 5)$
$x = 5$	Property of 1 for multiplication

D

CHECK YOUR UNDERSTANDING
What is the beginning point of deductive reasoning?

assumption

Deficient number

A number for which the sum of the proper factors (factors of the number except the number itself) is less than the number. For example, 9 is a deficient number. Its proper factors are 1 and 3. $1 + 3 < 9$.

See also Abundant number, amicable number, *and* perfect number.

CHECK YOUR UNDERSTANDING
Is 8 a deficient number?

yes; 1 + 2 + 4 = 7; 7 < 8

Degree

Of a monomial The degree of a term is the exponent of the variable.

$$3x^4 \qquad \text{The degree is 4.}$$

When a term has more than one variable, then its degree is the sum of the exponents of all the variables.

$$^-6x^2y^5 \qquad \text{The degree is } 2 + 5 \text{ or } 7.$$

Of a polynomial or equation The degree of a polynomial or of an equation in one variable is the degree of the term with the highest exponent.

$$5x^3 - 3x^2 + 1 \qquad\qquad y + 1 = 2y^5 - 3$$
$$\text{The degree is 3.} \qquad \text{The degree is 5.}$$

The degree of a polynomial with more than one variable is the highest sum of the exponents among the terms.

$$3x^2y - 5xyz^2$$
$$\underset{2+1=3}{} \quad \underset{1+1+2=4}{}$$

The degree is 4.

Of angle measure (°) A unit for measuring angles. One degree (°) is one three-hundred-sixtieth ($\frac{1}{360}$) of a complete revolution. A complete revolution has 360°. Another way to look at this unit is in terms of a circle. Think of a central angle that is one three-hundred-sixtieth of the entire circle. Then the measure of that central angle is 1°.

One degree is equal to 60 minutes ('): $1° = 60'$.
One minute is equal to 60 seconds (") : $1' = 60"$.

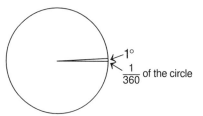

102

Of temperature A unit for measuring temperature. There are two kinds of units commonly used, Celsius (°C) and Fahrenheit (°F). Another unit, Kelvin, is used by scientists.

See also Celsius, Fahrenheit, *and* Kelvin.

D

Deka-

Also spelled deca-.

The prefix deka- means "ten".

Dekagram (dag) means "ten grams" (g).

$$1 \text{ dag} = 10 \text{ g}$$

A dekagram is a unit of mass in the metric system. The mass of ten peanuts is about 1 dg.

Dekaliter (daL) means "ten liters" (L).

$$1 \text{ daL} = 10 \text{ L}$$

A dekaliter is a unit of capacity in the metric system. A large punch bowl holds about 1 daL of soda.

Dekameter (dam) means "ten meters" (m).

$$1 \text{ dam} = 10 \text{ m}$$

A dekameter is a unit of length in the metric system. A dam is a little less than 11 yd.

Denial of a statement

Also called negation of a statement. In logic, the denial of statement *p* is *not p* (~p).

EXAMPLE

Statement: The product of 3 and 5 is 15 (p).

Denial: The product of 3 and 5 is not 15 (~p).

The truth table shows the two cases of truth values of a statement and its denial.

p	~p
T	F
F	T

So, the denial of a true statement is false. The denial of a false statement is true.

CHECK YOUR UNDERSTANDING
What is the denial of the statement,4 is an even number? Is the statement true? Is its denial true?

4 is not an even number; yes; no

Denominate number

A number used with a unit of measurement, such as 6 ft, 2 in., 5 gal, 8 lb.

CHECK YOUR UNDERSTANDING
Is 7 a denominate number?

no, it does not show a unit of measure

Denominator

The number named by the numeral below the fraction bar. In $\frac{3}{4}$ the denominator is 4.

CHECK YOUR UNDERSTANDING
What is the denominator in $\frac{5}{6}$?

6

Density property

A property that states that between any two fractions or any two rational numbers there is another fraction or another rational number, respectively. From this fact one can show that between any two rational numbers there is an infinite number of rational numbers.

D

Dependent equation

See System of equations.

Dependent event

In probability, an event whose outcome depends on the outcome of a previous event. For example, 6 slips of papers with letters A, B, C, D, E, F are placed in a hat. One slip is drawn and is not put back into the hat. Then a second slip is drawn. This is a dependent event, since the outcome of the second draw depends on the outcome of the first draw.

$$\boxed{A}\ \boxed{B}\ \boxed{C}\ \boxed{D}\ \boxed{E}\ \boxed{F}$$

P(C), the probability of drawing C, on the first draw is $\frac{1}{6}$, but the probability of drawing, say A, P(A), on the second draw is $\frac{1}{5}$, since there are now only 5 letters in the hat. The probability of drawing C then A, P(C, A) is $\frac{1}{6} \times \frac{1}{5}$ or $\frac{1}{30}$.

Dependent system of equations

See System of equations.

Dependent variable

In a function of two variables, one variable is dependent and the other independent. For example, in $y = 2x + 1$, y is the dependent variable. Its value depends on the value of x. If the value of x is 3, then the value of y is $y = 2 \cdot 3 + 1$ or 7.

CHECK YOUR UNDERSTANDING

In $y = 2x + 1$, what is the value of the dependent variable y, if the value of x is 2?

5

Derived equation

Any equation obtained from a given equation by performing the same operation on each side of the given equation.

EXAMPLE $2x = 3$ $4x^2 = 9$ is a derived equation. Each side of the equation $2x = 3$ was squared.

CHECK YOUR UNDERSTANDING

What is the derived equation obtained by adding 2 to each side of the equation $3x = 2$?

$3x + 2 = 4$

Descending order of a polynomial

The arrangement of terms of a polynomial from largest to smallest powers of the variable. The following polynomial is in descending order:

$$3x^4 - 2x^3 + 7x^2 - 5x^1 + 8.$$

CHECK YOUR UNDERSTANDING

Write the following polynomial in descending order:
$$x^2 + 3x^3 - x$$

$$3x^3 + x^2 - x$$

In a polygon A segment joining two nonconsecutive vertices. In the picture, segment AC is one diagonal.

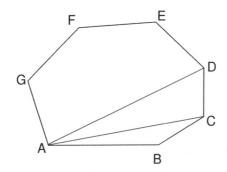

In a polyhedron A segment joining two vertices of a polyhedron that are in different faces of a polyhedron. In the picture, segment XY is one diagonal.

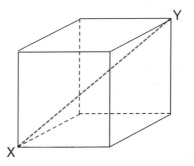

D

CHECK YOUR UNDERSTANDING
What is the other diagonal drawn in the polygon above?
segment AD

Diagram

See Venn diagram.

Diameter

Of a circle A segment connecting two points on the circle and passing through the center. AB is a diameter of circle O. The term is also used to denote the length of such a segment.

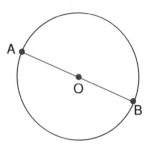

Of a sphere A segment connecting two points on a sphere and passing through the center.

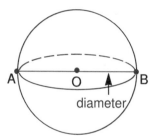

CHECK YOUR UNDERSTANDING
Is AO a diameter?

no

Difference

In arithmetic, a name of the result of subtraction.

$$8 - 3 = 5$$
↑
difference

CHECK YOUR UNDERSTANDING
Which number is the difference in $12 - 3 = 9$?

9

Difference of two squares

An algebraic expression of the form $x^2 - y^2$.
The difference of two squares can be factored as
shown below.

$$x^2 - y^2 = (x + y)(x - y)$$

NUMBER EXAMPLE $7^2 - 3^2 = (7 + 3)(7 - 3)$.

To verify that this is true, perform the operations:

$$7^2 - 3^2 \overset{?}{=} (7 + 3)(7 - 3)$$
$$49 - 9 \overset{?}{=} 10 \times 4$$
$$40 = 40$$

D

Digit

In the base-ten numeration system, any one of these
ten numerals: 0, 1, 2, 3, 4, 5, 6, 7, 8, 9.

CHECK YOUR UNDERSTANDING
How many digits are there in 32,408?

five

Dihedral angle

An angle formed by two half-planes intersecting in a
line. The half-planes are the faces of the
dihedral angle and the line of intersection
is the edge of the angle. Angle XYZ
is the plane angle of the
dihedral angle. It is formed
by rays YX and YZ perpendicular
to line ℓ and meeting in point Y.

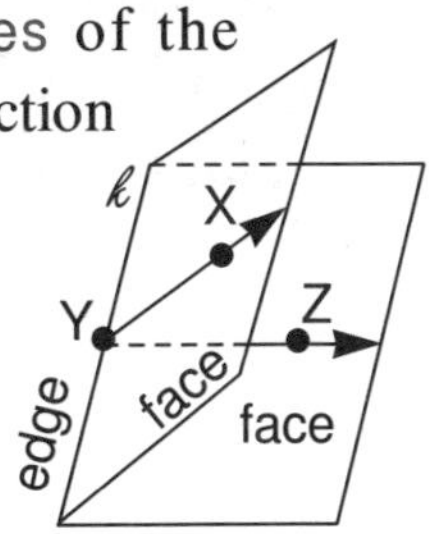

CHECK YOUR UNDERSTANDING
A dihedral angle is formed by the intersection of what two
geometric figures?

half-planes

Dimension

In coordinate geometry The number of coordinates required to represent a point. One number is needed to represent a point on a line. Therefore, a line has one dimension. Two numbers (a pair) are required to represent a point in a plane. Therefore, a plane has two dimensions. Three numbers (a triple) are needed to represent a point in space. Therefore, space has three dimensions.

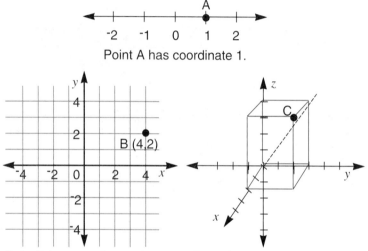

Point A has coordinate 1.

Point B has coordinates (4,2).   Point C has coordinates (2,3,4).

Of geometric figures The lengths of sides of geometric figures. For example, for the rectangle below, the dimensions are: length 3 cm, width 2 cm.

length 3 cm

width 2 cm

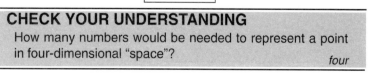

CHECK YOUR UNDERSTANDING
How many numbers would be needed to represent a point in four-dimensional "space"?

four

Direct variation

A linear function of the form $y = cx$, where c is the *constant of variation;* $c \neq 0$. We say that y is directly proportional to x. That is, y varies directly as x varies. If x is doubled, tripled or halved, then y is also doubled, tripled, or halved. If x increases 1 unit, then y increases c units.

Consider the direct variation $y = 5x$.

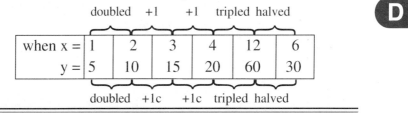

	doubled	+1	+1	tripled	halved
when x =	1	2	3	4	12	6
y =	5	10	15	20	60	30
	doubled	+1c	+1c	tripled	halved

CHECK YOUR UNDERSTANDING
Is $y = 9x$ a direct variation?

yes

Directed number

See Signed number.

Directly proportional

See Direct variation.

Discount

A reduction applied to a given price. A discount of 10% on an item costing $50 is $50 × 0.10 or $5. The discount of $5 reduces the price of the item by $5. The discount rate in this case is 10%. The discounted price or sale price is $45.

CHECK YOUR UNDERSTANDING
What is the dollar amount of discount of 5% on an item whose regular price is $100?

$5

Discrete Mathematics

That part of mathematics which commonly includes such concepts as sets, functions and relations, logic, combinations and permutations, graph theory, methods of proof, Boolean algebra, simple probability, and algorithms. Discrete mathematics deals with counting problems. For example, finding the number of two-digit odd numbers is a problem in discrete mathematics. The concept of discrete is opposite to that of continuous. For example, when solving a problem involving an aircraft in the process of landing, in discrete mathematics one would give a finite set of positions of the aircraft, rather than its continuous path.

CHECK YOUR UNDERSTANDING

Is the following a discrete mathematics problem?
You find the volume of a jar is 10 cups by filling it with10 cups of waters.

yes

Discriminant

For a quadratic equation of the form $ax^2 + bx + c = 0$, the *discriminant* is $b^2 - 4ac$.

Equation :	Discriminant :
$3x^2 - 4x + 1 = 0$	$b^2 - 4ac$
abc	$(^-4)^2 - (4)(3)(1)$ or 4.

The discriminant shows the nature of the solutions (roots).

$b^2 - 4ac \geq 0$.	Solutions are real numbers.
$b^2 - 4ac = 0$.	Solutions are equal (one solution).
$b^2 - 4ac < 0$.	Solutions are complex numbers.
$b^2 - 4ac$ is a perfect square.	Solutions are rational numbers.
$b^2 - 4ac$ is not a perfect square.	Solutions are irrational numbers.

CHECK YOUR UNDERSTANDING

What is the discriminant for the equation $3x^2 + 5x + 2 = 0$?

$5^2 - (4)(3)(2) = 1$

Disjoint sets

Sets that have no members (elements) in common. The intersection of disjoint sets is the empty (null) set. For example, {1, 3, 5} and {2, 4, 6, 8} are disjoint sets. They have no elements in common.

CHECK YOUR UNDERSTANDING
Are {1, 3} and {2, 3} disjoint sets?

no, they have the member 3 in common

D

Disjunction

A statement of the form *p or q*. Two simple statements are connected with *or*. An example of a disjunction is:

I will do my homework or I will go to the movies this afternoon.

Simple statement   Simple statement

In order to tell whether a disjunction is true or false, the truth value of each of the two simple statements needs to be known. The truth table lists all possible combinations of truth values of the simple statements and, in the last column, lists the truth values of the disjunction.

p	q	p or q
T	T	T
F	T	T
T	F	T
F	F	F

A disjunction is false only when both simple statements are false.

CHECK YOUR UNDERSTANDING
What is the truth value of the following disjunction?

$5 = 3 + 2$ or $7 = 9$

true

Distance formula

The formula used in coordinate geometry to find the distance between two points. Given two points with coordinates $A(x_1,y_1)$ and $B(x_2,y_2)$, the distance between them is given by the formula

$$d = \sqrt{(x_2 - x_1)^2 + (y_2 - y_1)^2}$$

Using this formula, the distance between two points with coordinates (3,1) and (5,2) can be found.

$$\underset{(x_1,y_1)}{\uparrow\ \uparrow}\qquad \underset{(x_2,y_2)}{\uparrow\ \uparrow}$$

$$d = \sqrt{(5 - 3)^2 + (2 - 1)^2} = \sqrt{2^2 + 1^2} = \sqrt{4 + 1} \text{ or } \sqrt{5}.$$

CHECK YOUR UNDERSTANDING
What is the distance between the points with coordinates (4,1) and (6,3)?

$\sqrt{8}$

Distributive property

The property of distributing one operation over another and the answer is the same.

Distributive Property of Multiplication over Addition

$$a(b + c) = ab + ac$$
$$2(4 + 1) \overset{?}{=} (2 \times 4) + (2 \times 1)$$
$$2\,(5) \overset{?}{=}\quad 8 \quad + \quad 2$$
$$10 = 10$$

Distributive Property of Multiplication over Subtraction

$$a(b - c) = ab - ac$$
$$4(5 - 2) \overset{?}{=} (4 \times 5) - (4 \times 2)$$
$$4\,(3) \overset{?}{=}\quad 20 \quad - \quad 8$$
$$12 = 12$$

Distributive Property of Division over Addition

$$\frac{b+c}{a} = \frac{b}{a} + \frac{c}{a}$$

$$\frac{4+6}{2} \overset{?}{=} \frac{4}{2} + \frac{6}{2}$$

$$5 \overset{?}{=} 2 + 3$$

$$5 = 5$$

Distributive Property of Division over Subtraction

D

$$\frac{b-c}{a} = \frac{b}{a} - \frac{c}{a}$$

$$\frac{9-3}{3} \overset{?}{=} \frac{9}{3} - \frac{3}{3}$$

$$\frac{6}{3} \overset{?}{=} 3 - 1$$

$$2 = 2$$

CHECK YOUR UNDERSTANDING

Is $a(b + c) = ab \times ac$ a statement of the distributive property of multiplication over addition?

no, a(b + c) = ab + ac is

Dividend

In division, the number that is being divided.

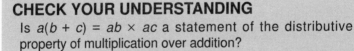

$$\underset{\uparrow}{a} \div b = c \qquad \underset{\uparrow}{6} \div 2 = 3 \qquad 2\overline{)8}^{\,4}$$

dividend   dividend   dividend

CHECK YOUR UNDERSTANDING

What is the dividend in $10 \div 2 = 5$?

10

Divisibility test

A rule that is used to tell whether one number is divisible by another. The following are some commonly used divisibility tests:

2: A number is divisible by 2 if the ones place is 0, 2, 4, 6, or 8. For example, 13,758 is divisible by 2.

3: A number is divisible by 3 if the sum of its digits is divisible by 3. For example, 327 → 3 + 2 + 7 = 12. 12 is divisible by 3, so 327 is divisible by 3.

4: A number is divisible by 4 if the number formed by its last two digits is divisible by 4. For example, the number formed by the last two digits of 924 (24) is divisible by 4, so 924 is divisible by 4.

5: A number is divisible by 5 if the ones digit is 0 or 5. For example, 89,235 is divisible by 5.

6: A number is divisible by 6 if it is divisible by 2 and by 3. For example, 32,784 is divisible by 2 (ones place is 4) and by 3 (3 + 2 + 7 + 8 + 4 = 24), so it is divisible by 6.

9: A number is divisible by 9 if the sum of its digits is divisible by 9. For example, 203,805 (2 + 0 + 3 + 8 + 0 + 5 = 18) is divisible by 9.

10: A number is divisible by 10 if its ones digit is 0. For example, 256,970 is divisible by 10.

11: A number is divisible by 11 if the alternating difference and sum, beginning with the ones digit, is divisible by 11. For example, 968,231 → 1 − 3 + 2 − 8 + 6 − 9 = $^-$11. $^-$11 is divisible by 11, so 968,231 is divisible by 11.

CHECK YOUR UNDERSTANDING
Is 216 divisible by 4?

yes, because 16 is divisible by 4.

Divisible

A number x is divisible by a number y if y divides x with a remainder of zero. Other ways of stating this are: A number x is divisible by y if y is a factor of x; x is divisible by y if the quotient is an integer.

EXAMPLE 26 is divisible by 13 but not by 4:
$$26 \div 13 = 2; \ 26 \div 4 = 6r2$$

CHECK YOUR UNDERSTANDING
Is 100 divisible by 25?

yes, $100 \div 25 = 4$

D

Division

One of the four basic operations of arithmetic. In the division statement $a \div b = c$, a is the dividend, b the divisor, and c is the quotient. Division is related to multiplication: if $a \div b = c$, then $cb = a$ and $bc = a$. For example, if $8 \div 2 = 4$, then $4 \times 2 = 8$ and $2 \times 4 = 8$.

Whole numbers If one number "goes into another", then division separates that number (dividend) into a group of equal numbers:
$$12 \div 4 = 3$$

3 groups of 4 each

OOOO / OOOO / OOOO

Another way to think about $12 \div 4$ is 4 subtracted repeatedly until the last difference is zero.

$$\begin{array}{r} 12 \\ -\ 4 \\ \hline 8 \end{array} \qquad \begin{array}{r} 8 \\ -\ 4 \\ \hline 4 \end{array} \qquad \begin{array}{r} 4 \\ -\ 4 \\ \hline 0 \end{array}$$

Since 3 groups of 4 were subtracted, $12 \div 4 = 3$.

Fractions $\frac{3}{4} \div \frac{5}{7} = \frac{3}{4} \times \frac{7}{5} = \frac{21}{20}$ or $1\frac{1}{20}$. In general, $\frac{a}{b} \div \frac{c}{d} = \frac{ad}{bc}$. That is, to divide one fraction by another, invert the divisor and multiply.

117

BASIC DIVISION FACTS

To do long division quickly, you need to know the basic division facts. If you have learned the basic multiplication facts, then you know the basic division facts, since division is related to multiplication. Any number divided by 1 is that number.

Basic division facts

$2\overline{)4}$	$2\overline{)6}$	$2\overline{)8}$	$2\overline{)10}$	$2\overline{)12}$	$2\overline{)14}$	$2\overline{)16}$	$2\overline{)18}$
2	3	4	5	6	7	8	9

$3\overline{)6}$	$3\overline{)9}$	$3\overline{)12}$	$3\overline{)15}$	$3\overline{)18}$	$3\overline{)21}$	$3\overline{)24}$	$3\overline{)27}$
2	3	4	5	6	7	8	9

$4\overline{)8}$	$4\overline{)12}$	$4\overline{)16}$	$4\overline{)20}$	$4\overline{)24}$	$4\overline{)28}$	$4\overline{)32}$	$4\overline{)36}$
2	3	4	5	6	7	8	9

$5\overline{)10}$	$5\overline{)15}$	$5\overline{)20}$	$5\overline{)25}$	$5\overline{)30}$	$5\overline{)35}$	$5\overline{)40}$	$5\overline{)45}$
2	3	4	5	6	7	8	9

$6\overline{)12}$	$6\overline{)18}$	$6\overline{)24}$	$6\overline{)30}$	$6\overline{)36}$	$6\overline{)42}$	$6\overline{)48}$	$6\overline{)54}$
2	3	4	5	6	7	8	9

$7\overline{)14}$	$7\overline{)21}$	$7\overline{)28}$	$7\overline{)35}$	$7\overline{)42}$	$7\overline{)49}$	$7\overline{)56}$	$7\overline{)63}$
2	3	4	5	6	7	8	9

$8\overline{)16}$	$8\overline{)24}$	$8\overline{)32}$	$8\overline{)40}$	$8\overline{)48}$	$8\overline{)56}$	$8\overline{)64}$	$8\overline{)72}$
2	3	4	5	6	7	8	9

$9\overline{)18}$	$9\overline{)27}$	$9\overline{)36}$	$9\overline{)45}$	$9\overline{)54}$	$9\overline{)63}$	$9\overline{)72}$	$9\overline{)81}$
2	3	4	5	6	7	8	9

LONG DIVISION

The algorithm for long division is estimate, multiply, subtract, bring down, repeat if necessary. See examples for dividing by one- and two-digit divisors below.

Dividing by a 1-Digit Number

$$591 \div 8$$

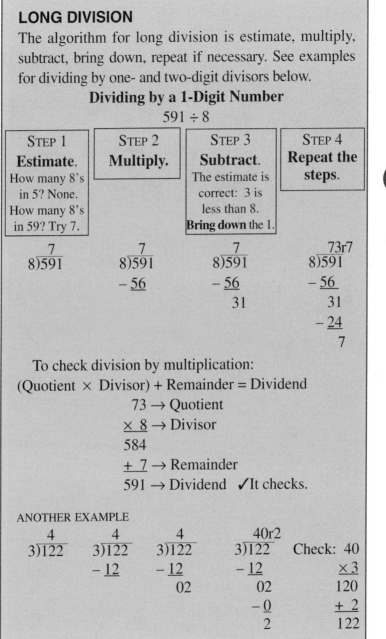

| STEP 1 Estimate. How many 8's in 5? None. How many 8's in 59? Try 7. | STEP 2 Multiply. | STEP 3 Subtract. The estimate is correct: 3 is less than 8. Bring down the 1. | STEP 4 Repeat the steps. |

```
      7            7            7           73r7
   8)591        8)591        8)591        8)591
              - 56         - 56         - 56
                            31           31
                                        - 24
                                          7
```

To check division by multiplication:
(Quotient × Divisor) + Remainder = Dividend

```
       73  → Quotient
     ×  8  → Divisor
      584
     +  7  → Remainder
      591  → Dividend   ✓It checks.
```

ANOTHER EXAMPLE

```
      4            4            4          40r2
   3)122        3)122        3)122        3)122       Check:  40
              - 12         - 12         - 12                ×  3
                            02           02                 120
                                        - 0                +  2
                                          2                 122
```

Dividing by a 2-Digit Number
621 ÷ 19

STEP 1 Estimate. How many 19's in 62? Try 3 in tens place.	STEP 2 Multiply.	STEP 3 Subtract. The estimate is correct: 5 < 19. Bring down the 1.	STEP 4 Repeat the steps.

```
      3              3              3            32r13
19)621         19)621         19)621         19)621
               - 57           - 57           - 57
                                51             51
                                              - 38
                                               13
```

To check division by multiplication:

(Quotient × Divisor) + Remainder = Dividend

```
      32  → Quotient
    × 19  → Divisor
    288
     32
    608
  +  13  → Remainder
    621  → Dividend   ✓It checks.
```

OTHER EXAMPLES

```
      305r15  Check: 305           300r132  Check: 300
87)26,550          × 87    254)76,332              × 254
 - 26 1           2135      - 76 2                 1200
    450           2440         13                  1500
  - 435          26535        - 0                   600
     15          + 15        132                  76200
                 26,550       - 0                 + 132
                             132                  76,332
```

120

A SHORT CUT IN DIVISION

When dividing by a number less then 10, use a shortcut.

Short form

Step 1
$$8\overline{)368} \quad \underline{4} \quad -\underline{32} \quad 4$$
$$8\overline{)36\!\!\!\!/8} \quad {}^{4}$$

Step 2
$$8\overline{)368} \quad \underline{46} \quad -\underline{32} \quad 48 \quad -\underline{48} \quad 0$$
$$8\overline{)36\!\!\!\!/8} \quad {}^{46}$$

D

ZERO IN DIVISION

Zero plays a special role in division. It is described by three separate cases.

Case 1. 0 divided by any non-zero number is 0.

$$0 \div 8 = 0 \qquad 0 \div 548 = 0 \qquad 0 \div {}^{-}26 = 0$$

Case 2. A non-zero number divided by 0 has no answer. Suppose $n \div 0 = k$ $(n \neq 0)$. Then $k \times 0 = n$. But the product of any number and 0 is 0. So, there is a contradiction and therefore division of a non-zero number by 0 is undefined.

Case 3. 0 divided by 0. Suppose $0 \div 0 = n$. Then $n \times 0 = 0$ for every number n. Thus, any number would be an answer to $0 \div 0$. Thus, $0 \div 0$ is meaningless.

CHECK YOUR UNDERSTANDING

Is the multiplication statement $4 \times 3 = 12$ related to the division statement $12 \div 3 = 4$?

yes

Division property of equations

Also called Division property of equality.

If $a = b$, then $\frac{a}{c} = \frac{b}{c}$, $c \neq 0$. For example, if $2x + 8 = 4$,

then $\frac{2x + 8}{2} = \frac{4}{2}$ or $x + 4 = 2$.

CHECK YOUR UNDERSTANDING
Use the division property of equations to simplify the equation $3x + 18 = 6$?

Divide each side by 3: $x + 6 = 2$

Division property of inequality

If $a > b$, then $\frac{a}{c} > \frac{b}{c}$ if c is positive and $\frac{a}{c} < \frac{b}{c}$ if c is negative. For example, if $12 > 8$, then $\frac{12}{4} > \frac{8}{4}$ or $3 > 2$

and $\frac{12}{-4} < \frac{8}{-4}$ or $^-3 < {}^-2$.

CHECK YOUR UNDERSTANDING
Use the division property of inequality to divide both sides of $25 > 15$ by $^-5$.

$^-5 < {}^-3$

Divisor

A number by which a number is being divided.

$$a \div \underset{\uparrow}{b} = c \qquad 34 \div \underset{\uparrow}{2} = 17$$

divisor　　　　　divisor　　　divisor $\rightarrow$ $8\overline{)48}$ ($\overset{6}{}$)

CHECK YOUR UNDERSTANDING
What is the divisor in $20 \div 4 = 5$?

4

122

Dodecagon

A polygon with 12 sides. It is a regular dodecagon if all of the sides are the same length and all of the angles have the same measure.

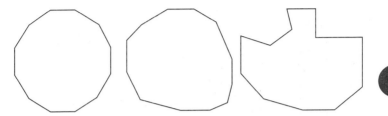

Regular dodecagon   Not regular dodecagons

D

CHECK YOUR UNDERSTANDING
The prefix *deca-* means ten? What number does the prefix *do-* add to ten?

two

Dodecahedron

A polyhedron with 12 faces. A dodecahedron has pentagons as faces. It is a regular dodecahedron if all the pentagons are regular (all of the sides are the same length and all of the angles have the same measure).

CHECK YOUR UNDERSTANDING
One-half of the faces of a dodecahedron are visible in the picture above. How many faces is that?

6

Domain of a function

The set of all first members (elements) of a function. Given the function $y = \{(1,5),(2,10),(3,15),(4,20),(5,25)\}$, its domain is $\{1,2,3,4,5\}$.

See also Range of a function.

CHECK YOUR UNDERSTANDING
What is the domain of the function $\{(2,4),(3,6),(4,8),(5,10)\}$?

{2,3,4,5}

Duodecimal numeration system

A system for naming numbers in base twelve. Base twelve numerals are called duodecimal numerals. It uses twelve digits: 1, 2, 3, 4, 5, 6, 7, 8, 9, t, e. t represents 11, e represents 12. Each place to the left has a value 12 times greater than the value of the place to the right. The following chart shows how the values of the digits in the duodecimal system are found.

1,728 12^3	144 12^2	12 12^1	1 12^0
1	1	1	1
		t	9
	8	6	7
1	t	5	e

To find what number is named by 1111 in base twelve, add the values of the five digits: $1 + 12 + 144 + 1{,}728 = 1{,}885$.

Thus, $1111_{\text{base twelve}} = 1{,}885_{\text{base ten}}$

t9 means ten twelves and 9 ones. $t9_{\text{base twelve}} = 129_{\text{base ten}}$

$867_{\text{base twelve}} = 7 + 72 + 1{,}152 = 1{,}231_{\text{base ten}}$

$1t5e_{\text{base twelve}} = 11 + 60 + 1{,}440 + 1{,}728 = 3{,}239_{\text{base ten}}$

CHECK YOUR UNDERSTANDING
What is $e5_{\text{base twelve}}$ written in base ten?

137

E

Edge

A line segment or line that is an intersection of two faces in a geometric figure in space.

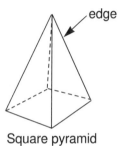

edge

Square pyramid

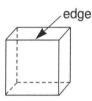

edge

Cube

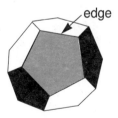

edge

Dodecahedron

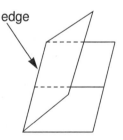

edge

Dihedral angle

See also Euler's formula *and* Space figures.

CHECK YOUR UNDERSTANDING
How many edges does a square pyramid have?

8

Egyptian numeration system

The numeration system developed by the Egyptians about 3000 B.C. They used hieroglyphics (picture writing). The base in the Egyptian system is the number 10. The seven basic hieroglyphic symbols are the following:

| | a vertical staff–stands for 1 or 10^0 |

a vertical staff–stands for 1 or 10^0

a heel bone–stands for 10 or 10^1

a scroll–stands for 100 or 10^2

a lotus flower–stands for 1,000 or 10^3

a pointing finger–stands for 10,000 or 10^4

a burbot fish–stands for 100,000 or 10^5

an astonished man–stands for 1,000,000 or 10^6

The Egyptian system is an additive system; that is, a symbol is repeated the required number of times and the values of the symbols are added. For example,

$$= 2,000,000 + 100,000 + 30,000 + 1,000 + 400 + 20 + 2$$
$$= 2,131,422$$

CHECK YOUR UNDERSTANDING
What number is shown?

23,401

126

Elapsed time

Time that passes between the beginning and end of an event. For example, you left home at 7:15 A.M. and arrived at school at 8:15 A.M. The elapsed time is 1 hour.

CHECK YOUR UNDERSTANDING
You left school at 3:15 P.M. and arrived at home at 4:30 P.M. What is the elapsed time?

1 hour 15 minutes

Element of a set

See Member of a set.

Elevation

See Angle of elevation.

Ellipse

A geometric figure such that, for each point P on it, the sum of the distances from P to two fixed points, F_1 and F_2, called foci, is constant: $a + b = c + d = e + f$.

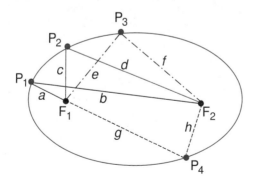

CHECK YOUR UNDERSTANDING
Is it true that, for the ellipse pictured above, $g + h = a + b$?

yes

Empty set

Also called Null set. The set that has no members (elements).

$$\{\ \}$$
Empty (null) set

$$\{0\}$$
This is not an empty set. It is a set with 0 as one member.

CHECK YOUR UNDERSTANDING
Is the set of whole numbers between 1 and 2 the empty set?

yes

Endpoint

The point at either extremity of a segment. The beginning point of a ray. Points A and B are the endpoints of segment AB. Point C is the endpoint of ray CD.

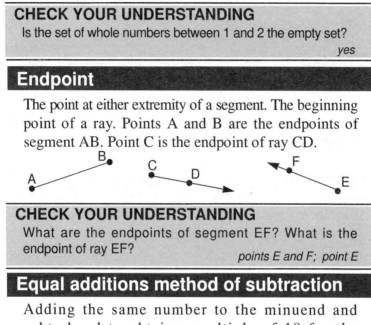

CHECK YOUR UNDERSTANDING
What are the endpoints of segment EF? What is the endpoint of ray EF?

points E and F; point E

Equal additions method of subtraction

Adding the same number to the minuend and subtrahend to obtain a multiple of 10 for the subtrahend. It is based on the property that adding the same number to the minued and the subtrahend does not change the answer. In general,

$$a - b = (a + n) - (b + n).$$

$$62 \longrightarrow (62 + 3) \longrightarrow 65$$
$$- 37 \longrightarrow - (37 + 3) \longrightarrow - 40$$
$$25$$

It is easier to subtract if the subtrahend is a multiple of 10.

CHECK YOUR UNDERSTANDING
Using the equal additions method, what would replace 46 − 18?

48 − 20

Equal fractions

Also called Equivalent fractions, Equal ratios, *or* Equivalent ratios. Two fractions that name the same number.

$$\frac{3}{4} = \frac{15}{20}$$

To tell whether two fractions are equal, use cross multiplication. If the cross products are equal, then the fractions are equal.

$$\frac{3}{4} \overset{?}{\underset{}{\bowtie}} \frac{15}{20}$$

$$3 \times 20 \overset{?}{=} 4 \times 15$$

$$60 = 60$$

The cross products are equal, so $\frac{3}{4} = \frac{15}{20}$.

E

CHECK YOUR UNDERSTANDING

Are $\frac{2}{7}$ and $\frac{12}{42}$ equal?

yes

Equality (=)

In mathematics to say that *a equals b, a is equal to b,* or *a = b* means that *a* and *b* are two names for the same number. For example, 7 = 3 + 4 means that 7 and 3 + 4 are two names for the same number.

CHECK YOUR UNDERSTANDING

Does *4 = 9 − 5* mean that *4* and *9 − 5* are two names for the same number?

yes

Equally likely outcomes

In probability, it means that two events have the same chance of occurring. For example, when tossing a coin H (heads) and T (tails) each has the same chance of landing up, or the probability $\frac{1}{2}$.

CHECK YOUR UNDERSTANDING

What is the probability of H (heads) landing up when tossing a coin?

$\frac{1}{2}$

Equation

A mathematical sentence with an equal sign (=).

EXAMPLES

Linear equations:

$$y = 5x \qquad \tfrac{x}{4} + 2 = 10 \qquad x + 3 = 9 \qquad 2x - 4 = 7x$$

The highest degree term is raised to the first power.

Quadratic (second-degree) equation:

$$y = x^2 + 1$$

The highest degree term is raised to the second power.

Cubic (third degree) equation:

$$4x^3 + 2x^2 + 2x + 6 = 8$$

The highest degree term is raised to the third power.

Fourth degree equation:

$$2x^4 + 4x^3 - 5x = 7$$

The highest degree term is raised to the fourth power.

SOLVING ONE-STEP EQUATIONS

To solve an equation, perform inverse operations to get the variable alone on one side of the equation.

$y - 5 = 7$

$y - 5 + 5 = 7 + 5$ Add 5 to each side of the equation.

$y = 12$ The solution of $y - 5 = 7$ is 12.

$x + 2 = 8$

$x + 2 - 2 = 8 - 2$ Subtract 2 from each side of the equation.

$x = 6$ The solution of $x + 2 = 8$ is 6.

$3z = 12$

$\dfrac{3z}{3} = \dfrac{12}{3}$ Divide each side of the equation by 3.

$z = 4$ The solution of $3z = 12$ is 4.

$\dfrac{a}{2} = 7$

$2(\tfrac{a}{2}) = 7 \cdot 2$ Multiply each side by 2.

$a = 14$ The solution of $\tfrac{a}{2} = 7$ is 14.

SOLVING TWO-STEP EQUATIONS

To solve a two-step equation, perform inverse operations to get the variable alone on one side by starting with operations farthest from the variable.

$$4y + 3 = 11$$
$$4y + 3 - 3 = 11 - 3 \quad \text{Subtract 3 from each side.}$$
$$4y = 8$$
$$\frac{4y}{4} = \frac{8}{4} \quad \text{Divide each side by 4.}$$
$$y = 2 \quad \text{The solution of } 4y + 3 = 11 \text{ is 2.}$$

$$\frac{x}{2} - 5 = 7$$
$$\frac{x}{2} - 5 + 5 = 7 + 5 \quad \text{Add 5 to each side of the equation.}$$
$$\frac{x}{2} = 12$$
$$2 \cdot \frac{x}{2} = 12 \cdot 2 \quad \text{Multiply each side by 2.}$$
$$x = 24 \quad \text{The solution of } \frac{x}{2} - 5 = 7 \text{ is 24.}$$

SOLVING EQUATIONS WITH VARIABLES ON BOTH SIDES

Perform operations to get the variable on one side of the equation.

$$4x - 7 = 2x + 3$$
$$4x - 7 - 2x = 2x + 3 - 2x \quad \text{Subtract } 2x \text{ from each side.}$$
$$2x - 7 = 3 \quad \text{Add 7 to both sides, then divide both sides by 2.}$$
$$x = 5 \quad \text{The solution of } 4x - 7 = 2x + 3 \text{ is 5.}$$

SOLVING EQUATIONS CONTAINING PARENTHESES

$$7y - 5(4 - 2y) = 31$$
$$7y - 20 + 10y = 31 \quad \text{Multiply to get parentheses out.}$$
$$17y - 20 = 31 \quad \text{Combine like terms.}$$
$$y = 3 \quad \text{The solution of } 7y - 5(4 - 2y) = 31 \text{ is 3.}$$

SOLVING EQUATIONS CONTAINING FRACTIONS

To get out fractions, multiply each side of the equation by the common denominator of all the fractions.

$$\frac{1}{4}z + \frac{7}{24} = \frac{1}{3}$$

$$24(\frac{1}{4}z + \frac{7}{24}) = 24 \cdot \frac{1}{3} \quad \text{Multiply by 24.}$$

$$24 \cdot \frac{1}{4}z + 24 \cdot \frac{7}{24} = 24 \cdot \frac{1}{3}$$

$$6z + 7 = 8 \quad \text{Subtract 7 from both sides.}$$

$$6z = 1 \quad \text{Divide both sides by 6.}$$

$$z = \frac{1}{6} \quad \text{The solution of}$$

$$\frac{1}{4}z + \frac{7}{24} = \frac{1}{3} \text{ is } \frac{1}{6}.$$

SOLVING EQUATIONS CONTAINING DECIMALS

To get out decimals, multiply each side of the equation by a power of 10 so all decimals are whole numbers.

$$1.6x - 0.08 = 0.4$$

$$100(1.6x - 0.08) = 100(0.4) \quad \text{Multiply by 100.}$$

$$160x - 8 = 40 \quad \text{Divide each side by 8.}$$

$$20x - 1 = 5 \quad \text{Add 1 to each side.}$$

$$20x = 6 \quad \text{Divide each side by 20.}$$

$$x = 0.3 \quad \text{The solution of}$$

$$1.6x - 0.08 = 0.4 \text{ is } 0.3.$$

SOLVING A LITERAL EQUATION

A literal equation is an equation that contains only variables. EXAMPLE $ax + b = c$

To solve $ax + b = c$ for x, perform the inverse operations to get the x alone on one side by starting with operations farthest from the variable.

$$ax + b = c$$

$$ax + b - b = c - b \quad \text{Subtract } b \text{ from each side.}$$

$$ax = c - b$$

$$\frac{ax}{a} = \frac{c - b}{a} \quad \text{Divide each side by } a.$$

$$x = \frac{c - b}{a}$$

SOLVING QUADRATIC EQUATIONS

By using the quadratic formula To solve a quadratic equation of the form $ax^2 + bx + c = 0$, use the quadratic formula: $x = \frac{-b \pm \sqrt{b^2 - 4ac}}{2a}$

To solve $15x^2 - 13x + 2 = 0$, substitute in the formula: $a = 15, b = {}^-13, c = 2$.

$$x = \frac{13 \pm \sqrt{(-13)^2 - 4 \cdot 15 \cdot 2}}{2 \cdot 15} = \frac{13 \pm \sqrt{169 - 120}}{30} = \frac{13 \pm \sqrt{49}}{30}$$

$$\frac{13 + 7}{30} = \frac{20}{30} = \frac{2}{3} \qquad \frac{13 - 7}{30} = \frac{6}{30} = \frac{1}{5}$$

There are two solutions, $\frac{2}{3}$ and $\frac{1}{5}$.

By factoring This method of factoring quadratic equations is a reversal of the FOIL method of multiplying binomials. To solve $3x^2 - 8x - 3 = 0$:
Factor $3x^2 - 8x - 3$ into two binomials.

$(3x\ ?\ 1)(1x\ ?\ 3)$ — Try $3x$ and $1x$ as factors of $3x^2$.

Try 3 and 1 as factors of 3.

$(3x + 1)(1x - 3)$ — To give ⁻3 one sign must be positive, the other negative. Try + in first and – in second. Check by multiplying. It works.

$3x + 1 = 0 \qquad x - 3 = 0$ — Set each factor equal to 0.

$3x = {}^-1 \qquad\qquad x = 3$

$\frac{3x}{3} = \frac{{}^-1}{3}$

$x = \frac{{}^-1}{3}$

The solutions are $\frac{{}^-1}{3}$ and 3.

E

See also Addition property for equations, Derived equations, Division property for equations, Equation of a line, Equivalent equations, Multiplication property for equations, Subtraction property for equations, *and* Systems of equations.

Equation of a line

Also called Linear equation. An equation of this form or an equation that can be put into this form:

$$ax + by + c = 0 \text{ where } a \text{ and } b \neq 0$$

For example, the equation $5x + 3y - 15 = 0$ is a linear equation in two variables. The graph of this equation is a line. To graph this equation, we need to find just two points on this line.

Let $x = 0$, then $y = 5$. So, one point on the line is $(0,5)$.

Let $y = 0$, then $x = 3$. So, another point on the line is $(3,0)$.

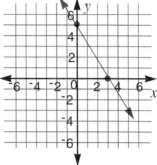

Graph of the linear equation $5x + 3y - 15 = 0$.

TWO-POINT FORM OF AN EQUATION OF A LINE

An equation of the form: $y - y_1 = \frac{y_2 - y_1}{x_2 - y_1} (x - x_1)$.

If you know two points, you can use this form to find the equation of the line containing the two points. Two points on the line on the graph above are $(0,5)$ and $(3,0)$.
$$\underset{x_1 \, y_1}{} \qquad \underset{x_2 \, y_2}{}$$

Substituting the values in the general formula above will give the equation for the line.

$$y - 5 = \frac{0 - 5}{3 - 0}(x - 0)$$

$$y - 5 = \frac{^-5}{3}(x - 0)$$

$$y - 5 = \frac{^-5x}{3}$$

$$3(y - 5) = {}^-5x$$

$$3y - 15 = {}^-5x \quad \rightarrow 5x + 3y - 15 = 0$$

EQUATIONS OF VERTICAL AND HORIZONTAL LINES

The equation of a horizontal line is $y = c$ where c is a constant. For example, $y = 2$ is an equation of a horizontal line parallel to the x-axis, 2 units up from the origin. The equation for a vertical line is $x = c$ where c is a constant. For example, $x = {}^-4$ is the graph of a vertical line parallel to the y-axis and 4 units to the left of it.

See also Intercept form, Point-slope form, Slope-intercept form, *and* Slope of a line through two points.

E

Equiangular polygon

A polygon in which each angle has the same measure.

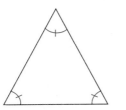

Equiangular triangle   Every rectangle is equiangular
(all right angles)

Equidistant

At the same distance. For example, point C is equidistant from points A and B.

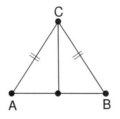

Equilateral polygon

A polygon with all sides the same length (all sides congruent).

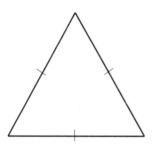 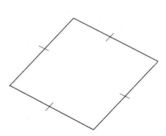

Equilateral triangle

Every rhombus is an equilateral polygon.

Equivalence relation

A relation between the members of a set that have the following three properties.

1. *Reflexive*: a R a, that is, each member has this relation to itself. R stands for the relation whatever it is.
2. *Symmetric*: if a R b, then b R a.
3. *Transitive*: if a R b and b R c, then a R c.

The relation *is equal to* (=) is an equivalence relation in the set of real numbers. It has the three properties.

Reflexive: $a = a$, that is every number is equal to itself.

Symmetric: if $a = b$, then $b = a$, for every number a and b.

Transitive: if $a = b$, and $b = c$, then $a = c$, for every number a, b, and c.

E

CHECK YOUR UNDERSTANDING
Is the relation *is greater than* (>) an equivalence relation?

no; 3 is not greater than 3.

Equivalent equations

Equations that have the same solution. For example, $2x = 8$ and $3x = 12$ are equivalent equations. Each has 4 as its solution.

CHECK YOUR UNDERSTANDING
Are $4x = 20$ and $3x = 15$ equivalent equations?

yes; each has 5 as its solution.

Equivalent fractions

See Equal fractions.

Equivalent sets

Two finite sets are equivalent if they have the same number of members. Two infinite sets are equivalent if there is a one-to-one correspondence between the sets.

CHECK YOUR UNDERSTANDING
Are the sets {1,3,5} and {2,4,6} equivalent?

yes

Equivalent system of equations

Two or more systems of equations that have the same solution. For example, the system of equations $\{2x + y = 4, x + y = 3\}$ and the system $\{4x + y = 6, 5x - 2y = 1\}$ are equivalent. Each has $(1, 2)$ as its solution.

CHECK YOUR UNDERSTANDING
Are the system of equations $\{x + y = 0, 2x - y = 3\}$ and the system $\{3x + y = 2, x - 3y = 4\}$ equivalent ?

yes; the solution of each system is (1,⁻1)

Estimate

An approximate number that is close to the desired number. For example, you might say:

I am estimating the distance from my house
to school to be about 4 miles.

ESTIMATION STRATEGIES
Here are some strategies for finding estimates in various situations.

Rounding. Round numbers so that you can quickly
see what the approximate answer will be.

$$
\begin{array}{rcl}
435 &\rightarrow& 400 \\
628 &\rightarrow& 600 \\
589 &\rightarrow& 600 \\
+\ 778 &\rightarrow& +\ 800 \\
\hline
&& 2400
\end{array}
\qquad
\begin{array}{rcl}
28.7 &\rightarrow& 29 \\
\times\ 2.05 &\rightarrow& \times\ 2 \\
\hline
&& 58
\end{array}
$$

$$
\begin{array}{rcl}
16\frac{5}{8} &\rightarrow& 17 \\
-9\frac{7}{8} &\rightarrow& -10 \\
\hline
&& 7
\end{array}
\qquad
2.5\overline{)94.32} \rightarrow 3\overline{)90}
\quad
\text{About 30}
$$

138

Front-end Add or subtract the leftmost digits and adjust by looking at the sum or difference of what is left.

$3.47 ⟍
8.74 ⟍ ⤫ $1
6.27 ⟋ ⤫
+ 5.51 ⟋ $1

Front-end:
$3 + $8 + $6 +$5 = $22
Adjust: $22 + $2 = $24
About $24

6432 ⟍
− 4897 ⟋ ⟶ 1400 − 900 = 500
2000

Front-end: 6000 − 4000 = 2000
432 < 897; regrouping is needed
Adjust: 1400 − 900 is 500
2000 − 500 = 1500
About 1500

Range of Values   Find the upper bound by rounding up and multiplying. Find the lower bound by rounding down and multiplying.

879	900	800
× 542	× 600	× 500
	540,000	400,000

The exact answer is between 400,000 and 540,000.

Clustering

When numbers are close to one rounded number, use that rounded number to estimate.

38,147   These numbers
44,918   cluster around
43,180   40,000.
37,490   40,000
33,819   ×   6
+ 42,150   240,000
About 240,000

Sometimes it is convenient to cluster numbers to make them easier to add.

38,217 ⟍
24,017 ⟶ About 50,000
25,384 ⟋ About 50,000
+ 10,019 ⟋
About 100,000

E

Compatible Numbers Think of a basic fact that is close to the numbers.

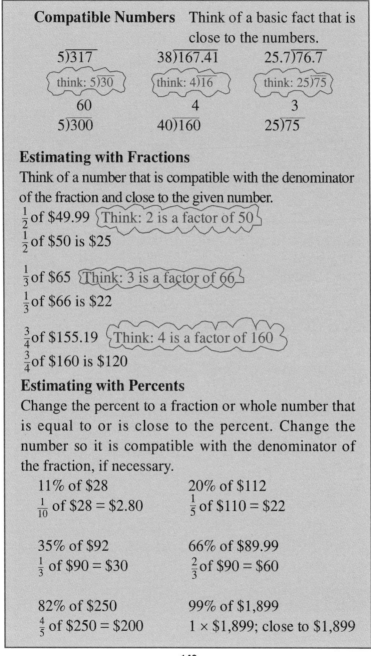

$5\overline{)317}$ $38\overline{)167.41}$ $25.7\overline{)76.7}$

think: $5\overline{)30}$ think: $4\overline{)16}$ think: $25\overline{)75}$

60 4 3

$5\overline{)300}$ $40\overline{)160}$ $25\overline{)75}$

Estimating with Fractions

Think of a number that is compatible with the denominator of the fraction and close to the given number.

$\frac{1}{2}$ of $49.99 Think: 2 is a factor of 50

$\frac{1}{2}$ of $50 is $25

$\frac{1}{3}$ of $65 Think: 3 is a factor of 66

$\frac{1}{3}$ of $66 is $22

$\frac{3}{4}$ of $155.19 Think: 4 is a factor of 160

$\frac{3}{4}$ of $160 is $120

Estimating with Percents

Change the percent to a fraction or whole number that is equal to or is close to the percent. Change the number so it is compatible with the denominator of the fraction, if necessary.

11% of $28 20% of $112
$\frac{1}{10}$ of $28 = $2.80 $\frac{1}{5}$ of $110 = $22

35% of $92 66% of $89.99
$\frac{1}{3}$ of $90 = $30 $\frac{2}{3}$ of $90 = $60

82% of $250 99% of $1,899
$\frac{4}{5}$ of $250 = $200 $1 \times $1,899$; close to $1,899

To estimate 5% of a number, estimate 10% and take one-half of the answer. Use compatible numbers, if necessary.

5% of $11.67

Think: 10% of $12 is $1.20   5% of $11.67 is about $0.60

To estimate 15% of a number, estimate 10% and add one-half of that amount to it. Use compatible numbers, if necessary.

15% of $20.49

Think: 10% of $20 is $2.00   15% of $20.49 is about $3.00

E

CHECK YOUR UNDERSTANDING
About how many miles is (12.8 + 11.7 + 3.4) miles?

about 28 miles

Euler's formula

A formula that relates the number of vertices, faces, and edges in polyhedra.

number of vertices + number of faces – number of edges = 2

$$V + F - E = 2$$

A triangular pyramid has 4 vertices, 4 faces, 6 edges:

$$4 + 4 - 6 = 2$$

CHECK YOUR UNDERSTANDING
A cube has 8 vertices and 6 faces. Use the formula to find the number of edges.

8 + 6 – E = 2; E = 12

Evaluate

See Expression-EVALUATING AN ALGEBRAIC EXPRESSION.

Even number

A number that is divisible by 2; that is, the quotient of the number and 2 is a whole number. For example, 14 is an even number, because the quotient $14 \div 2 = 7$, and 7 is a whole number.

CHECK YOUR UNDERSTANDING
Is 29 an even number?

no

Event

In probability, a subset of a sample space for a given experiment. For example, for the experiment of rolling a die the sample space is $\{1, 2, 3, 4, 5, 6\}$. One event is rolling a number less than 4, which is $\{1, 2, 3\}$. This event is a subset of the sample space.

CHECK YOUR UNDERSTANDING
What subset of the sample space given above is the event of rolling a number 3 or greater?

{3,4,5,6}

Expanded form

When a numeral is expressed as a sum of the products of each digit and its place value. The expanded form of 34,592.78 is
$(3 \times 10,000) + (4 \times 1000) + (5 \times 100) + (9 \times 10) + (2 \times 1) + (7 \times \frac{1}{10}) + (8 \times \frac{1}{100})$.
The place values can also be shown as powers of ten:
$(3 \times 10^4) + (4 \times 10^3) + (5 \times 10^2) + (9 \times 10^1) + (2 \times 10^0) + (7 \times 10^{-1}) + (8 \times 10^{-2})$.

CHECK YOUR UNDERSTANDING
What is the expanded form of 253.6?

$(2 \times 100) + (5 \times 10) + (3 \times 1) + (6 \times \frac{1}{10})$

Expanded numeral

See Expanded form.

Exponent

In the expression x^n (read: x to the nth power), n is the exponent. In 3^4 (read: 3 to the 4th power), 4 is the exponent. An exponent tells how many times the base is used as a factor.

5^2 Read: 5 to the second power or 5 squared

$5 \times 5 = 25$

4^3 Read: 4 to the third power or 4 cubed

$4 \times 4 \times 4 = 64$

A number with an exponent of 1 is the number itself: $8^1 = 8$. A non-zero number with an exponent of 0 is 1: $99^0 = 1$.

E

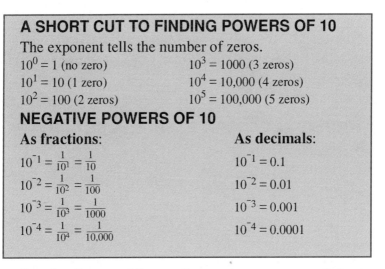

A SHORT CUT TO FINDING POWERS OF 10

The exponent tells the number of zeros.

$10^0 = 1$ (no zero) $10^3 = 1000$ (3 zeros)
$10^1 = 10$ (1 zero) $10^4 = 10,000$ (4 zeros)
$10^2 = 100$ (2 zeros) $10^5 = 100,000$ (5 zeros)

NEGATIVE POWERS OF 10

As fractions:

$10^{-1} = \frac{1}{10^1} = \frac{1}{10}$

$10^{-2} = \frac{1}{10^2} = \frac{1}{100}$

$10^{-3} = \frac{1}{10^3} = \frac{1}{1000}$

$10^{-4} = \frac{1}{10^4} = \frac{1}{10,000}$

As decimals:

$10^{-1} = 0.1$

$10^{-2} = 0.01$

$10^{-3} = 0.001$

$10^{-4} = 0.0001$

See also Base *and* Power of a number-PROPERTIES OF A POWER (LAW OF EXPONENTS).

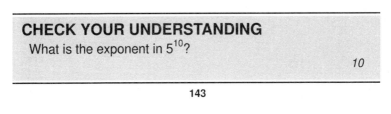

CHECK YOUR UNDERSTANDING

What is the exponent in 5^{10}?

10

Expression

Algebraic An algebraic expression consists of one or more variables. It usually contains some constants and one or more operations.

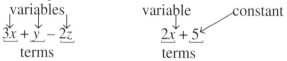

Each part of the expression between operation signs is called a term. If the terms contain the same variable(s), then they are called like terms or similar terms. For example, $5xy$ and ^-7xy are similar terms. If the terms differ in at least one variable, then they are called unlike terms.

Numerical A combination of numerals and operation symbols. Each of the following is a numerical expression:

$$7 \cdot 5 - 3 \qquad \frac{8-6}{2} \qquad 7\,(5-3)+4 \qquad 6^2 - 10$$

WRITING ALGEBRAIC EXPRESSIONS FOR WORD PHRASES

Use a letter to represent an unknown number or variable. Use key words to write the correct symbol.

Word phrase	Variable *	Expression
4 *less than* a number	a	$a-4$
A number *decreased by* 9	b	$b-9$
50 *minus* a number	z	$50-z$
A number *more than* 5	x	$5+x$
A number *increased by* 7	y	$y+7$
The *sum of* 6 and a number	c	$6+c$
3 *plus* a number	k	$3+k$

* can be any letter

Word phrase	Variable *	Expression
The *difference of* a number and 8	n	$n - 8$
7 *times* a number	m	$7m$
The *product of* 12 and a number	t	$12t$
$\frac{3}{5}$ of a number	k	$\frac{3}{5}k$
A number *times* 8	d	$d \cdot 8$ or $d \times 8$
A number divided by 2	y	$\frac{y}{2}$ or $y \div 2$
6 divided by a number	s	$\frac{6}{s}$ or $6 \div s$

* can be any letter

EVALUATING AN ALGEBRAIC EXPRESSION

To evaluate an algebraic expression, substitute the values given for the variables and perform the operations according to the order of operations.

Evaluate $z^2 + 5xy - (x + y)$, for $x = 2$, $y = 3$, and $z = 4$

$$4^2 + 5(2)(3) - (2 + 3) =$$
$$16 + 30 - 5 = 41$$

SIMPLIFYING AN ALGEBRAIC EXPRESSION

Remove parentheses and change the signs of the terms within the parentheses since subtraction is used.

$$7x - (3x + 3) + 1$$
$$7x - 3x - 3 + 1 \qquad \text{Combine like terms.}$$
$$4x - 2$$

Remove parentheses preceded by multiplication.

$4 - [2(y + 2) - 7(y - 3)]$ Work with innermost parentheses first.

$4 - [2y + 4 - 7y + 21]$ Multiply by number outside inner parentheses.

$4 - [^-5y + 25]$ Combine like terms.

$4 + 5y - 25$ Remove brackets and change signs.

$5y - 21$

REDUCING AN ALGEBRAIC EXPRESSION
Find an algebraic expression that is equivalent to a given expression but in a simpler form. For example, by combining like terms the algebraic expression
$$2x^3 - 2x^2 + 3 + 2x^2 - 4$$
can be reduced to its equivalent simpler expression:
$$2x^3 - 1$$

CHECK YOUR UNDERSTANDING
Is $3x + 2z$ an algebraic expression? If yes, how many terms does it have? Is 2 x 3 + 6 x 7 a numerical expression?

yes; 2; yes

Exterior

Of an angle Points outside an angle. The shaded part is the exterior of angle A. It extends without end. The angle itself is not part of the exterior.

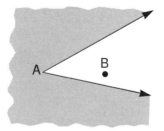

Of a simple closed curve All of the points that are on the outside of a simple closed curve. The shaded part is the exterior of the pictured curve. It extends without end. Point A is in the exterior of the simple closed curve in the picture.

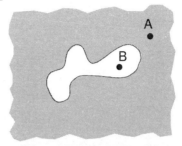

CHECK YOUR UNDERSTANDING
Is point B in the exterior of angle A on page 146? Is point B in the exterior of the simple closed curve above?

no; no

Exterior angle

An angle that is outside a polygon. Angle 1 is an exterior angle of triangle ABC.

CHECK YOUR UNDERSTANDING
Is angle 2 in the picture above another exterior angle of triangle ABC?

yes

Externally tangent circles

See Tangent circles.

147

Extracting a root

Computing a root of a number. Calculators have a $\sqrt{}$ (square root). For example, entering 6, then the $\sqrt{}$ sign gives the display 2.4494897. Thus $\sqrt{6} = 2.449489$ to six decimal places.

See also Square root.

CHECK YOUR UNDERSTANDING
Enter 7, then the $\sqrt{}$ sign. What is the display?

2.645751

Extraneous root

Also called Extraneous solution. A root of a derived equation that is not a root of the original equation. To see how it can occur, consider the equation $x = 4$. Its root is 4. Now square both sides of the equation $x = 4$: $x^2 = 16$. The derived equation has two roots, 4 and $^-4$, since $4^2 = 16$ and $(^-4)^2 = 16$. Thus, $^-4$ is an extraneous root of the original equation.

CHECK YOUR UNDERSTANDING
The equation that is derived from $x = 3$ by squaring both sides is $x^2 = 9$. What is the extraneous root in this case?

$^-3$

Extremes in a proportion

The first and fourth terms of a proportion. (The means are the second and third terms of a proportion.) In the proportion $\frac{a}{b} = \frac{c}{d}$, a and d are the extremes, and b and c are the means.

CHECK YOUR UNDERSTANDING
What are the extremes in the proportion $\frac{m}{n} = \frac{p}{q}$?

m and q

Face

A flat side of a solid figure.

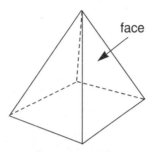

Square pyramid

CHECK YOUR UNDERSTANDING

How many faces of the pyramid pictured above are triangles?

4

Factor in multiplication

A number in a multiplication statement. In the statement $3 \times 5 = 15$, 3 and 5 are the factors.

CHECK YOUR UNDERSTANDING

What are the factors in $7 \times 4 = 28$?

7 and 4

Factor of a number

A number that divides exactly into a given number. For example, all factors of 12 are 1, 2, 3, 4, 6, and 12. Each of these divides 12: $12 \div 1 = 12$, $12 \div 2 = 6$, $12 \div 3 = 4$, and so on.

See also Common factor.

CHECK YOUR UNDERSTANDING
List all factors of 8.

1, 2, 4, and 8

Factor of a polynomial

A polynomial by which a given polynomial is divisible. For example, $x - 1$ is one factor of $2x^2 + 3x - 5$, because $(2x^2 + 3x - 5) \div (x - 1) = 2x + 5$. That is, $2x^2 + 3x - 5$ is divisible by $x - 1$. Polynomials can have factors that are monomials or polynomials.

FACTORING POLYNOMIALS
Factoring Trinomials of the Form $x^2 + bx + c$

Factor $x^2 - 7x + 10$. Think: $(x + a)(x + b) = x^2 + (a + b)x + ab$

$(x\ \ )(x\ \ )$ Look for two numbers whose sum is ⁻7 and product is 10. By trial and error, we find that ⁻2 and ⁻5 will give a sum of ⁻7 and a product of 10.

$(x - 2)(x - 5) = x^2 - 7x + 10$

$x - 2$ and $x - 5$ are the two linear binomial factors of the trinomial $x^2 - 7x + 10$.

Factoring Trinomials of the Form $ax^2 + bx + c$

Factor $6x^2 + 13x - 5$.

$$\text{Think: } (ax + b)(cx + d) = acx^2 + (ad + bc)x + bd$$

$(x \quad)(x \quad)$ Look for two numbers whose product is 6 and two other numbers whose product is ⁻5. By trial and error, we find that 3 and 2 will give a product of 6 for the first pair and ⁻1 and 5 will give a product of ⁻5 for the second pair.

$$(3x - 1)(2x + 5) = 6x^2 + 13x - 5$$

$3x - 1$ and $2x + 5$ are the two linear binomial factors of the trinomial $6x^2 + 13x - 5$.

Special Cases of Factoring

There are two special cases of factoring:

Difference of Two Squares

In general, $x^2 - y^2 = (x + y)(x - y)$

EXAMPLE $7^2 - 3^2 \stackrel{?}{=} (7 + 3)(7 - 3)$

$$49 - 9 \stackrel{?}{=} 10 \times 4$$
$$40 = 40$$

Perfect Square Trinomials

$$x^2 + 2xy + y^2 = (x + y)^2 \qquad\qquad x^2 - 2xy + y^2 = (x - y)^2$$

EXAMPLES

$3^2 + 2(3)(6) + 6^2 \stackrel{?}{=} (3 + 6)^2$ $8^2 - 2(8)(5) + 5^2 \stackrel{?}{=} (8 - 5)^2$

$9 + 36 + 36 \stackrel{?}{=} 9^2$ $64 - 80 + 25 \stackrel{?}{=} 3^2$

$81 = 81$ $9 = 9$

F

CHECK YOUR UNDERSTANDING

$6x^2 + 13x - 5 = (3x - 1)(2x + 5)$. Is $3x - 1$ a factor of $6x^2 + 13x - 5$?

yes

Factor tree

A diagram that shows the prime factorization of a number.

Factorial (!)

The product of all the positive integers through the given integer.

EXAMPLE   ┌──— Read "five factorial"

$5! = 1 \times 2 \times 3 \times 4 \times 5 = 120.$

Factorization

See Prime factorization.

Fahrenheit (°F) scale

A scale for measuring temperature. On this scale 32°F is assigned to the freezing point of water and 212°F is assigned to the boiling point of water. There are 100 degrees between the freezing and boiling points of water on the Celsius scale. There are 180 degrees between the freezing and boiling points of water on the Fahrenheit scale: 1.8°F = 1°C.

HOW TO CONVERT TEMPERATURE READINGS

The following formulas can be used to convert temperature readings.

Fahrenheit to Celsius	**Celsius to Fahrenheit**
$C = \frac{5}{9}(F - 32)$	$F = \frac{9}{5}C + 32$
What is 50°F in °C?	What is 35°C in °F ?
$C = \frac{5}{9}(F - 32)$	$F = \frac{9}{5}C + 32$
$= \frac{5}{9}(50 - 32)$	$= \frac{9}{5} \times 35 + 32$
$= \frac{5}{9} \times 18$ or 10°C	$= 63 + 32$ or 95°F

CHECK YOUR UNDERSTANDING

On the Fahrenheit scale, between what two numbers are the temperatures that fall between the freezing and the boiling points of water?

32° F and 212° F

F

Fathom

A unit of length used in England during the 12th century for measuring the depth of water. One fathom is the same length as 2 yards.

CHECK YOUR UNDERSTANDING

How many fathoms are there in 10 yards?

5

Fibonacci numbers

Also called Fibonacci sequence. Numbers in the sequence 1, 1, 2, 3, 5, 8, 13, 21, 34, ... Each number in the sequence after the second number is the sum of the two previous numbers. It is an infinite sequence.

CHECK YOUR UNDERSTANDING

What number follows 34 in the sequence of Fibonacci numbers?

55

A set of numbers with two operations that have these properties:

Closure Property under Addition and under Multiplication
This means that the sum and the product of any two real numbers is also a real number.

Commutative Property of Addition and of Multiplication
$x + y = y + x$ and $xy = yx$

Associative Property of Addition and of Multiplication
$(x + y) + z = x + (y + z)$ and $(xy)z = x(yz)$

Distributive Property of Multiplication over Addition
$x(y + z) = (xy) + (xz)$

Property of Zero for Addition
$x + 0 = 0 + x = x$

Property of One for Multiplication
$x \cdot 1 = 1 \cdot x = x$

Property of Additive Inverse
$x + (-x) = 0$

Property of Multiplicative Inverse
$x \cdot \dfrac{1}{x} = 1$

EXAMPLE The set of real numbers (rational and irrational numbers) together with the operations of addition and multiplication constitutes a field, because the above properties hold for all real numbers.

CHECK YOUR UNDERSTANDING
Why is the set of whole numbers not a field?
no Property of additive inverse and no Property of multiplicative inverse

Figurate numbers

Numbers that are represented by using dots in various geometric shapes.

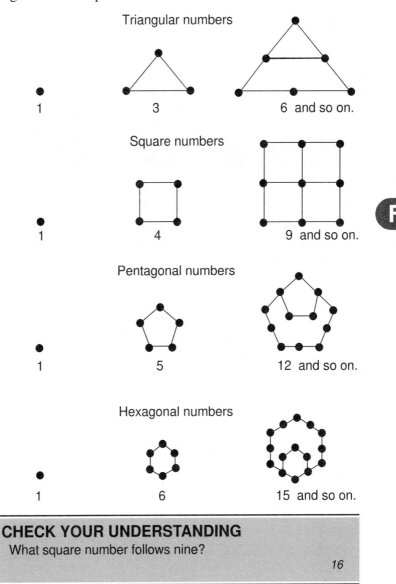

Triangular numbers

1   3   6 and so on.

Square numbers

1   4   9 and so on.

Pentagonal numbers

1   5   12 and so on.

Hexagonal numbers

1   6   15 and so on.

CHECK YOUR UNDERSTANDING
What square number follows nine?

16

Finite set

A set that has a specific number of members.

EXAMPLE $\{1,2,3,4,5,6,7,8,9,10\}$

The set of whole numbers from 1 through 10 is finite. It has 10 members.

CHECK YOUR UNDERSTANDING
Is the set of members of your family finite?

yes

Flip

Also called Reflection. A move of a figure over a line as if the line were a mirror reflection, the image of the figure. The size and shape of the figure stay the same.

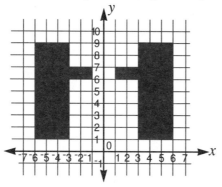

The following points correspond:

($^-$3,9) and (3,9), ($^-$1,7) and (1,7), ($^-$6,1) and (6,1)

See also Slide *and* Turn.

CHECK YOUR UNDERSTANDING
What point corresponds to (4,1)

($^-$4,1)

156

Flow chart

Also called Flow diagram. A display for communicating a logical sequence of operations to be performed in a specified order. Flow charts are often used to diagram a sequence of steps for a computer to follow. The flow chart below gives directions for counting down from 20 to 8 by 2's.

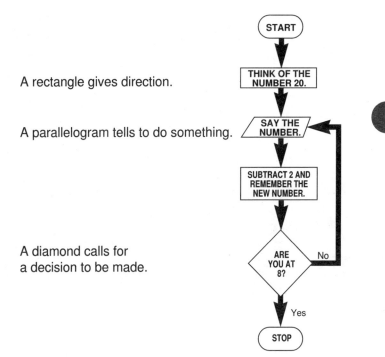

A rectangle gives direction.

A parallelogram tells to do something.

A diamond calls for
a decision to be made.

F

CHECK YOUR UNDERSTANDING
According to the flow chart above, what number would you say in order to go to Stop?

8

Fluid ounce (fl oz)

A unit of liquid measure. There are 8 fluid ounces in 1 cup.

CHECK YOUR UNDERSTANDING

How many fluid ounces are there in 4 cups?

32

Focus   *plural* foci

See Ellipse.

FOIL method of factoring trinomials

FOIL stands for *First-Outer-Inner-Last.* This method of factoring trinomials is a reversal of the FOIL method of multiplying binomials.

Factor $x^2 + 10x + 21$ into two binomials.

$(1x + 3)(1x + 7)$ Use $1x$ and $1x$ as factors of x^2.
Try 3 and 7 as factors of 21.
$(3 + 7 = 10,$ the coefficient of the middle term)

CHECK YOUR UNDERSTANDING

What would be the first terms of the binomials that are factors of $a^2 + 3a + 2$?

a and a

FOIL method of multiplying binomials

FOIL stands for *First-Outer-Inner-Last.* This method of multiplying binomials specifies the order in which the products of terms are found, as in this case:

$$(2x + 3)(x - 4y) = 2x^2 - 8xy + 3x - 12y$$

$$\quad\quad\quad F \quad O \quad I \quad L$$

CHECK YOUR UNDERSTANDING

Using the FOIL method of multiplying binomials, what will be the first product when multiplying $(a + b)(c + d)$?

ac

Formula

An equation that shows a mathematical relationship.

EXAMPLE The formula for the perimeter of a square is $p = 4s$, where s is the length of each side of the square.

If the length of each side of the square is 5 cm, then $p = 4(5)$ or 20 cm.

See page 456 for a list of formulas.

CHECK YOUR UNDERSTANDING
The length of a rectangle is ℓ, the width, w. What formula shows the perimeter?

$P = 2(\ell + w)$ or $P = 2\ell + 2w$

F

Four-color problem

The problem of showing that it is sufficient to have four colors in order to color any map so that no adjacent regions are colored with the same color. (This was proved to be true by two mathematicians, Kenneth Appel and Wolfgang Haken, at the University of Illinois, with the aid of computers, in July 1976.)

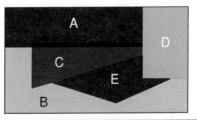

CHECK YOUR UNDERSTANDING
Could you use five colors to color a map so that no two adjacent regions are of the same color?

yes

Fractals

A geometric shape that is self-similar and has fractional dimension. Natural phenomena, such as formation of snowflakes, clouds, mountain ranges, and landscapes involve patterns. Their pictorial representations are fractals. Pictorial representations of the pattern are usually generated by computers.

CHECK YOUR UNDERSTANDING

Can a coastline be pictured or described by a fractal?

yes

Fraction

A number that can be expressed in the form $\frac{a}{b}$, where a and b are whole numbers ($b \neq 0$).

EXAMPLES

$$\frac{3}{7} \qquad 0.12 = \frac{12}{100} \text{ or } \frac{3}{25} \qquad 3\frac{1}{3} = \frac{10}{3}$$

THINKING ABOUT FRACTIONS

Fractions are used to name part of a whole or part of a set. What part is shaded grey? What part are triangles?

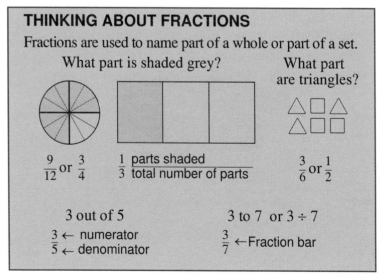

$\frac{9}{12}$ or $\frac{3}{4}$ $\frac{1 \text{ parts shaded}}{3 \text{ total number of parts}}$ $\frac{3}{6}$ or $\frac{1}{2}$

3 out of 5   3 to 7 or 3 ÷ 7

$3 \leftarrow$ numerator
$\overline{5} \leftarrow$ denominator

$\frac{3}{7} \leftarrow$ Fraction bar

160

Some fractions have special names:

Improper Fraction   **Mixed number**

$\frac{7}{3}$ Numerator is larger $2\frac{4}{5}$ A whole number
       than denominator.   and a fraction.

Equal fractions

Fractions that name the same number can be simplified to the same fraction. For example, $\frac{9}{12}$ and $\frac{12}{16}$.

$$\frac{9 \div 3}{12 \div 3} = \frac{3}{4} \qquad \frac{12 \div 4}{16 \div 4} = \frac{3}{4}$$

So $\frac{9}{12}$ and $\frac{12}{16}$ are equal fractions.

Remember these two rules about fractions:

1. A fraction is not changed in value if both the numerator and denominator are multiplied by the same number. $\frac{2}{3} = \frac{10}{15}$ because 2 and 3 are both multiplied by 5.

2. A fraction is not changed in value if both the numerator and denominator are divided by the same number: $\frac{10}{16} = \frac{5}{8}$ because 10 and 16 are both divided by 2.

If the same number is added to both the numerator and denominator or subtracted from both the numerator and denominator, the value of the fraction **is changed**.

EXAMPLES $\frac{5}{6} \rightarrow \frac{5-2}{6-2} = \frac{3}{4}$ $\frac{3}{4} \neq \frac{5}{6}$, since $3 \times 6 \neq 4 \times 5$
$18 \neq 20$

$\frac{7}{9} \rightarrow \frac{7+3}{9+3} = \frac{10}{12}$ $\frac{10}{12} \neq \frac{7}{9}$, since $10 \times 9 \neq 12 \times 7$
$90 \neq 84$

WRITING FRACTIONS IN LOWEST TERMS (SIMPLEST FORM)

A fraction is in lowest terms (simplest form) if the greatest common factor (GCF) of the numerator and denominator is 1.

Look at the numerator and denominator for common factors greater than 1.	5 is a common factor of the numerator and denominator.	Is the fraction in lowest terms? No, there is another common factor of 3.
$\dfrac{15}{75}$	$\dfrac{15 \div 5}{75 \div 5} = \dfrac{3}{15}$	$\dfrac{3 \div 3}{15 \div 3} = \dfrac{1}{5}$

FINDING COMMON DENOMINATORS

The least common denominator (LCD) is the least common multiple (the smallest number that both denominators will divide into evenly).

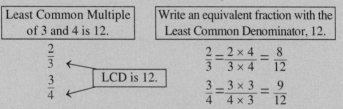

Least Common Multiple of 3 and 4 is 12.	Write an equivalent fraction with the Least Common Denominator, 12.
$\dfrac{2}{3}$ ← LCD is 12. $\dfrac{3}{4}$ ←	$\dfrac{2}{3} = \dfrac{2 \times 4}{3 \times 4} = \dfrac{8}{12}$ $\dfrac{3}{4} = \dfrac{3 \times 3}{4 \times 3} = \dfrac{9}{12}$

COMPARING FRACTIONS

If fractions have the same denominators, compare the numerators.

Compare $\dfrac{8}{9}$ and $\dfrac{5}{9}$. $8 > 5$, so $\dfrac{8}{9} > \dfrac{5}{9}$.

If fractions have different denominators, write equivalent fractions with the same denominator and compare numerators.

Compare $\dfrac{2}{3}$ and $\dfrac{5}{6}$. The LCD of 3 and 6 is 6.

$$\dfrac{2}{3} = \dfrac{2 \times 2}{3 \times 2} = \dfrac{4}{6} \qquad \dfrac{5}{6} = \dfrac{5 \times 1}{6 \times 1} = \dfrac{5}{6}$$

$$\dfrac{4}{6} < \dfrac{5}{6} \text{ so } \dfrac{2}{3} < \dfrac{5}{6}$$

See also Cross multiplication.

WRITING AN IMPROPER FRACTION AS A MIXED NUMBER

An improper fraction can be written as a mixed number by dividing the denominator into the numerator and writing the remainder over the denominator (divisor).

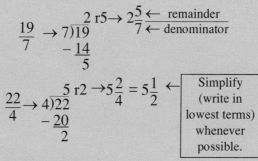

$$\frac{19}{7} \rightarrow 7\overline{)19} \quad \begin{array}{c} 2\ r5 \rightarrow 2\frac{5}{7} \leftarrow \text{remainder} \\ \ \ \leftarrow \text{denominator} \\ -\underline{14} \\ 5 \end{array}$$

$$\frac{22}{4} \rightarrow 4\overline{)22} \quad \begin{array}{c} 5\ r2 \rightarrow 5\frac{2}{4} = 5\frac{1}{2} \leftarrow \\ -\underline{20} \\ 2 \end{array}$$

Simplify (write in lowest terms) whenever possible.

F

WRITING A MIXED NUMBER AS AN IMPROPER FRACTION

Here is a shortcut for writing a mixed number as an improper fraction.

Write $3\frac{5}{7}$ as an improper fraction.

STEP 1	STEP 2	STEP 3
Multiply the denominator by the whole number:	Add the numerator of the fraction to the answer:	Write the result over the denominator:
$7 \times 3 = 21$	$21 + 5 = 26$	$\dfrac{26}{7}$

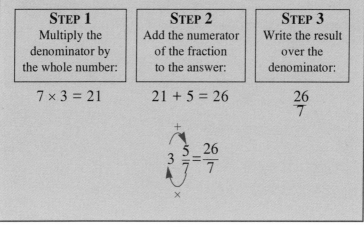

$$3\frac{5}{7} = \frac{26}{7}$$

ADDING AND SUBTRACTING FRACTIONS AND MIXED NUMBERS WITH LIKE DENOMINATORS

To add fractions and mixed numbers with the same denominators, add the numerators of the fractions, keep the denominator the same. Add the whole numbers. Simplify, if possible.

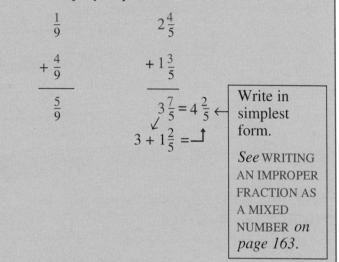

$$\frac{1}{9}$$

$$+\frac{4}{9}$$

$$\frac{5}{9}$$

$$2\frac{4}{5}$$

$$+1\frac{3}{5}$$

$$3\frac{7}{5}=4\frac{2}{5} \leftarrow$$

$$3+1\frac{2}{5}=$$

Write in simplest form.

See WRITING AN IMPROPER FRACTION AS A MIXED NUMBER *on page 163.*

To subtract fractions and mixed numbers with the same denominators, subtract the numerators of the fractions, keep the denominator the same. Subtract any whole numbers. Simplify, if possible.

$$\frac{7}{8}$$

$$-\frac{5}{8}$$

$$\frac{2}{8}=\frac{1}{4}$$

$$9\frac{7}{10}$$

$$-5\frac{4}{10}$$

$$4\frac{3}{10}$$

ADDING AND SUBTRACTING FRACTIONS AND MIXED NUMBERS WITH UNLIKE DENOMINATORS

Fractions must have the same denominators before they can be added or subtracted. To add fractions with different denominators, find equivalent fractions with a common denominator, then add or subtract as shown on page 164.

$$\frac{5}{8} = \frac{15}{24}$$
$$-\frac{5}{12} = -\frac{10}{24}$$
$$\frac{5}{24}$$

$$7\frac{3}{5} = 7\frac{6}{10}$$
$$+2\frac{7}{10} = +2\frac{7}{10}$$
$$9\frac{13}{10} = 10\frac{3}{10}$$

SUBTRACTING FRACTIONS AND MIXED NUMBERS WHEN REGROUPING IS NEEDED

F

Sometimes it is necessary to rename (regroup or borrow) before you can subtract.

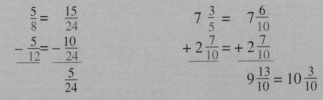

Think: $3 = 2\frac{5}{5}$

$3 + \frac{1}{5} = 2\frac{5}{5} + \frac{1}{5} = 2\frac{6}{5}$

$$3\frac{1}{5} = 2\frac{6}{5}$$
$$-1\frac{4}{5} = -1\frac{4}{5}$$
$$1\frac{2}{5}$$

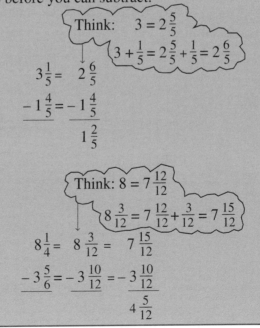

Think: $8 = 7\frac{12}{12}$

$8\frac{3}{12} = 7\frac{12}{12} + \frac{3}{12} = 7\frac{15}{12}$

$$8\frac{1}{4} = 8\frac{3}{12} = 7\frac{15}{12}$$
$$-3\frac{5}{6} = -3\frac{10}{12} = -3\frac{10}{12}$$
$$4\frac{5}{12}$$

MULTIPLYING FRACTIONS AND MIXED NUMBERS

Multiply numerators. Multiply denominators. Simplify the answer (write in lowest terms) when possible.

Cancel if possible.

$$\frac{2}{3} \times \frac{5}{7} = \frac{10}{21}$$

$$\frac{7}{\underset{3}{\cancel{9}}} \times \frac{\overset{1}{\cancel{3}}}{5} = \frac{7}{15}$$

Change mixed fractions to improper fractions (see p. 163). Then multiply the numerators. Multiply the denominators. Simplify the answer (write in lowest terms) when possible.

$$1\frac{2}{5} \times 10 =$$

$$\frac{7}{\underset{1}{\cancel{5}}} \times \frac{\overset{2}{\cancel{10}}}{1} = \frac{14}{1} = 14$$

$$4\frac{2}{3} \times 2\frac{3}{5} =$$

$$\frac{14}{3} \times \frac{13}{5} = \frac{182}{15} = 12\frac{2}{15}$$

DIVIDING FRACTIONS AND MIXED NUMBERS

Find the reciprocal of the divisor. Then multiply the numerators. Multiply the denominators. Simplify the answer (write in lowest terms) when possible.

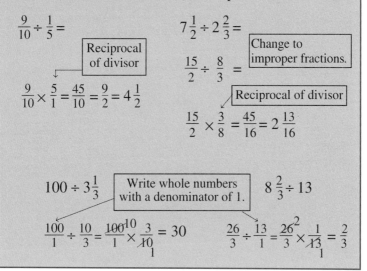

$$\frac{9}{10} \div \frac{1}{5} =$$

Reciprocal of divisor

$$\frac{9}{10} \times \frac{5}{1} = \frac{45}{10} = \frac{9}{2} = 4\frac{1}{2}$$

$$7\frac{1}{2} \div 2\frac{2}{3} =$$

Change to improper fractions.

$$\frac{15}{2} \div \frac{8}{3} =$$

Reciprocal of divisor

$$\frac{15}{2} \times \frac{3}{8} = \frac{45}{16} = 2\frac{13}{16}$$

$$100 \div 3\frac{1}{3}$$

Write whole numbers with a denominator of 1.

$$\frac{100}{1} \div \frac{10}{3} = \frac{\overset{10}{\cancel{100}}}{1} \times \frac{3}{\underset{1}{\cancel{10}}} = 30$$

$$8\frac{2}{3} \div 13$$

$$\frac{26}{3} \div \frac{13}{1} = \frac{\overset{2}{\cancel{26}}}{3} \times \frac{1}{\underset{1}{\cancel{13}}} = \frac{2}{3}$$

FRACTIONS TO DECIMALS

Divide the denominator into the numerator to find a decimal for a fraction.

terminating decimal

$$\frac{4}{5} = 5\overline{)\begin{array}{r} 0.8 \\ 4.0 \\ -4\,0 \\ \hline 0 \end{array}} \quad \text{zero remainder}$$

repeating decimal

$$\frac{2}{3} = 3\overline{)\begin{array}{r} 0.666\ldots \\ 2.000 \\ -1\,8 \\ \hline 20 \\ -18 \\ \hline 20 \\ -18 \\ \hline 2 \end{array}} \quad \begin{array}{l}\text{The digit} \\ \text{6 repeats} \\ \text{without end.}\end{array}$$

Write a bar over any digits or group of digits that repeat in a repeating decimal.

$$0.666\ldots = 0.\overline{6} \qquad\qquad 0.727272\ldots = 0.\overline{72}$$

FRACTIONS TO PERCENTS

First change the fraction to a decimal, then to a percent.

$$\frac{1}{2} = 2\overline{)\begin{array}{r} 0.5 \\ 1.0 \end{array}} \to 0.50 = 50\%$$

$$\frac{7}{8} = 8\overline{)\begin{array}{r} 0.875 \\ 7.000 \\ -6\,4 \\ \hline 60 \\ -56 \\ \hline 40 \\ -40 \end{array}} \to 0.875 \to 0.875 = 87.5\%$$

You may need to express a remainder as a fraction or round a quotient to express a fraction as a percent.

$$\frac{2}{3} = 3\overline{)\begin{array}{r} 0.66 \\ 2.00 \\ -1\,8 \\ \hline 2\,0 \\ -1\,8 \\ \hline 2 \end{array}} = 66\tfrac{2}{3}\%$$

$$\frac{5}{9} = 9\overline{)\begin{array}{r} 0.555 \\ 5.000 \\ -4\,5 \\ \hline 50 \\ -45 \\ \hline 50 \\ -45 \end{array}} \approx 0.56 \to 56\%$$

F

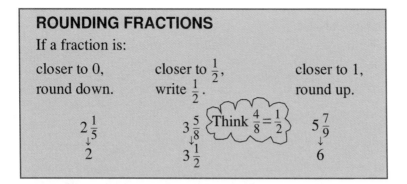

CHECK YOUR UNDERSTANDING
What is the simplest fractional name for 0.1?

$\dfrac{1}{10}$

Fractional equation

An equation that contains fractions.

EXAMPLE $\dfrac{1}{3}x + \dfrac{5}{6} = \dfrac{2}{3}$

SOLVING FRACTIONAL EQUATIONS

Solve $\dfrac{1}{3}x + \dfrac{5}{6} = \dfrac{2}{3}$

$6(\dfrac{1}{3}x + \dfrac{5}{6}) = 6 \cdot \dfrac{2}{3}$ Multiply each side of the equation by the Least Common Denominator, 6.

$2x + 5 = 4$

$2x + 5 - 5 = 4 - 5$ Subtract 5 from each side.

$2x = {}^-1$

$x = \dfrac{{}^-1}{2}$ Divide each side by 2.

Check: $\dfrac{1}{3}x + \dfrac{5}{6} = \dfrac{1}{3} \cdot \dfrac{{}^-1}{2} + \dfrac{5}{6} = \dfrac{4}{6} = \dfrac{2}{3}$

So, the solution of $\dfrac{1}{3}x + \dfrac{5}{6} = \dfrac{2}{3}$ is $\dfrac{{}^-1}{2}$.

CHECK YOUR UNDERSTANDING
Solve: $\dfrac{1}{2}x + \dfrac{2}{3} = \dfrac{5}{6}$.

$\dfrac{1}{3}$

Frequency

The number of times something occurs or the number in a particular category in a set of data. For example, 100 people were surveyed about pet ownership. 34 people had cats, 56 had dogs, 2 had birds, and 8 had horses. The frequency of horses is 8.

See also Frequency table *and* Relative frequency.

CHECK YOUR UNDERSTANDING
What is the frequency of dogs in the survey?

56

Frequency diagram

See Histogram.

Frequency table

A method of summarizing data. The ages in the sample below are summarized by tallying them in intervals of ten years and writing the total in the frequency column.

AGES OF A SAMPLE OF 35 PEOPLE				
38	8	68	17	11
15	45	10	57	27
29	84	20	25	40
23	49	76	77	48
28	31	36	5	39
45	23	48	18	48
33	22	55	41	43

FREQUENCY TABLE		
Interval	Tally	Frequency
0-9	//	2
10-19	𝖳𝖧𝖫	5
20-29	𝖳𝖧𝖫 ///	8
30-39	𝖳𝖧𝖫	5
40-49	𝖳𝖧𝖫 ////	9
50-59	//	2
60-69	/	1
70-79	//	2
80-89	/	1

CHECK YOUR UNDERSTANDING
According to the frequency table, how many people in the sample were from 20 to 29 years old?

8

Function

Also called Mapping. A set of ordered pairs such that no two ordered pairs have the same first member. These ordered pairs can be numbers or other things.

WAYS OF SHOWING FUNCTIONS

As a table

STUDENT'S NAME	STUDENT'S HEIGHT
Olivia	5'8"
Evan	5'2"
Julia	5'9"
Steven	4'11"

As a mapping

Olivia — 5'9"
Evan — 5'2"
Julia — 5'8"
Steven — 4'11"

Olivia is mapped into 5'8'', Evan into 5'2'', Julia into 5'9'', Steven into 4'11''.

As a set of ordered pairs

{(Olivia, 5'8"), (Evan, 5'2"), (Julia, 5'9"), (Steven, 4'11")}
Braces are used to indicate that it is a set.

As an equation

$y = 2x + 3$ or $f(x) = 2x + 3$
In this function, a number is multiplied by 2 and 3 is added to the product to find the value of the function.

As a graph

Graph of the function $f(x) = x + 2$.

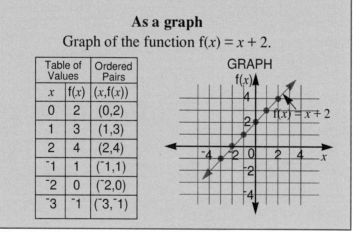

Table of Values		Ordered Pairs
x	$f(x)$	$(x, f(x))$
0	2	(0,2)
1	3	(1,3)
2	4	(2,4)
⁻1	1	(⁻1,1)
⁻2	0	(⁻2,0)
⁻3	⁻1	(⁻3,⁻1)

GRAPH
$f(x) = x + 2$

See also Domain of a function, Range of a function, Relation, *and* Vertical-line test for function.

Fundamental counting principle

Also called Basic counting principle. A general rule that states that if a choice can be made in x different ways and for each of these choices a second choice can be made in y different ways, then the choices can be made in xy different ways.

Joe's House   Stephanie's House   School

2 routes   3 routes

Multiply the number of choices at each stage: $2 \times 3 = 6$. So, there are 6 different routes from Joe's House to School by way of Stephanie's House.

F

CHECK YOUR UNDERSTANDING

If the first choice can be made in 4 different ways and the second choice in 5 different ways, then in how many ways can the choices be made?

20

Fundamental theorem of arithmetic

Also called Unique factorization theorem. Theorem that states that any counting number greater than 1 is prime or can be written as a unique product of prime numbers, except for the order of factors. The number has exactly one prime factorization except for the order of factors.

EXAMPLE 220 is factored as $2 \times 2 \times 5 \times 11$.

CHECK YOUR UNDERSTANDING

What is the prime factorization of 42?

$2 \times 3 \times 7$

Gallon

Liquid measure of capacity. One gallon contains 4 quarts.

CHECK YOUR UNDERSTANDING
How many quarts are there in 5 gallons?

20

General equation

A form of an equation using letters only. A general quadratic equation in one variable might be shown as
$$ax^2 + bx + c = 0.$$

Generalization

A statement that expresses some relationship that is true for all numbers in a specified set.

EXAMPLE

Each of the following numbers is divisible by 3:

Number	Divided by 3	Sum of its digits
12	$12 \div 3 = 4$	$1 + 2$ or 3
36	$36 \div 3 = 12$	$3 + 6$ or 9
78	$78 \div 3 = 26$	$7 + 8$ or 15 and $1 + 5 = 6$

The sum of the digits of the number is also divisible by 3. Generalization: If the sum of the digits of a number is divisible by 3, then the number is divisible by 3.

CHECK YOUR UNDERSTANDING
Is the following generalization true?
If a number ends in 2, then it is not divisible by 3.

no, 12 is divisible by 3

Geoboard

A device used for exploring properties of geometric figures. It can be made from a flat piece of wood by driving nails into it. The nails can be arranged in squares or circles, thus making either a square or a circular geoboard. A triangle can be shown using a rubber band. In a similar way many other geometric figures can be shown.

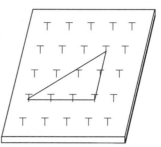

Square geoboard

CHECK YOUR UNDERSTANDING

On a geoboard like the one described above, what things suggest points?

nails

G

Geometric figure

A *figure* means a "set of points". Such sets of points can be line segments, triangles, other polygons, circles, and so on. There are plane figures (two-dimensional). There are also solid or space figures (three-dimensional), such as cubes, other rectangular solids, spheres, and so on. Pictures of these sets of points are also considered to be geometric figures.

CHECK YOUR UNDERSTANDING

Is a triangle a geometric figure?

yes

Geometric mean

The geometric mean of two numbers is the square root of their product. The geometric mean of 4 and 9 is $\sqrt{4 \times 9}$ or $\sqrt{36}$ or 6. In general, the geometric mean of n numbers is the nth root of the product of these numbers.

CHECK YOUR UNDERSTANDING
What is the geometric mean of 5 and 20?

$$\sqrt{5 \times 20} = \sqrt{100} \text{ or } 10$$

Geometric progression

Also called Geometric sequence. It is a sequence of numbers in which each succeeding term is obtained by multiplying the preceding term by the same number. That number is called the ratio or common ratio of the geometric progression. The following is a geometric progression: 1, 2, 4, 8, 16, 32, . . .
The common ratio for this geometric progression is 2.

CHECK YOUR UNDERSTANDING
What term follows 32 in the geometric progression above?

64

Geometric sequence

See Geometric progression.

Geometric series

The indicated sum of the terms of a geometric sequence. The geometric series corresponding to the geometric sequence 1, 2, 4, 8, 16, 32 is $1 + 2 + 4 + 8 + 16 + 32$.
See also Partial sum in an infinite series.

CHECK YOUR UNDERSTANDING
What is the sum of the first three terms in the series above?

7

Geometry

The study of sets of points, called geometric figures, and their shapes, sizes, and properties. There are several kinds of geometries. The type studied in high school is called Euclidean geometry, developed by Euclid, a Greek mathematician of about 300 B.C.

CHECK YOUR UNDERSTANDING
Is the study of properties of triangles included in geometry?

yes

Goldbach's conjecture

Named after the mathematician Christian Goldbach, who in 1742 observed that every even integer greater than 2 can be represented as a sum of two prime numbers. For example: $4 = 2 + 2$, $16 = 3 + 13$, $28 = 11 + 17$, and so on. It is called a conjecture because no one has been able to prove that it is true, yet no one has been able to find an example of an even number greater than 2 for which the conjecture is not true.

G

CHECK YOUR UNDERSTANDING
How can 8 be written as a sum of two prime numbers?

3 + 5

Golden ratio

The ratio $\frac{1 + \sqrt{5}}{2}$. It is claimed that the shape of a rectangle with this ratio of length to width is most pleasing to the eye. An approximation of this ratio is 8 to 5.

CHECK YOUR UNDERSTANDING
A rectangle has a width of 10 cm and a length of 16 cm. Is the ratio of length to width close to the golden ratio?

yes

Golden rectangle

A rectangle in which the ratio of length to width is approximately 8 to 5. The exact ratio is $\dfrac{1+\sqrt{5}}{2}$ and is called a golden ratio. It is claimed that the shape of such a rectangle is most pleasing to the eye.

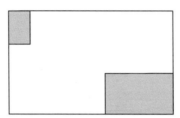

CHECK YOUR UNDERSTANDING
What is the ratio of length to width in a golden rectangle?

1 + √5 to 2

Golden section

A line segment divided into two segments in the ratio of the longer segment to shorter segment $\dfrac{1+\sqrt{5}}{2}$ or approximately 8 to 5.

CHECK YOUR UNDERSTANDING
A line segment is divided so one part measures 24 in. and the other measures 15 in. Do the two segments form a golden section?

yes

Gram (g)

A unit of mass in the metric system. There are 1000 grams in 1 kilogram: 1 kg = 1000 g.

CHECK YOUR UNDERSTANDING
How many grams are there in 3 kilograms?

3000

Graph

A pictorial representation of some mathematical relationship. It can be a point on a number line, which is a graph of a real number. It can be a point in a coordinate system, which is a graph of an ordered pair of real numbers. It can be a line in a coordinate system which is a graph of a linear (first degree) equation. It can be a part of a plane, which is a graph of an inequality.

GRAPHING A REAL NUMBER ON A NUMBER LINE

Graphs of some real numbers:

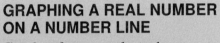

Graph of 1: point A.   Graph of $-1\frac{1}{2}$: point B.

Graph of $\sqrt{2}$: point C.   Graph of $-3\frac{1}{3}$: point D.

GRAPHING INEQUALITIES ON A NUMBER LINE

Graph of $x < 2$:

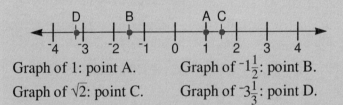

The graph is an infinite set of points. The hollow circle around 2 indicates that 2 does not belong to the solution set.

Graph of $x \geq 3$:

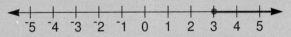

The graph is an infinite set of points. The solid dot at 3 indicates that 3 belongs to the solution set.

GRAPHING ORDERED PAIRS OF NUMBERS IN A COORDINATE SYSTEM

Graphs of some ordered number pairs:

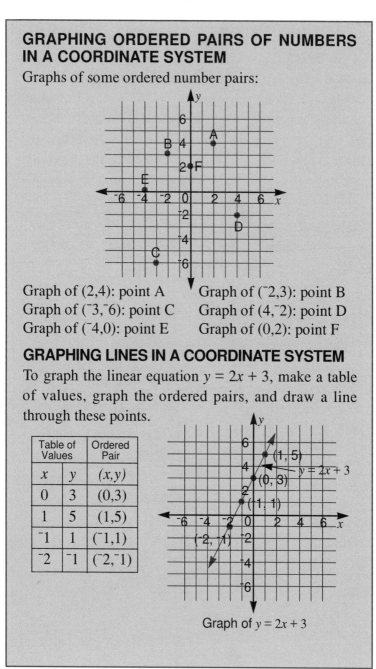

Graph of (2,4): point A   Graph of (⁻2,3): point B
Graph of (⁻3,⁻6): point C   Graph of (4,⁻2): point D
Graph of (⁻4,0): point E   Graph of (0,2): point F

GRAPHING LINES IN A COORDINATE SYSTEM

To graph the linear equation $y = 2x + 3$, make a table of values, graph the ordered pairs, and draw a line through these points.

Table of Values		Ordered Pair
x	y	(x,y)
0	3	(0,3)
1	5	(1,5)
⁻1	1	(⁻1,1)
⁻2	⁻1	(⁻2,⁻1)

Graph of $y = 2x + 3$

GRAPHING INEQUALITIES IN A COORDINATE SYSTEM

To graph the inequality $y > 2x + 3$, use the graph of the equation $y = 2x + 3$ from page 178. Try a pair of numbers to see whether they satisfy the inequality. Try (0,5). $5 > 2(0) + 3$. Since $5 > 3$ is true, the point (0,5) lies in the desired half-plane. Thus, the graph of the inequality $y > 2x + 3$ is that part of the half-plane that contains point (0,5). The half-plane that is the graph of $y > 2x + 3$ is shaded grey. The line is dashed to indicate that the points on the line do not belong to the half-plane.

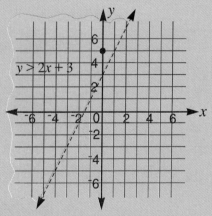

Graph of the inequality $y > 2x + 3$

CHECK YOUR UNDERSTANDING
Does the point (2,1) belong to the graph of $y > 2x + 3$?

no

Grating method of multiplication

See Multiplication.

Greater than (>)

An inequality relation such as 7 > 2. Read: 7 is greater than 2.

CHECK YOUR UNDERSTANDING
Is the inequality 2 > 7 true?

no

Greater than or equal to (≥)

An inequality relation that also includes equality, as in the true statement 4 ≥ 4. Read: 4 is greater than or equal to 4.

CHECK YOUR UNDERSTANDING
Is 7 ≥ 7 true?

yes

Greatest Common Factor (GCF)

Also called Greatest Common Divisor (GCD). The greatest positive integer that is a common factor of two or more numbers. The GCF of 12 and 18 is 6, written as GCF (12,18) = 6, because 12 ÷ 6 = 2 and 18 ÷ 6 = 3 and 6 is the greatest positive integer that divides both 12 and 18.

FINDING THE GREATEST COMMON FACTOR (GCF)
By finding all the factors
Find the Greatest Common Factor (GCF) of 16 and 24:
1. List all the factors of each number:
    16: 1 , 2 , 4 , 8 , 16
    24: 1 , 2 , 3 , 4 , 6 , 8 , 12, 24
2. Circle the factors common to both numbers (1, 2, 4, 8).
3. List the common factors: 1, 2, 4, 8
The greatest factor common to 16 and 24 is 8. So, the GCF (16,24) = 8.

By using prime factorization

Find the prime factorization of each number:
$$16 = 2 \times 2 \times 2 \times 2$$
$$24 = 2 \times 2 \times 2 \times 3$$
Multiply the prime factors that are common to both numbers:
$$2 \times 2 \times 2 = 8$$
So, GCF (16,24) = 8.

CHECK YOUR UNDERSTANDING
What is GCF (6,9)?

3

Greatest Possible Error (GPE)

One half the unit used for measuring.

EXAMPLES

Unit used for measuring	GPE
1 in.	$\frac{1}{2}$ in. or 0.5 in.
1 cm	$\frac{1}{2}$ cm or 0.5 cm
1 km	$\frac{1}{2}$ km or 0.5 km

CHECK YOUR UNDERSTANDING
What is the greatest possible error if the unit used for measuring is 1 mile?

$\frac{1}{2}$ *mile or 0.5 mile*

Gross

Twelve dozen or 144.

CHECK YOUR UNDERSTANDING
How many dozen are there in 2 gross?

24

Gross income

Income before any expenses and deductions are subtracted.

Grouping property

See Associative property.

Grouping symbols

Symbols used to indicate the grouping of numbers or terms. They also serve the function of indicating in what order operations should be performed. It is common practice to use parentheses, ( ),when only one kind of grouping symbol is needed. When a second kind of symbol is needed, then brackets, [ ], are used. If a third kind of grouping symbol is required, then braces, { }, are used. The common rule is to perform the operations within parentheses first, then within brackets, and last within braces.

EXAMPLE

$(2 + 3)\{[(7 - 1)(4 + 1) - 2] [(5 - 3) - (9 - 8)]\}$

$5 \quad \{ \quad [6 \times 5 - 2] \quad [2 - 1]\} \leftarrow$ Perform the operations within parentheses first.

$5 \quad \{28 \times 1\} \leftarrow$ Then perform the operations within the brackets.

$5 \cdot 28 \quad \leftarrow$ Finally, perform the operations within the braces.

$5 \cdot 28 = 140$

CHECK YOUR UNDERSTANDING

What is the following equal to? $4 + [(9 - 6) (3 + 1) - 3]$

13

Half-line

See Ray.

Half-plane

Given a line, the set of all points on each side of the line is a half-plane. If the line is included in the half plane, then the half-plane is said to be closed. If the line is not included, then the half-plane is said to be open.

CHECK YOUR UNDERSTANDING

Into how many half-planes does a line divide a plane?

2

Hectare

A unit for measuring area. One hectare is the area of a square with sides 100 meters long.

1 hectare = (100×100) m^2 or 10,000 m^2

One hectare would be equal to about two football fields.

CHECK YOUR UNDERSTANDING

How many hectares are there in 50,000 m^2?

5

Hecto-

The prefix hecto means "one hundred" (100).

Hectogram (hg) means "one hundred grams" (g).
$$1 \text{ hg} = 100 \text{ g}$$
A hectogram is a unit of mass in the metric system.

Hectoliter (hL) means "one hundred liters" (L).
$$1 \text{ hL} = 100 \text{ L}$$
A hectoliter is a unit of capacity in the metric system.

Hectometer (hm) means "one hundred meters" (m).
$$1 \text{ hm} = 100 \text{ m}$$
A hectometer is a unit of length in the metric system.

CHECK YOUR UNDERSTANDING
What would hectopound mean if it were a word?

100 pounds

Height of a triangle

The length of an altitude in a triangle.

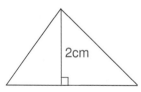

One height of the triangle is 2 cm.

CHECK YOUR UNDERSTANDING
If one altitude in a triangle is 5 cm long, what is one height?

5 cm

Hemisphere

Half of a sphere. It is obtained by cutting the sphere with a plane containing the center of the sphere. Usually the circle, which is part of the plane, is included in the hemisphere.

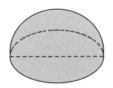

Hemisphere

CHECK YOUR UNDERSTANDING
If a plane does not pass through the center of the sphere, does it cut off a hemisphere?

no

Heptagon

H

A polygon with seven sides.

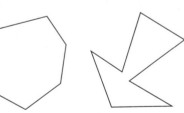

Regular heptagon   Not regular heptagons

CHECK YOUR UNDERSTANDING
How many angles does a heptagon have?

7

Heron's formula

Also called Hero's formula. A formula for the area of a triangle. It was derived by Heron, an Egyptian mathematician with Greek schooling.

$$A = \sqrt{s(s-a)(s-b)(s-c)}$$

where s is one-half the perimeter of the triangle and a, b, and c are the lengths of the sides of the triangle.

CHECK YOUR UNDERSTANDING
Using Heron's formula, find the area of a triangle whose sides are 5 cm, 7 cm, and 8 cm long.
$$s = \frac{5+7+8}{2} = 10; \quad A = \sqrt{10(10-5)(10-7)(10-8)} = \sqrt{10 \times 5 \times 3 \times 2}$$
$$= \sqrt{300} = \sqrt{3 \times 100} \text{ or } 10\sqrt{3} \text{ cm}^2$$

Hexagon

A polygon with six sides.

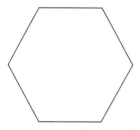 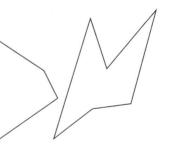

Regular hexagon   Not regular hexagons

CHECK YOUR UNDERSTANDING
How many angles does a hexagon have?

6

Hexagonal number

A number that can be represented using dots and hexagons as shown below. The first five hexagonal numbers are shown. The general formula for obtaining hexagonal numbers is $n(2n - 1)$ where n is a counting number that indicates the position of the number in the sequence. To find the third hexagonal number, substitute 3 for n in the formula: $3(6 - 1) = 15$.

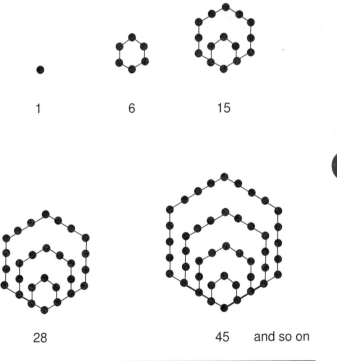

1   6   15

28   45   and so on

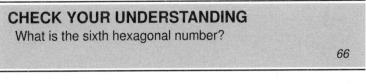

CHECK YOUR UNDERSTANDING
What is the sixth hexagonal number?

66

Hieroglyphic numerals

See Egyptian numeration system.

Hindu-Arabic numeration system

Our commonly used base-ten numeration system in which ten digits are used: 0, 1, 2, 3, 4, 5, 6, 7, 8, and 9.

CHECK YOUR UNDERSTANDING

What is the value of 1 in 126 in the Hindu-Arabic numeration system?

one hundred

Histogram

A pictorial way of representing data. Given a set of scores, one can display the frequency of the scores by making a histogram. For example, the bar representing the 81-90 score range shows a frequency of 13. This means 13 scores were in this range.

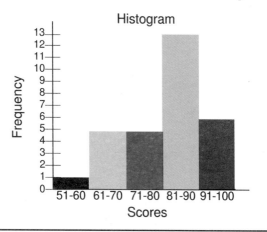

CHECK YOUR UNDERSTANDING

In the histogram above, how many scores fall in the interval 51-60?

one

See x-axis.

Hypotenuse

The side opposite the right angle in a right triangle. It is always the longest side of a right triangle. $\overline{AB}$ is the hypotenuse.

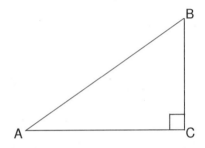

CHECK YOUR UNDERSTANDING

Is the hypotenuse opposite the largest angle in a right triangle?

*yes; each of the other two angles measures less than 90°
because the sum of the three angles in a triangle is 180°*

H

Hypothesis

See Axiom.

Icosahedron

A polyhedron with twenty faces. A regular icosahedron has 20 congruent equilateral triangles for its faces.

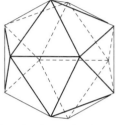

Regular icosahedron

CHECK YOUR UNDERSTANDING
What plane geometric figure is each face of a regular icosahedron?

an equilateral triangle

Identical

The term used mostly in geometry to refer to congruent figures, that is, figures that have the same shape and size.

CHECK YOUR UNDERSTANDING
Does saying "identical triangles" mean "congruent triangles"?

yes

Identity

An equality, denoted by $\equiv$, that is true for all values of the variable(s), such as $2(x - y) \equiv 2x - 2y$. The equality sign (=) is often used in place of the identity sign ($\equiv$).

CHECK YOUR UNDERSTANDING
Is $4(a + b) = 4a + 4b$ an identity?

yes

Identity element

A number, say e, in a set of numbers so that, given an operation, the result of performing that operation on any number and e results in that number. If e is the identity element, then for every number n in a given set and for operation $*$, $n * e = e * n = n$.

CHECK YOUR UNDERSTANDING
If, in some set of numbers, for every number k in the set and operation #, $k \# h = h \# k = k$, is h an identity element?

yes

Identity for addition

Also called Additive identity. The identity for addition is the number 0. It is called the identity, because 0 added to any number is equal to that number: $a + 0 = 0 + a = a$.

CHECK YOUR UNDERSTANDING
What is $^-6 + 0$ equal to?

$^-6$

I

Identity for multiplication

Also called Multiplicative identity. The identity for multiplication is the number 1, because 1 multiplied by any number is equal to that number: $a \cdot 1 = 1 \cdot a = a$.

CHECK YOUR UNDERSTANDING
What is $^-14 \cdot 1$ equal to?

$^-14$

Identity property for addition

Also called Zero property. It states that zero plus any number is that number. Using the variable n, $n + 0 = 0 + n = n$.

CHECK YOUR UNDERSTANDING
What is $z + 0$ equal to?

z

Identity property for multiplication

Also called Property of one for multiplication. It states that one times any number is that number. Using the variable n, $n \cdot 1 = 1 \cdot n = n$.

CHECK YOUR UNDERSTANDING
What is $z \cdot 1$ equal to?

z

If-then statement

See Conditional.

Imaginary number

Also called pure imaginary number. A complex number a + bi is an imaginary number when a = 0, b ≠ 0, and i = $\sqrt{-1}$. Thus, an imaginary number is of the form bi, where b is a real number (b ≠ 0).

EXAMPLES $\frac{1}{3}i$ 5i   ⁻2i $\sqrt{2}i$

CHECK YOUR UNDERSTANDING
Is ⁻$\sqrt{3}$i an imaginary number?

yes

Implication

See Conditional.

Impossible event

In probability, an event that cannot take place. The probability of such an event is 0.

EXAMPLE   Choosing a negative number from a set of positive numbers is an impossible event.

CHECK YOUR UNDERSTANDING
Is choosing an odd integer from a set of even integers an impossible event?

yes

Improper fraction

A fraction in which the numerator is greater than or equal to the denominator, such as in $\frac{5}{5}$ and $\frac{6}{5}$. Thus, an improper fraction is either equal to 1 or is greater than 1.

CHECK YOUR UNDERSTANDING
Is $\frac{6}{7}$ an improper fraction?

no

Incenter

The center of a circle that is inscribed in a triangle. The incenter is the point of intersection of the three angle bisectors of the triangle. In the picture, point I is the incenter.

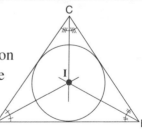

CHECK YOUR UNDERSTANDING
What is the least number of angle bisectors required to locate the incenter of a circle?

2, because two intersecting segments determine a unique point

Inclination angle

See Angle of inclination.

Included angle

An angle formed by two sides of a polygon is the included angle of the two sides. In triangle STR, angle T is the included angle of sides $\overline{ST}$ and $\overline{RT}$.

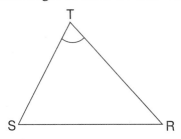

CHECK YOUR UNDERSTANDING

In triangle STR above, angle R is the included angle of which two sides?

$\overline{SR}$ and $\overline{TR}$

Included side

A side of a polygon whose endpoints are vertices of two angles. In triangle STR, side SR is the included side of angles S and R.

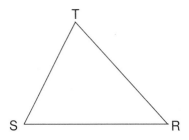

CHECK YOUR UNDERSTANDING

In triangle STR above, side $\overline{TR}$ is the included side of which two angles?

angles T and R

Incommensurable

Also called Incommensurate.

Line segments Two line segments are incommensurable if there is no line segment that would go into each of the two segments a whole number of times. For example, line segments of 4 in. and $4\sqrt{2}$ in. are incommensurable because there is no line segment that will go into each a whole number of times.

Numbers Two numbers are incommensurable if there is no rational number that would go into each of the two numbers a whole number of times. For example, 1 and $\sqrt{2}$ are incommensurable numbers.

CHECK YOUR UNDERSTANDING
Are $\frac{1}{3}$ and $\frac{1}{6}$ incommensurable?

no; $\frac{1}{6}$ goes into $\frac{1}{3}$ two times and into $\frac{1}{6}$ one time

Inconsistent system of equations

A system of two or more equations that has no common solution.

EXAMPLE $x + y = 3$ and $2x + 2y = 7$

To see that the two equations have no common solution, divide each side of the second equation by 2. Result: $x + y = 3\frac{1}{2}$. The sum of two numbers cannot be both 3 and $3\frac{1}{2}$.

CHECK YOUR UNDERSTANDING
Is the following an inconsistent system of equations?
$x - y = 4$ and $2x - 2y = 10$

yes, $x - y$ cannot be both 4 and 5

Independent equations

See System of equations.

Independent events

In probability, when the outcome of one event does not depend on the outcome of another event. For example, in two tosses of a coin, the outcome of the second toss does not depend on the outcome of the first toss. In each toss the probability of tails landing up is $\frac{1}{2}$ and the probability of heads landing up is $\frac{1}{2}$.

See also Dependent event.

CHECK YOUR UNDERSTANDING
Are two rolls of a die independent events?

yes

Independent system of equations

A system of two or more equations that have a common solution.

> EXAMPLE $x + y = 7$ and $x - y = 1$
> The ordered pair (4,3) is the solution of this system.

CHECK YOUR UNDERSTANDING
Is the following system of two equations an independent system? If yes, give the common solution. $x + y = 8$ and $x - y = 2$

yes; 5 and 3

Independent variable

In a function of two variables, one variable is dependent and the other independent. For example, in $y = 2x + 1$, x is the independent variable. The value of y depends on the value of x. If the value of x is 3, then the value of y is $y = 2 \cdot 3 + 1$ or 7.

CHECK YOUR UNDERSTANDING
In $y = 2x + 1$, what is the value of the dependent variable y, if the value of x is 2?

5

Index
plural **indexes or indices**

The number used to indicate the root. For example, in $\sqrt[3]{2}$, the index is 3. When writing a square root, such as $\sqrt{6}$, the index is not written. It is a common understanding that the index in such cases is 2. In general, the index in the nth root, $\sqrt[n]{a}$, is n.

CHECK YOUR UNDERSTANDING
What is the index in $\sqrt[5]{7}$?

5

Indirect measurement

Finding distances without directly measuring them. For example, the distance between the points A and B on opposite sides of the river can be found by measuring accessible distance AC and angle C. Angle A is made to be a right angle. Trigonometry can then be used to compute the distance.

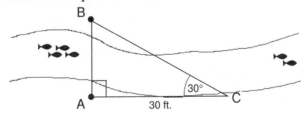

$\frac{AB}{AC}$ = tan 30°. Tan 30° is approximately 0.6 *(See table on page 455)*. AB = AC × tan 30° = 30 × 0.6 or about 18 ft.

CHECK YOUR UNDERSTANDING
For purposes of indirect measurement, what kind of a triangle do you need to make?

a right triangle

Inductive reasoning (or thinking)

Reaching a conclusion on the basis of a number of observations that form a pattern. For example, multiplying counting numbers by 2, one observes that the product in each case is an even number.

$2 \times 1 = 2, 2 \times 2 = 4, 2 \times 3 = 6, 2 \times 4 = 8, 2 \times 5 = 10, \ldots$

The conclusion reached by inductive reasoning is that the product of any counting number and 2 is an even number.

CHECK YOUR UNDERSTANDING
Dividing randomly selected nonzero numbers by themselves gives the same result. One reaches a conclusion that a nonzero number divided by itself is 1. Is this conclusion reached by inductive reasoning?

yes

Inequality

A sentence that contains > (is greater than), < (is less than), ≥ (is greater than or equal to), ≤ (is less than or equal to), or ≠ (is not equal to). Such sentences are of the following forms:

$a > b$ a is greater than b
$a < b$ a is less than b
$a \geq b$ a is greater than or equal to b
$a \leq b$ a is less than or equal to b
$a \neq b$ a is not equal to b

EXAMPLES OF INEQUALITIES THAT ARE TRUE STATEMENTS
$7 > 3$ $6 < 8$ $4 \geq 4$ $7 \leq 9$ $2 \neq 1$

198

SOLVING INEQUALITIES AND GRAPHING THE SOLUTION SETS

Solve and graph the solution set: $x + 4 < 6$

$$x + 4 - 4 < 6 - 4 \quad \text{Subtract 4 from each side}$$
$$x < 2$$

The solution set is the set of all numbers less than 2. It is an infinite set.

Graph of $x < 2$:

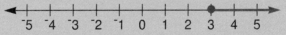

The hollow circle around 2 indicates that 2 does not belong to the solution set.

Solve and graph the solution set: $x - 5 \geq {}^-2$

$$x - 5 + 5 \geq {}^-2 + 5 \quad \text{Add 5 to each side.}$$
$$x \geq 3$$

The solution set is the set of all numbers greater than or equal to 3. It is an infinite set.

Graph of $x \geq 3$:

The solid dot at 3 indicates that 3 belongs to the solution set.

Solve and graph the solution set: $\frac{1}{2}x + 1 > {}^-1$

$$2(\tfrac{1}{2}x + 1) > {}^-1 \cdot 2 \quad \text{Multiply each side by 2.}$$
$$x + 2 > {}^-2 \quad \text{Subtract 2 from each side.}$$
$$x > {}^-4$$

Graph of $x > {}^-4$:

Solve and graph the solution set: $^-3x \leq 6$

$(^-3x) \div {^-3} \geq 6 \div {^-3}$ Divide each side by $^-3$.

$x \geq {^-2}$ **Multiplying or dividing each side of an inequality by a negative number reverses the inequality sign.**

Graph of $x \geq {^-2}$:

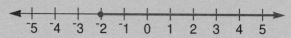

Combining Inequalities: Conjunction

Solve and graph the solution set of the conjunction:

$$x > 3 \text{ and } x > {^-2}$$

Numbers that are greater than 3 are also greater than $^-2$. So, the solution set of the conjunction $x > 3$ and $x > {^-2}$ is the intersection of the two sets described by the two inequalities.

Graph of $x > 3$ and $x > {^-2}$:

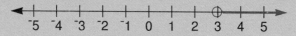

Combining Inequalities: Disjunction

Solve and graph the solution set of the disjunction:

$$x > 3 \text{ or } x < 1$$

Numbers that are greater than 3 or less than 1 are in the solution set. So, the solution set of the disjunction $x > 3$ or $x < 1$ is the union of the two sets described by the two inequalities.

Graph of $x > 3$ or $x < 1$:

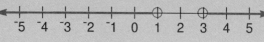

SOLVING SYSTEMS OF INEQUALITIES BY GRAPHING

Solve the system by graphing: $-x + y < 1$
$$x + y \geq {}^-3$$

Step 1 Graph the lines $-x + y = 1$ and $x + y = {}^-3$

Step 2 Locate one point on one side of the graph of $-x + y = 1$ to see whether its coordinates satisfy the inequality $-x + y < 1$. If they do, then the half-plane in which this point lies is the graph of the inequality. If they do not, then the other half-plane is the graph. Test $(4,2)$: ${}^-4 + 2 < 1$ is true, so the half-plane containing the point $(4,2)$ is the graph of $-x + y < 1$.

Step 3 Perform the same test for the half-planes determined by the graph of $x + y = {}^-3$. (The half-plane together with the boundary line in which the graph of $(2,0)$ is located is the graph of $x + y \geq {}^-3$.

The graph of the solution set of the system $-x + y < 1$ and $x + y \geq {}^-3$ consists of the points in the intersection of the graphs of the two inequalities. It is shaded grey in the graph below.

The dashed line in the graph indicates that the boundary does not belong to the solution set, while the solid line indicates that it does.

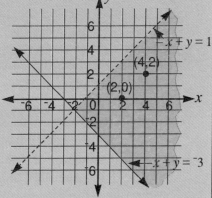

CHECK YOUR UNDERSTANDING

Why is the boundary of the graph of $x + y \geq {}^-3$ included in the solution set of the inequality?

because the inequality has the symbol $\geq$

Inference

Also called Syllogism. A conclusion that logically follows from premises. The standard form involves two premises and an inference.

EXAMPLE All men are mortal. (major premise)

Fernando is a man. (minor premise)

Fernando is mortal. (conclusion or inference)

CHECK YOUR UNDERSTANDING
What conclusion about C follows from the following premises?
All circles are round. (major premise) C is a circle. (minor premise)
C is round.

Infinite

Without end. Endless.

EXAMPLE The set of counting numbers: 1,2,3,4,5,6, … is infinite. Three dots are written to indicate that a set continues without end.

CHECK YOUR UNDERSTANDING
Is the set of all fractions infinite?
yes

Infinite decimal

See Nonterminating decimal.

Infinity (∞)

A concept of something that extends beyond any given value. If a sequence of numbers increases beyond any bound, it is said that the sequence tends toward infinity. The counting numbers tend toward infinity.

CHECK YOUR UNDERSTANDING
Does the set of all even numbers tend toward infinity?
yes

Inscribed angle

An angle is inscribed in a circle when its vertex is on the circle and its sides are chords of the circle. Angle ABC is inscribed in circle O.

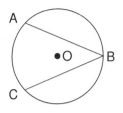

Inscribed circle

A circle is inscribed in a polygon if each side of the polygon is tangent to the circle. In a circle inscribed in a triangle, the center of the circle is the intersection of the angle bisectors of the triangle. Circle O is inscribed in triangle ABC.

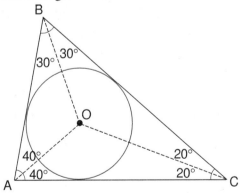

Inscribed polygon

A polygon is inscribed in a circle if each vertex of the polygon is on the circle. Triangle ABC is inscribed in circle O. Circle O is said to be circumscribed about the triangle. The center of the circle which is circumscribed about triangle ABC is the point of intersection of perpendicular bisectors of the sides of the triangle.

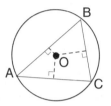

CHECK YOUR UNDERSTANDING

Is each vertex of triangle ABC on circle O?

yes

Integers

Positive and negative whole numbers and 0:

..., ⁻4, ⁻3, ⁻2, ⁻1, 0, +1, +2, +3, +4, ...

The set of integers is infinite, extending without end to the left and to the right of 0 on the number line. An integer has both a magnitude (how much) and direction (positive or negative). It is common practice not to write the + sign with positive integers. It is simply understood that an integer with no sign is a positive integer.

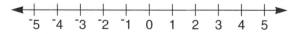

Number line showing some integers

204

USING INTEGERS

There are many situations in which integers can be used.

EXAMPLES temperature of 23°C above 0°: $^+23°C$

temperature of 10°C below 0°: $^-10°C$

gain of $10: $^+10$ dollars

loss of $5: $^-5$ dollars

being $15 "in the hole": $^-15$ dollars

being $20 "out of the hole": $^+20$ dollars

gain of 15 yards in football: $^+15$ yards

loss of 10 yards in football: $^-10$ yards

INTEGERS AS POINTS ON A NUMBER LINE

Each integer has a point on a number line corresponding to it. The integer is the coordinate of that point. The point corresponding to 0 is called the *origin*.

EXAMPLES   Point A: $^-5$ Point D: 3

        ↑   ↑

  coordinate of point A   coordinate of point D

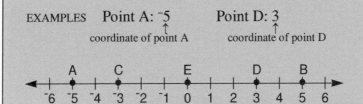

I

Each integer has an opposite integer. Points corresponding to opposite integers are the same distance from the origin.

EXAMPLES Points A and B are the same distance from zero.
$^-5$ and 5 are opposites.

Points C and D are the same distance from zero.
$^-3$ and 3 are opposites.

0 is its own opposite.

COMPARING AND ORDERING INTEGERS

You can use a number line to compare integers and arrange them in order. The ordering of integers is shown on the number line. The integers become greater as you move from left to right along the number line.

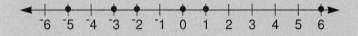

$^-5 < {}^-3$ because $^-5$ is to the left of $^-3$ on the number line.
  ↑— is less than

$0 > {}^-5$ because 0 is to the right of $^-5$ on the number line.
  ↑— is greater than

$0 < 4$ because 0 is to the left of 4 on the number line.

$1 > {}^-2$ because 1 is to the right of $^-2$ on the number line.

$^-2 < 6$ because $^-2$ is to the left of 6 on the number line.

ABSOLUTE VALUE OF AN INTEGER

Absolute value of an integer is its distance from zero on a number line.

EXAMPLES $|5| = 5$ $|0| = 0$ $|^-6| = 6$

ADDING INTEGERS

The sum of two positive integers is positive.
$$2 + 3 = 5$$
The sum of two negative integers is negative.
$$^-7 + {}^-5 = {}^-12$$
The sum of a positive and negative integer is:
positive if the positive integer has the greater absolute value.
negative if the negative integer has the greater absolute value.
zero if the absolute value of the integers is the same.

To add a positive and a negative integer, find the difference of the absolute values of the numbers and use the sign of the integer with the greater absolute value.

$$^-5 + 9 = ?$$ $$^-8 + 5 = ?$$
$$9 - 5 = 4$$ $$8 - 5 = 3$$
$^-5 + 9 = 4$ ← $|9| > |^-5|$ So, the sum is positive. $^-8 + 5 = {}^-3$ ← $|^-8| > |5|$ So, the sum is negative.

The sum is zero if the absolute value of the integers is the same.
$$^-6 + 6 = 0$$

The sum of 0 and any integer is that integer.
$$5 + 0 = 5$$ $$^-8 + 0 = {}^-8$$

SUBTRACTING INTEGERS

To subtract integers, add the opposite of the subtrahend (the integer being subtracted).

EXAMPLES
$$8 - 3 = 8 + {}^-3 = 5$$
$$9 - {}^-5 = 9 + 5 = 14$$
$$^-8 - 3 = {}^-8 + {}^-3 = {}^-11$$
$$^-7 - {}^-2 = {}^-7 + 2 = {}^-5$$
$$^-4 - {}^-4 = {}^-4 + 4 = 0$$

Zero subtracted from an integer is that integer.
$$9 - 0 = 9$$ $$^-6 - 0 = {}^-6$$

MULTIPLYING INTEGERS
The product of two positive integers is positive.
$$3 \times 5 = 15$$
The product of two negative integers is positive.
$$^-4 \times ^-5 = 20$$
The product of a positive and a negative integer is negative.
$$^-3 \times 6 = ^-18$$
Zero multiplied by any integer is 0.
$$0 \times ^-8 = 0$$

DIVIDING INTEGERS
The quotient of two positive integers is positive.
$$15 \div 5 = 3$$
The quotient of two negative integers is positive.
$$^-20 \div ^-5 = 4$$
The quotient of a positive and a negative integer is negative.
$$^-18 \div 6 = ^-3$$
Zero divided by any nonzero integer is 0.
$$0 \div ^-8 = 0$$
Division by 0 is undefined.

The set of integers under division does not have the Closure property. This means that the quotients of some integers are not integers. Example: $6 \div 5$ is not an integer.

CHECK YOUR UNDERSTANDING
Is there an integer between any two consecutive integers?

no; example: there is no integer between 5 and 6

Intercept

In coordinate geometry, the point at which a graph intersects the x-axis or the y-axis. The point of intersection with the x-axis is called x-intercept and the point of intersection with the y-axis, y-intercept. On the graph shown, the x-intercept is point $(1,0)$ and the y-intercept is point $(0,^-1)$.

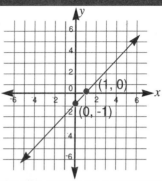

CHECK YOUR UNDERSTANDING

In the graph above, does the x-intercept lie on the y-axis?

no

Intercept form

The intercept form of an equation of a line is $\frac{x}{a}+\frac{y}{b}= 1$, where a is the x-intercept and b is the y-intercept. The point of intersection with the x-axis and y-axis can be read directly from the equation. For example, write the equation of the line $y = 3x - 2$ in intercept form.

$3x - y = 2$

$\frac{3x}{2}-\frac{y}{2} = 1$ Divide both sides by 2 to get 1 on the right side.

$\frac{3x}{2}$ is the same as $\frac{x}{\frac{2}{3}}$ and $-\frac{y}{2}$ is the same as $+\frac{y}{^-2}$, so

$\frac{x}{\frac{2}{3}}+\frac{y}{^-2} = 1$. The x-intercept is $\frac{2}{3}$. The y-intercept is $^-2$.

To graph the equation using this form, mark a point at $(\frac{2}{3},0)$ and $(0,^-2)$ and connect with a line.

CHECK YOUR UNDERSTANDING

What is the intercept form of the equation of the line $y = 2x + 1$?

$-2x + y = 1; \dfrac{x}{\frac{^-1}{2}} + \dfrac{y}{1}= 1$

Intercepted arc

An arc that lies in the interior of an angle with one endpoint on each side of the angle. Arc CB is the intercepted arc of inscribed angle CAB.

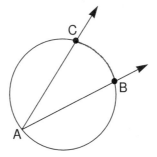

Interest

An amount of money paid for the use of money. The percent of the invested or borrowed amount on which the interest is based is called the rate of interest. The amount invested or borrowed is called the principal. If $100 is invested at the annual rate of 6% simple interest, then at the end of one year the investment will earn $100 × 0.06 or $6 in interest.

See also Compound interest *and* Simple interest.

Interior angle of a polygon

An angle formed by two sides of a polygon.

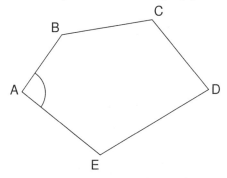

Angle BAE is an interior angle.

See also Exterior angle of a polygon.

Interior of an angle

Points inside an angle. The shaded part of angle A is the interior of angle A. It extends without end.

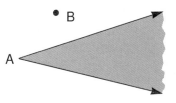

Interior of a polygon

The points inside a polygon. The shaded part is the interior of triangle ABC. The sides of the triangle do not belong to the interior.

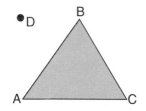

CHECK YOUR UNDERSTANDING
Is point D in the interior of triangle ABC?

no

Interpolation

Given a table of numerical values, such as a table of square roots, interpolation is a procedure for estimating values between those found in the table.

EXAMPLE

$\sqrt{20.2} = ?$

Since 20.2 is one-fifth of the way from 20 to 21, $\sqrt{20.2}$ is one-fifth of the way from 4.472 to 4.583:

$\frac{4.583 - 4.472}{5} = 0.0222$

$4.472 + 0.0222 = 4.4942$

So, $\sqrt{20.2} = 4.4942$

No.	Square root
20	4.472
21	4.583
22	4.690
23	4.796
24	4.899
25	5.000
26	5.099
27	5.196

$\sqrt{20.2} \to$ 20

CHECK YOUR UNDERSTANDING
Using the table above, find $\sqrt{26.5}$ by interpolation.

5.1475

Intersect

To cross. Line segment AB intersects line segment CD at point E. Line segment AB intersects the circle at two points, F and G.

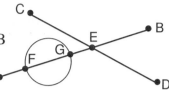

Intersecting geometric figures

Geometric figures that have points in common.

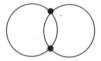

Intersecting lines   Intersecting circles

Intersection of sets

A set consisting of all those members that belong to two or more sets. The intersection of {1, 3, 5} and {3, 4, 5, 6} is {3, 5}.

See also Union of sets.

Interval

For numbers A set of numbers between two given numbers. For example, the set of numbers between 5 and 9 is an interval. If the numbers 5 and 9 are not included in the interval, then it is an open interval. It is described by the inequality $5 < n < 9$ (Read: five is less than n and n is less than nine or n is between five and nine). If 5 and 9 are included in the interval, then it is a closed interval. It is described by the inequality $5 \leq n \leq 9$ (Read: five is less than or equal to n and n is less than or equal to nine).

For segments A set of points between two points. If the endpoints of the segment are not included in the interval, then it is an open interval. If the endpoints are included, it is a closed interval.

CHECK YOUR UNDERSTANDING
Does the inequality $3 < n < 10$ describe a closed interval?

no

Inverse of a function

A function obtained by reversing the order of elements in the ordered pairs. Given the function $\{(a_1,b_1), (a_2,b_2), (a_3,b_3), (a_4,b_4)\}$, its inverse is the function with the the first and the second elements in the ordered pairs reversed:

$$\{(b_1,a_1), (b_2,a_2), (b_3,a_3), (b_4,a_4)\}$$

CHECK YOUR UNDERSTANDING
What is the inverse of the function $\{(1,2), (3,4)\}$?

{(2,1),(4,3)}

Inverse of a relation

A relation obtained by reversing the order of elements in the ordered pairs. Given the relation {(1,5), (1,6), (2,6), (2,7)}, its inverse is {(5,1), (6,1), (6,2), (7,2)}.

CHECK YOUR UNDERSTANDING
What is the inverse of the following relation? {(0,3),(0,7)}

{(3,0),(7,0)}

Inverse of a statement

The inverse of a conditional *if p then q* is *if not p then not q*. The inverse of a true conditional can be false.

Conditional	Inverse
If two angles are right angles, then they are congruent. (true)	If two angles are not right angles, then they are not congruent. (false)

CHECK YOUR UNDERSTANDING
Is the inverse of this statement true?
If two angles measure 30° each, then they are congruent.

no

Inverse operation

An operation that undoes another operation. Subtraction is the inverse operation of addition: $3 + 4 - 4 = 3$. Division is the inverse operation of multiplication: $8 \times 5 \div 5 = 8$.
Subtraction can be defined in terms of addition:
If $a + b = c$, then $c - b = a$ and $c - a = b$.
Division can be defined in terms of multiplication:
If $ab = c$, then $c \div b = a$ and $c \div a = b$.

CHECK YOUR UNDERSTANDING
What two subtraction statements follow from the addition statement, $5 + 1 = 6$?

$6 - 1 = 5$ and $6 - 5 = 1$

Inverse property of addition

Also called Additive inverse property. The sum of a number and its opposite (additive inverse) is equal to 0 (the additive identity or identity for addition). For every number a, $a + (-a) = 0$.

CHECK YOUR UNDERSTANDING
What is 6 + ⁻6 equal to?

0

Inverse property of multiplication

Also called Multiplicative inverse property. The product of a number and its reciprocal (multiplicative inverse) is equal to 1 (the identity for multiplication or multiplicative identity).

CHECK YOUR UNDERSTANDING
What is the multiplicative inverse of 5?

$\frac{1}{5}$

Inverse variation

A variation stated in the form $y = \frac{k}{x}$, where k is the constant of variation. In this equation the values of y get smaller as the values of x get greater. It is said that x and y are inversely proportional.

CHECK YOUR UNDERSTANDING
Why is $y = \frac{5}{x}$ an inverse variation?

because the values of one variable get smaller as the values of the other variable get larger

Inversely proportional

See Inverse variation.

Irrational number

A number that cannot be written in the form $\frac{a}{b}$, where a and b are whole numbers, $b \neq 0$.

EXAMPLES $\sqrt{2}$ 0.313113111311113 . . .

Any infinite nonrepeating decimal is an irrational number. The union of the set of rational numbers and the set of irrational numbers is the set of real numbers.

CHECK YOUR UNDERSTANDING
Is the infinite decimal 0.10203040. . ., where no block of digits repeats, an irrational number?

yes

Irreducible polynomial

Also called Prime polynomial. A polynomial that cannot be factored into polynomials of lower degree.

EXAMPLES $x + 1$ $2x - 3$

CHECK YOUR UNDERSTANDING
Is $x + 3$ an irreducible polynomial?

yes

I

Isosceles trapezoid

A trapezoid in which the two nonparallel sides are the same length (congruent).

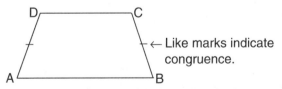

← Like marks indicate congruence.

CHECK YOUR UNDERSTANDING
What two sides are the same length in the trapezoid above?

$\overline{AD}$ and $\overline{BC}$

Isosceles triangle

A triangle with at least two sides of the same length (congruent).

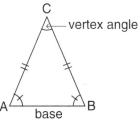

Iteration

A process of repeating the same steps within a sequence of calculations. Repetition.

EXAMPLE

Computing products of successive whole numbers starting with 2 and ending with 1000. These steps will be repeated: take a number, add 1, multiply the numbers beginning with the first number. The first four repetitions will give the following results:

take a number	add 1	multiply the numbers
2	3	$2 \times 3 = 6$
3	4	$2 \times 3 \times 4 = 24$
4	5	$2 \times 3 \times 4 \times 5 = 120$
5	6	$2 \times 3 \times 4 \times 5 \times 6 = 720$

Joint variation

A variation in which the value of one variable depends on the values of two or more variables, as in $w = kxyz$. The value of w varies directly as the values of x, y, and z. The constant of variation is k.

CHECK YOUR UNDERSTANDING

Is $x = 4yz$ a joint variation? If $y = 1$ and $z = 2$, what is x equal to?

yes; 8

Kelvin (°K)

Also called Absolute temperature.

A scale for measuring temperature devised by Lord Kelvin, a British physicist of the late nineteenth and early twentieth centuries. Absolute zero in the Kelvin scale is 0°K and is equivalent to ⁻273.15°C.

	Fahrenheit	Celsius (centigrade)	Kelvin (absolute temperature)
Steam			
Water boils →	+212°	+100°	+373.15
Liquid water			
Water freezes →	+32°	0°	+273°
Solid water (ice)			
	⁻459.7°	⁻273.15°	0° Absolute Zero

J-K

CHECK YOUR UNDERSTANDING

What is 100°C equal to in Kelvin scale?

373.15°K

Kilo-

The prefix kilo means "one thousand" (1,000).

Kilogram (kg) means one thousand grams.

$$1 \text{ kg} = 1000 \text{ g}$$

A kilogram is a unit of mass in the metric system. It is equivalent to about 2.2 pounds in the customary system.

Kiloliter (kL) means "one thousand liters" (L).

$$1 \text{ kL} = 1000 \text{ L}$$

A kiloliter is a unit of capacity in the metric system.

Kilometer (km) means "one thousand meters" (m).

$$1 \text{ km} = 1000 \text{ m}$$

A kilometer is a unit of length in the metric system.

Kilowatt (kW) means "one thousand watts" (W).

$$1 \text{ kW} = 1000 \text{ W}$$

A kilowatt is a unit for measuring electricity.

CHECK YOUR UNDERSTANDING

What would *kilodollar* mean if it were a word?

$1000

Kilowatt-hour (kWh)

A unit for measuring electricity. It is equal to the amount of electricity used to operate a 1000-watt appliance for 1 hour. If you burn a 100-watt light bulb for 10 hours, you will use 1 kilowatt-hour of electricity.

CHECK YOUR UNDERSTANDING

How many kilowatt-hours will be used when operating a 1000-watt appliance for 5 hours?

5 kWh

Kite

In geometry, a quadrilateral (polygon with four sides), in which there are two pairs of consecutive congruent sides.

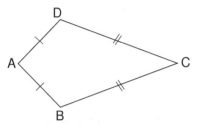

CHECK YOUR UNDERSTANDING
In the kite above, $\overline{AB}$ and $\overline{AD}$ is one pair of congruent sides. What is the second pair of congruent sides?

$\overline{BC}$ and $\overline{DC}$

K

Lateral area

The area of the surface, excluding the bases of a geometric figure.

The lateral area (L) of a right prism is the product of the perimeter of the base and the height.

$L = ph$

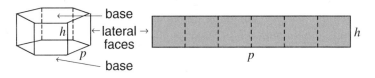

The lateral area of a right cylinder is the product of the circumference of the base and the height.

$L = 2\pi rh$

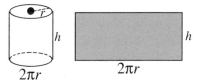

The lateral area of a cone is $\frac{1}{2}$ the product of the circumference and the slant height.

$L = \frac{1}{2} \cdot 2\pi rl$

Least common denominator (LCD)

The least common multiple of the denominators of two or more fractions.

EXAMPLE Find the LCD for $\frac{3}{8}$ and $\frac{5}{12}$.

The denominators of the fractions are 8 and 12.

The least common multiple of 8 and 12 is 24.

So, the LCD for the fractions $\frac{3}{8}$ and $\frac{5}{12}$ is 24.

$$\frac{3}{8} = \frac{9}{24} \text{ and } \frac{5}{12} = \frac{10}{24}$$

HOW TO FIND THE LCD OF TWO FRACTIONS

Find the least common denominator of $\frac{2}{5}$ and $\frac{3}{4}$.

1. List multiples of each denominator:

   5: 5, 10, 15, 20, 25, 30, 35, 40, . . .

   4: 4, 8, 12, 16, 20, 24, 28, 32, 36, 40, . . .

2. Circle multiples common to both numbers (20, 40).

3. List the common denominators: 20, 40

   The least common multiple is 20, so 20 is the least common denominator. If there are no numbers common to both, find the next several multiples for each. There will always be one common multiple for the two numbers and that is the product of the two numbers.

4. Write $\frac{2}{5}$ and $\frac{3}{4}$ as equivalent fractions with denominators of 20.

$$\frac{2 \times 4}{5 \times 4} = \frac{8}{20} \qquad \frac{3 \times 5}{4 \times 5} = \frac{15}{20}$$

HOW TO FIND THE LCD OF TWO RATIONAL EXPRESSIONS

To find the least common denominator of two rational expressions, look for the missing factors that will make the denominators the same.

See next page for an example.

L

223

EXAMPLE $\dfrac{4}{(x-1)(x+2)}$ $\dfrac{(x+3)}{(x+2)(2x-5)}$

The factor $2x - 5$ is needed in the first expression. The factor $x - 1$ is needed in the second expression. So, multiply the numerator and denominator of the first expression by $2x - 5$ and the numerator and denominator of the second expression by $x - 1$.

$\dfrac{4(2x-5)}{(x-1)(x+2)(2x-5)}$ $\dfrac{(x+3)(x-1)}{(x+2)(2x-5)(x-1)}$

Now the denominators are the same.

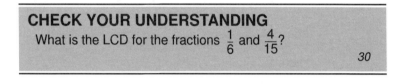

CHECK YOUR UNDERSTANDING
What is the LCD for the fractions $\dfrac{1}{6}$ and $\dfrac{4}{15}$?

30

Least common multiple (LCM)

The least number that is a common multiple of two or more numbers.

EXAMPLE Find the LCM of 4 and 6.

The least number that is a common multiple of 4 and 6 is 12.

So, 12 is the LCM of 4 and 6, written as LCM(4,6) = 12.

See also Common multiple.

CHECK YOUR UNDERSTANDING
What is the LCM of 5 and 4?

20

Leg of a right triangle

Each of the two sides of the right angle in a right triangle. In right triangle ABC, $\overline{AC}$ is one of the legs.

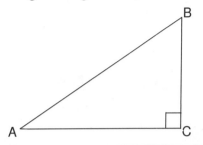

CHECK YOUR UNDERSTANDING
What is the other leg in the right triangle ABC?

BC

Length

Of a segment A number that tells how many units there are in a segment. Length is expressed in linear units. For example, a yard is a linear unit.

Of a rectangle The measure of the longer of two adjacent sides in a rectangle that is not a square. In rectangle ABCD below, the length is the measure of $\overline{CD}$, or 3.2 cm.

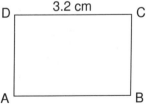

CHECK YOUR UNDERSTANDING
Is an inch a linear unit? The length of rectangle ABCD is 3.2 cm. How long is side AB?

yes; 3.2 cm

L

Less than (<)

An inequality relation, as in 3 < 8. Read: 3 is less than 8.

CHECK YOUR UNDERSTANDING
Is the statement 8 < 3 true?

no

Less than or equal to (≤)

An inequality relation that also includes equality, as in the true statement 6 ≤ 6. Read: 6 is less than or equal to 6.

CHECK YOUR UNDERSTANDING
Is 9 ≤ 9 true?

yes

Light-year

The distance that light travels in one year in a vacuum. Light travels at an average speed of 186,000 miles per second. A light-year is 5,878,000,000,000 miles or about 6 trillion miles.

CHECK YOUR UNDERSTANDING
A star is 10 light-years away. About how many miles is that?

about 60 trillion miles

Like fractions

Also called Similar fractions. Fractions that have the same denominator. $\frac{3}{7}$ and $\frac{5}{7}$ are like fractions. Each has the denominator 7.

CHECK YOUR UNDERSTANDING
Are $\frac{2}{5}$ and $\frac{2}{7}$ like fractions?

no; they have different denominators

Like radicals

Two or more radicals that have the same index. For example, $\sqrt[3]{4}$ and $\sqrt[3]{5}$ are like radicals. Each has the index 3.

CHECK YOUR UNDERSTANDING
Are $\sqrt{2}$ and $\sqrt{7}$ like radicals? What is the index of each?

yes; 2

Like terms

Also called Similar terms. Two or more terms that contain the same variable(s). For example, $5xy$ and ^-7xy are similar terms. If the terms differ in at least one variable, then they are called unlike terms.

CHECK YOUR UNDERSTANDING
Are $3x$ and $4x$ like terms?

yes

Limit

A central concept of calculus indicating a number that a sequence of numbers approaches. For example, the infinite sequence of numbers, $1, \dfrac{1}{2}, \dfrac{1}{3}, \dfrac{1}{4}, \dfrac{1}{5}, \dfrac{1}{6}, \cdots$ approaches the number 0 as its limit, since the fractions are becoming smaller and smaller. We say that the limit of this sequence is 0.

L

CHECK YOUR UNDERSTANDING
Does the following infinite sequence have the limit 0?

$$1, \frac{1}{2}, \frac{1}{4}, \frac{1}{8}, \frac{1}{16}, \frac{1}{32}, \cdots$$

yes

Line

A set of points that form a straight path extending infinitely in two directions. The directions are opposite of each other.

This line can be labeled $\overleftrightarrow{AB}$. Read: line AB.

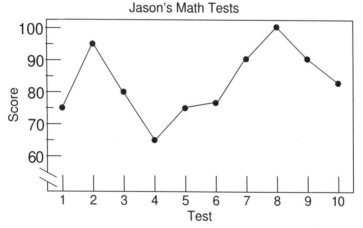

See also Equation of a line.

CHECK YOUR UNDERSTANDING
Can a line be measured?

no, it extends infinitely in both directions

Line graph

A method of displaying data using a broken line.

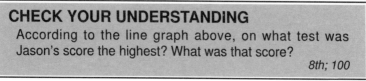

The graph shows that Jason's score on the 3rd test was 80.

CHECK YOUR UNDERSTANDING
According to the line graph above, on what test was Jason's score the highest? What was that score?

8th; 100

228

Line of reflection

A line through which a geometric figure is reflected, so that a copy of the figure appears on the other side of the line.

Line *s* is a line of reflection.

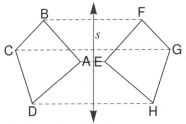

The two quadrilaterals are symmetric to each other with respect to line *s*.

CHECK YOUR UNDERSTANDING
Is quadrilateral EFGH a reflection of quadrilateral ABCD?

yes

Line of symmetry

Also called Axis of symmetry. A line such that if a figure is folded about the line, then one half of the figure matches the other half.

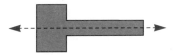

Some figures may have more than one line or axis of symmetry. A figure that has a line of symmetry is said to have line or reflectional symmetry.

CHECK YOUR UNDERSTANDING
Is the dashed line a line of symmetry in the figure above?

yes

Line segment

A part of a line that has two endpoints and a definite length.

A $\bullet$————————$\bullet$ B $\quad \overline{AB}$ Read: line segment AB

Points A and B are the endpoints of line segment AB.

CHECK YOUR UNDERSTANDING
Is line segment AB the same as line segment BA?

yes

Linear equation

An equation in which the variables are raised to the first power. A linear equation may have one variable or several variables. An equation in one variable can be of the form $ax + b = 0$ where x is the variable. An equation in four variables can be of the form $aw + bx + cy + dz + e = 0$ where w, x, y, and z are variables.

CHECK YOUR UNDERSTANDING
Is $3x + 4y + 7z + 1 = 0$ a linear equation? How many variables does it have?

yes; three

Linear function

A function that can be expressed in the form of a linear equation (an equation in which a variable is raised to the first power).

EXAMPLE $\{(1,2), (2,3), (3,4), (4,5), \ldots\}$
The three dots indicate that the function has an infinite number of members (ordered pairs). Expressed as an equation, this function is $y = x + 1$ (the second member of each ordered pair is 1 greater than the first member).

CHECK YOUR UNDERSTANDING
Write an equation for the following linear function, using x and y.
$\{(1,3), (2,4), (3,5), (4,6), \ldots\}$

$y = x + 2$

Linear inequality

An inequality in which the variables are raised to the first power. A linear inequality in one variable can be of the form $ax + b > 0$, or $ax + b < 0$, or $ax + b \geq 0$, or $ax + b \leq 0$ where x is the variable. A linear inequality in two variables can have similar forms with the first form being $ax + by + c > 0$ where x and y are variables.

CHECK YOUR UNDERSTANDING

Is $3x - 4y + 7 > 0$ a linear inequality? How many variables does it have?

yes; two

Linear interpolation

See Interpolation.

Linear polynomial

See Polynomial.

Linear term

A first-degree term (raised to the first power) in an algebraic expression.

EXAMPLE Algebraic expression: $2x + y^2 - 3$

$2x$ is a linear term, since x is raised to the first power.

CHECK YOUR UNDERSTANDING

What is the linear term in $m^2 + 4n + 6$?

4n

L

Liter (L)

A metric unit for measuring volume or capacity. A liter is a little more than a quart.

CHECK YOUR UNDERSTANDING

Is one quart a little less than a liter?

yes

Literal equation

An equation in which the coefficients of the variables are letters, *also called* literal numbers, rather than specific numbers.

EXAMPLE $ax + by = c$ is a literal equation.

literal coefficients or literal numbers — constant

CHECK YOUR UNDERSTANDING
Is $3x - 5y = 2$ a literal equation?

no

Literal number

See Literal equation.

Logarithm

The logarithm of a positive number is the exponent indicating the power to which it is necessary to raise a given number, the base, to produce the positive number.

$$\underset{\text{base}}{\log_2} 8 = 3 \qquad 2^{\underset{\text{exponent (logarithm)}}{3}} = 8$$

positive number

Read: *The logarithm, with base 2, of 8 is 3.*

CHECK YOUR UNDERSTANDING
What is the logarithm in $\log_m k = z$ or $m^z = k$?

z

Logic

The study of laws governing valid thinking patterns and of the structure of statements.

CHECK YOUR UNDERSTANDING
Are ways of thinking a subject of study in logic?

yes

Long division

See Division.

Loss

In business or personal finances, when expenditures exceed income.

CHECK YOUR UNDERSTANDING
Company X's income for December was $23,563 and expenditures were $23,978. Did the company have a loss for the month of December? How much?

yes; $415

Lower quartile

See Quartile.

Lowest terms of a fraction

Also called Simplest form of a fraction. A fraction in which the numerator and denominator are relatively prime (they have no common factors greater than 1).

EXAMPLES $\frac{1}{2}$ $\frac{3}{4}$ $\frac{7}{8}$ $\frac{9}{10}$

An example of a fraction that is **not** in lowest terms is $\frac{2}{4}$. Both the numerator and denominator can be divided by 2.

$$\frac{2 \div 2}{4 \div 2} = \frac{1}{2} \quad \leftarrow\text{fraction in lowest terms}$$

CHECK YOUR UNDERSTANDING
Why is $\frac{3}{15}$ not in lowest terms?

there is a common factor of 3 for the numerator and denominator

L

233

M

Magic square

A square array of numbers arranged so that the sum of numbers in each row, column, and diagonal is the same. The sum in each row, column, and diagonal is called the magic sum. The number of rows or columns is called the rank of the magic square.

4	9	2
3	5	7
8	1	6

Magic square
of rank 3

$a+c$	$a-b-c$	$a+b$
$a+b-c$	a	$a-b+c$
$a-b$	$a+b+c$	$a-c$

General formula for
creating a 3-by-3 magic square

CHECK YOUR UNDERSTANDING
What is the magic sum for each magic square above?

15; 3a

Map scale

Numbers that tell what distance is represented on the map by a given length. For example, "1 inch = 25 miles" means that the length of one inch on the map represents the actual distance of 25 miles.

CHECK YOUR UNDERSTANDING
On a map with a scale "1 inch = 25 miles", how many inches will represent an actual distance of 200 miles?

8 inches

Mapping

See Function.

Markdown

A reduction in the price of an item. "Every item marked down 30%" means that the price of every item is reduced by 30% of its regular price.

CHECK YOUR UNDERSTANDING
If the regular price of an item is $60, what is its price after a 30% markdown?

$42

Markup

A percent increase in the cost of an item to cover expenses and profit. The percent markup is called the markup rate.

CHECK YOUR UNDERSTANDING
A markup on tennis shoes is 60% of their cost. A pair of tennis shoes costs the retailer $40. What is the price after the markup?

$64

Mass

The amount of matter in an object. This measure remains the same regardless of the object's location. For example, an astronaut's mass is the same on earth as it is on the moon. Mass should not be confused with weight. Weight is subject to the force of gravity. For example, the weight of an astronaut on the moon is about one-sixth of the weight on earth. The most often used units of mass are the gram (g) and the kilogram (kg).

M

CHECK YOUR UNDERSTANDING
The mass of a person on earth is 70 kilograms. What is the mass of this person on the moon?

70 kilograms

Mathematical expectation

The product of the probability of an event occurring and the amount of money one receives if the event occurs. For example, suppose someone will receive $1.20 if a 6 comes up on a roll of a die. Since the probability of 6 coming up is $\frac{1}{6}$, the mathematical expectation is $\frac{1}{6} \times \$1.20$ or $.20. This means that rolling a die many times will lead to an average winning of $.20.

CHECK YOUR UNDERSTANDING
One will receive $6 if 3 comes up on a roll of a die. What is the mathematical expectation?

$1

Mathematical expression

See Algebraic expression.

Mathematical sentence

An equation or inequality that has one or more variables.

EXAMPLES $\qquad 2x + 5 = 0 \qquad\qquad x + y > 4$

CHECK YOUR UNDERSTANDING
Is $2x - 3y < 2$ a mathematical sentence?

yes

Matrix 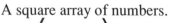 *plural* **matrices**

A square array of numbers.

$$\begin{pmatrix} 3 & 4 \\ \\ {}^-2 & 5 \end{pmatrix} \qquad \begin{pmatrix} a_1 & b_1 & c_1 \\ a_2 & b_2 & c_2 \\ a_3 & b_3 & c_3 \end{pmatrix}$$

Matrix of order 2 or 2-by-2 matrix
It has four numbers.

A general 3-by-3 matrix
It has nine entries.

CHECK YOUR UNDERSTANDING
How many entries will a matrix of order 5 contain?

25

Maximum point

In a coordinate system, the point on a graph of a curve with the largest (greatest) y-coordinate. In the graph of the curve below, the maximum point has the coordinates (4,2).

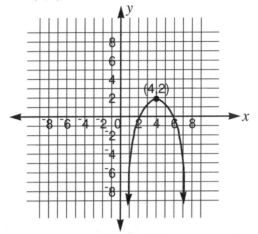

CHECK YOUR UNDERSTANDING

What is the y-coordinate of the maximum point in the graph above? Is there a point on the graph that has a y-coordinate greater than 2?

2; no

Maximum value

The highest (largest, greatest) value. For example, the maximum value of the function $f(x) = -x^2 + 8x + 1$ is 17. It will occur when $x = 4$. For any other value of x the value of the function will be less than 17.

M

CHECK YOUR UNDERSTANDING

Will the value of the function $f(x) = -x^2 + 8x + 1$ be less than 17 for $x = 5$? What is the value?

yes; 16

Mayan numeration system

Developed by the Mayas as one of the earliest positional numeration systems. It is based on 20. The twenty basic Mayan symbols are:

0 ⬭	5 ▬	10 ▬▬	15 ▬▬▬
1 •	6 •/▬	11 •/▬▬	16 •/▬▬▬
2 ••	7 ••/▬	12 ••/▬▬	17 ••/▬▬▬
3 •••	8 •••/▬	13 •••/▬▬	18 •••/▬▬▬
4 ••••	9 ••••/▬	14 ••••/▬▬	19 ••••/▬▬▬

To write names for larger numbers, the Mayas stacked the "numerals" on top of each other. The "numeral" on top indicated the number by which twenty was to be multiplied and then the number at the bottom was added.

EXAMPLE $\underline{\bullet\bullet}$ 7 × 20 or 140
$\underline{\bullet\bullet\bullet}$ 8

$(7 \times 20) + 8 = 148$

CHECK YOUR UNDERSTANDING
What does $\overset{\bullet}{\underset{\bullet}{\underline{}}}$ in the Mayan system stand for?

131

Mean

Arithmetic mean *Also called* Average. The sum of given numbers divided by the number of numbers used in computing the sum.

EXAMPLE The arithmetic mean of 3, 7, 17, and 33 is:

Sum of the numbers → $\dfrac{3 + 7 + 17 + 33}{4} = \dfrac{60}{4} = 15.$
Number of numbers →

238

Geometric mean The geometric mean of two numbers is the square root of their product. The geometric mean of 4 and 9 is $\sqrt{4 \times 9}$ or $\sqrt{36}$ or 6.

Statistical mean The same as Arithmetic mean.

EXAMPLE   The mean for 8, 9, 10, 11, 10, 12 is 10.

$$\frac{8 + 9 + 10 + 11 + 10 + 12}{6} = \frac{60}{6} = 10$$

CHECK YOUR UNDERSTANDING
What is the arithmetic mean of these bowling scores: 110, 120, 115? What is the geometric mean of 4 and 25?

115; $\sqrt{4 \times 25} = \sqrt{100}$ or 10

Means in a proportion

The second and third terms of a proportion. (The extremes are the first and fourth terms.) In the proportion $\frac{a}{b} = \frac{c}{d}$, b and c are the means, and a and d are the extremes.

CHECK YOUR UNDERSTANDING
What are the means in the proportion $\frac{m}{n} = \frac{p}{q}$?

n and p

Measurement

Using various units to assign numerical values to properties of objects, such as length, weight, and so on. There are two basic systems of measurement in use in the United States, customary and metric.

See also Table of Measures *on pages 448-449 and* Precision of measurement.

M

Measures of central tendency

The mean, median, and mode of statistical data are all measures of central tendency.

Median

In geometry In a triangle, a line segment from a vertex to the midpoint of the opposite side. In a trapezoid, a line segment connecting the midpoints of the two nonparallel sides.

The three medians in a triangle

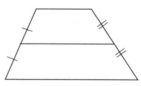

Median of a trapezoid

Within the same figure, line segments of the same length have like markings.

In statistics For a set of an odd number of data arranged in order, it is the middle number. The median of {2, 7, 15, 56, 89} is 15 (the middle number). For an even number of data arranged in order, it is the average of the two middle numbers. The median of {3, 5, 10, 12, 20, 25} is $\frac{10 + 12}{2}$ or 11.

Mega-

Used as a prefix to mean "one million". For example, the prefix is used when referring to the power of the atomic bomb. An atomic bomb of 10 megatons has an explosive power equal to that of 10 million tons of TNT.

CHECK YOUR UNDERSTANDING
How many tons are 5 megatons?

5 million

Member of a set

Also called Element of a set. Any one thing that belongs to a set. For example, the number 6 is a member of the set of all counting numbers.

CHECK YOUR UNDERSTANDING
Is 7 a member of the set of all even counting numbers?

no

Mental math

Performing computations in one's head without writing anything down.

MENTAL MATH STRATEGIES
With basic facts To solve $x + 6 = 20$
Think: What number plus 6 is 20? Answer: 14
So, the solution is 14.
In adding To add $36 + 49$
Add: $30 + 40 = 70$
Add: $6 + 9 = 15$
Add: $70 + 15 = 85$
So, $36 + 49 = 85$.

M

In subtracting To subtract $75 - 48$

Add 2 to each number so 48 is a multiple of ten: $77 - 50 = 27$

So, $75 - 48 = 27$

In multiplying: Using the Distributive Property

Multiply: 58×9

$58 \times 9 = (50 + 8) \times 9 = (50 \times 9) + (8 \times 9)$

$\qquad\qquad = 450 + 72$ or 522

To add $450 + 72$, think: $(450 + 50) + 22$

In using percents

When finding a percent of a number, sometimes it is easier to multiply by a fraction .

Remember these:

$12\frac{1}{2}\% = \frac{1}{8}$ $25\% = \frac{1}{4}$ $33\frac{1}{3}\% = \frac{1}{3}$ $50\% = \frac{1}{2}$ $75\% = \frac{3}{4}$

Find $12\frac{1}{2}\%$ of $160.

> Think: $\frac{1}{8}$ of 160 is 20. So, $12\frac{1}{2}\%$ of $160 is $20.

Find 25% of $400.

> Think: $\frac{1}{4}$ of 400 is 100, so 25% of $400 is $100.

Find $33\frac{1}{3}\%$ of $150.

> Think: $\frac{1}{3}$ of 150 is 50, so $33\frac{1}{3}\%$ of $150 is $50.

Find 50% of $120.

> Think: $\frac{1}{2}$ of 120 is 60, so 50% of $120 is $60.

Find 75% of $400.

> Think: $\frac{1}{4}$ of 400 is 100, then $\frac{3}{4}$ of 400 is 300.
> So, 75% of $400 is $300.

In computing tips (15%)

Remember 10% is $\frac{1}{10}$ and 5% is one-half of that.

The bill comes to $25.

> Think: $\frac{1}{10}$ of $25 is $2.50.
> Half of that is $1.25.

So, a 15% tip on $25 is $2.50 + $1.25 = $3.75.

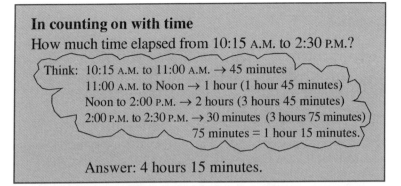

In counting on with time

How much time elapsed from 10:15 A.M. to 2:30 P.M.?

Think: 10:15 A.M. to 11:00 A.M. → 45 minutes
11:00 A.M. to Noon → 1 hour (1 hour 45 minutes)
Noon to 2:00 P.M. → 2 hours (3 hours 45 minutes)
2:00 P.M. to 2:30 P.M. → 30 minutes (3 hours 75 minutes)
75 minutes = 1 hour 15 minutes.

Answer: 4 hours 15 minutes.

Meter (m)

The basic unit of length in the metric system of measurement. It is about 3 inches longer than a yard. Most doorways are about 2 meters high.

See Table of Measures *on page 448.*

CHECK YOUR UNDERSTANDING

About how wide are most doorways to the nearest meter ?

about 1 m

Metric system

A system of measurement developed in 1790 by the French Academy of Sciences. The basic units in the metric system are the following: for length–the meter, for mass–the gram, for capacity–the liter. Other units in the metric system are related to the basic units in terms of powers of 10; therefore, it is a decimal system. For example, 1 kilometer = 1000 meters or 10^3 meters.

See Table of Measures *on page 448.*

M

CHECK YOUR UNDERSTANDING

What number is the metric system based on?

10

Metric ton (t)

A unit of mass in the metric system that is approximately equal to 1.1 U.S. tons or 2200 lb.

CHECK YOUR UNDERSTANDING
Approximately how many U.S. tons are there in 3 metric tons?

3.3

Microsecond

One-millionth of a second.

CHECK YOUR UNDERSTANDING
What fraction of a second are 5 microseconds?

5 millionths

Midpoint formula

The formula for finding the coordinates of the midpoint of a segment in the coordinate system. If the coordinates of the endpoints of a segment are (x_1, y_1) and (x_2, y_2), then the coordinates of the midpoint of that segment are $\left(\dfrac{x_1 + x_2}{2}, \dfrac{y_1 + y_2}{2} \right)$.

CHECK YOUR UNDERSTANDING
The coordinates of the endpoints of a segment are (4,7) and (8,9). What are the coordinates of the midpoint?

(6,8)

Midpoint of a segment

A point that divides a segment into two congruent segments (segments of the same length).
See also **Construction** *and* **Midpoint formula**.

CHECK YOUR UNDERSTANDING
Point M is the midpoint of segment AB that is 8 cm long. How long is each segment into which M divides segment AB?

4 cm

Mile (mi)

A unit of length (distance) in the customary system. A mile is equal to 5280 feet.

CHECK YOUR UNDERSTANDING
How many feet are there in 2 miles?

10,560

Milli-

The prefix milli means "one-thousandth".

Milligram (mg) means "one-thousandth of a gram" (g).

$$1 \text{ mg} = \frac{1}{1000} \text{ g}$$

A milligram is a unit of mass in the metric system. A small seed weighs about 1 mg.

Milliliter (mL) means "one-thousandth of a liter" (L).

$$1 \text{ mL} = \frac{1}{1000} \text{ L}$$

A milliliter is a unit of capacity in the metric system. A teaspoon holds about 5 mL of liquid.

Millimeter (mm) means "one-thousandth of a meter" (m).

$$1 \text{ mm} = \frac{1}{1000} \text{ m}$$

A millimeter is a unit of length in the metric system. A quarter is about 2 mm thick.

CHECK YOUR UNDERSTANDING
How many milligrams are the same as two thousandths of a gram?

2

Million (M)

One thousand thousand or 1,000,000 (one million).

M

CHECK YOUR UNDERSTANDING
How many millions is five thousand thousand?

5

Minimum point

In a coordinate system, the point on a graph of a curve with the smallest (least) y-coordinate. In the graph of the curve below, the minimum point has the coordinates $(1,^-4)$.

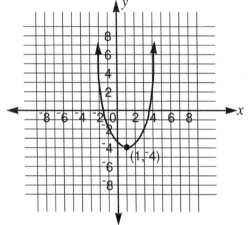

Minimum value

The smallest (least) value. For example, the minimum value of the function $f(x) = x^2 - 4x + 9$ is 5. It will occur for $x = 2$. For any other value of x the value of the function will be greater than 5.

Minor arc

See Arc.

Minuend

A number from which another number is being subtracted.

EXAMPLE $12 - 7 = 5$

∟ minuend

CHECK YOUR UNDERSTANDING
What is the minuend in $8 - 3 = 5$?

8

Minus sign (–)

The symbol $-$. It has three different meanings in mathematics:

In $7 - 5 = 2$ it means subtract.

In $^-4$ it means negative.

In $-x$ it means opposite (additive inverse of).

CHECK YOUR UNDERSTANDING
What does the symbol $-$ in $-y$ mean?

opposite (additive inverse of)

Minute

A unit of time or a unit of angle measurement. There are 60 minutes in one hour. There are 60 minutes in one degree of angle measure.

CHECK YOUR UNDERSTANDING
How many minutes are there in 2 degrees of angle measure?

120

Mixed number

A whole number and a fraction. For example, $2\frac{3}{4}$ is a mixed number.

M

CHECK YOUR UNDERSTANDING
Is $5\frac{1}{2}$ a mixed number? What is its whole number?

yes; 5

Möbius strip

A strip of paper turned over to form a half twist, then joined at the ends. The Möbius strip, discovered by August Möbius in 1858, is a one-sided figure.

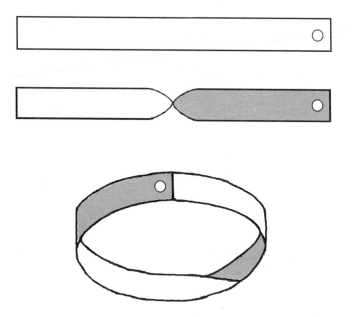

If you start at any point on the strip and draw a line down the middle of the strip, you will end up back at the same point without crossing an edge. If you cut the strip on this line, you will end up with just one strip, not two as you may expect. If you make another Möbius strip and cut it parallel to the edge, one third of the way from the edge you will get two linked strips. The study of such properties of figures belongs to the field of topology.

Mode

One of the three basic measures of central tendency. It is the number or numbers that occur most often in a set of data. In the set of data {45, 56, 75, 75, 80}, 75 is the mode. In the set of data {25, 45, 25, 65, 45, 75}, 25 and 45 are the modes. If no number occurs most often, the set of data has no mode.

CHECK YOUR UNDERSTANDING
What is the mode in {34, 45, 67, 87, 97, 97}?

97

Modular arithmetic

Adding by using only a given set of numbers for the sum. For example, in modulo seven arithmetic, this set of numbers is used: $\{0,1,2,3,4,5,6\}$. In modulo five, this set of numbers is used: $\{0,1,2,3,4\}$.

EXAMPLES

Modulo seven

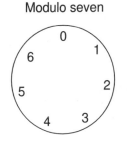

Modulo five

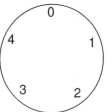

$5 + 2 = 0$ modulo seven

$6 + 4 = 3$ modulo seven

$4 + 4 = 3$ modulo five

$4 + 1 = 0$ modulo five

M

CHECK YOUR UNDERSTANDING
What is 3 + 3 modulo 5 equal to?

1

249

Monomial

An expression that can be a constant, a variable, or a product of a constant and one or more variables. Each of the following is a monomial:

5 (a constant) x (a variable)

^-3z (a product of a constant and one variable)

$6xyz$ (a product of a constant and more than one variable)

MULTIPLYING MONOMIALS

$$a^4 \times a^3 = a^{4+3} = a^7$$

In general, $a^n \times a^m = a^{n+m}$

$$2a^4 \times (^-5a^3) = (2 \cdot {}^-5)(a^4 a^3) = {}^-10a^7$$

MULTIPLYING A POLYNOMIAL AND A MONOMIAL

$$5x(x + 3) = 5x^2 + 15x$$

$$^-4x(^-2x^2 + 3x - 5) = 8x^3 - 12x^2 + 20x$$

CHECK YOUR UNDERSTANDING

Is ^-2xy a monomial?

yes

Multiple of a number

A number that is the product of the given number and a counting number.

EXAMPLE 12 is a multiple of 4, because $3 \times 4 = 12$.

See also Common multiple *and* Least common multiple.

CHECK YOUR UNDERSTANDING

Is 13 a multiple of 5?

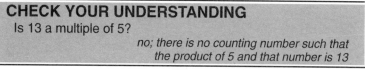

no; there is no counting number such that the product of 5 and that number is 13

Multiplication

One of the four basic operations. It can be thought of as repeated addition: 4×3 can be interpreted to mean four 3's or $3 + 3 + 3 + 3 = 12$.

There are three ways to show multiplication:

$^-5 \times 3$	$^-5 \cdot 3$	$(^-5)(3)$
with a multiplication sign	with a dot	with parentheses

USING THE MULTIPLICATION ALGORITHM

Multiply $\;\;357 \longleftarrow$ multiplicand
$\underline{\times \;\; 49} \longleftarrow$ multiplier
$3213 \longleftarrow 9 \times 357$ ⎱ partial products
$\underline{+ \; 1428} \longleftarrow 4 \times 357$ ⎰
$17{,}493 \longleftarrow$ product

GRATING METHOD OF MULTIPLICATION

The number to be multiplied is written across the top of the grates. The multiplier is written down the right side. The product of each pair of digits is written in a cell. The ones are written in the lower portion and any tens are written in the upper portion. The diagonal strips are then added from right to left as if they were vertical columns.

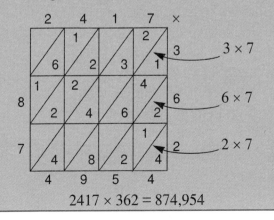

$$2417 \times 362 = 874{,}954$$

HALVING AND DOUBLING METHOD OF MULTIPLICATION

To multiply by halving and doubling, place the numbers in two columns. Halve the one in the left-hand column. Discard the remainder of 1 when necessary. Double the number in the right-hand column. Add the numbers in the right-hand column that are opposite odd numbers in the left-hand column to get the answer. Here's an example of multiplying 27 by 31.

27*	31	
13*	62	
6	124	
3*	248	
1*	496	$31 + 62 + 248 + 496 = 837$

* odd numbers

CHECK YOUR UNDERSTANDING
What is the addition interpretation of 3 × 4?

three 4's or 4 + 4 + 4

Multiplication property of equations

Also called Multiplication property of equality.

If each side of an equation is multiplied by the same number, the new equation has the same solution. Equations with the same solution are called equivalent equations.

EXAMPLE $x + 3 = 5$

$2(x + 3) = 2 \cdot 5$ or $2x + 6 = 10$

Each equation has the solution 2.

$x + 3 = 5$ and $2x + 6 = 10$ are equivalent equations.

In general: If $a = b$, then $ac = bc$.

CHECK YOUR UNDERSTANDING
By what number is each side of the equation $x - 4 = 5$ multiplied to obtain the equation $3x - 12 = 15$?

3

Multiplication property of inequality

If each side of an inequality is multiplied by the same positive number, the resulting inequality has the same solutions. The same sense of inequality holds for both inequalities.

> (is greater than) remains >

EXAMPLE $x > 5$

$3x > 3 \cdot 5$

$3x > 15$

The solution set of each inequality is the set of all numbers greater than 3. The inequalities $x > 5$ and $3x > 15$ are equivalent.

If each side of an inequality is multiplied by a negative number, the sense of inequality changes.

> changes to <, < changes to >

EXAMPLE $x < 6$

$^-2x > ^-2 \cdot 6$

$^-2x > ^-12$

The solution set of each inequality is the set of all numbers less than 6. The inequalities $x < 6$ and $^-2x > ^-12$ are equivalent.

CHECK YOUR UNDERSTANDING
By what number is each side of the inequality $x - 4 < 3$ multiplied to obtain the inequality $5x - 20 < 15$?

5

M

Multiplication property of one

See Identity property for multiplication.

Multiplication property of reciprocals

The product of any nonzero number and its multiplicative inverse (reciprocal) is equal to the multiplicative identity or 1. That is, for any nonzero number x, $x \cdot \frac{1}{x} = 1$.

EXAMPLES $\quad 5 \cdot \frac{1}{5} = 1 \qquad \frac{3}{5} \times \frac{5}{3} = 1$

In general, $\frac{a}{b} \cdot \frac{b}{a} = 1$ $(a \neq 0, b \neq 0)$

CHECK YOUR UNDERSTANDING

What is the product $\frac{7}{10} \times \frac{10}{7}$ equal to?

1

Multiplication table

See Basic facts.

Multiplicative identity

See Identity for multiplication.

Multiplicative inverse

See Reciprocal.

Multiplicative inverse property

See Inverse property of multiplication.

Mutually exclusive events

In probability, two events that cannot take place at the same time. For example, when rolling a die, 2 and 3 cannot occur at the same time.

CHECK YOUR UNDERSTANDING

Are heads and tails coming up on one toss of a coin mutually exclusive events?

yes

Natural numbers

Also called Counting numbers.
The numbers 1, 2, 3, 4, 5, . . .

CHECK YOUR UNDERSTANDING
Is 0 a natural number?

no

Necessary condition

The condition C_1 is necessary for condition C_2 if C_2 is true whenever C_1 is true. For example, in order for a triangle to be an equilateral triangle (C_2), it must have three congruent sides (C_1). Thus, the condition three congruent sides is necessary for a triangle to be an equilateral triangle. This condition happens to also be a sufficient condition. That is, it is sufficient for a triangle to have three congruent sides to be an equilateral triangle. In order for a quadrilateral to be a rhombus, it is necessary that opposite sides be parallel, but not sufficient. The sides must also be congruent.

CHECK YOUR UNDERSTANDING
Is having one right angle a necessary condition for a triangle to be a right triangle? Is it a sufficient condition?

yes; yes

Negation of a statement

See Denial of a statement.

Negative number

Also called Minus number *or* Signed number. A number that is less than 0. For example, $^-5, \frac{^-3}{4}, ^-2$ are negative numbers. Negative numbers are used for recording temperatures below 0°, being "in the hole", a loss on a share of stock, a withdrawal from a bank account, the depth of a submarine below sea level, and others.

CHECK YOUR UNDERSTANDING

Can a negative number be used to record a loss of yardage in a football game?

yes

Negative sign

A sign that shows a number is less than 0. For example, the negative sign in these numbers show they are numbers less than 0, or negative numbers: $^-2.1, \frac{^-1}{4}, ^-3.$

CHECK YOUR UNDERSTANDING

Is the sign in the expression 7 – 5 a negative sign?

no, it is a minus sign indicating subtraction

Net

A pattern to be cut and folded to make a solid shape. This net can be folded to make a triangular pyramid.

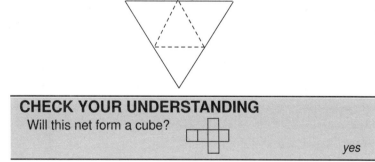

CHECK YOUR UNDERSTANDING

Will this net form a cube?

yes

Net income

The amount left after the expenses and deductions have been subtracted from the total or gross income.

Nonagon

A polygon with nine sides.

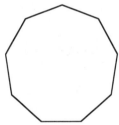
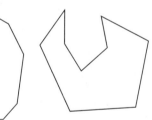

Regular nonagon   Not regular nonagons

N

Noncollinear points

Points that cannot be contained in one line.

Three noncollinear points   Five collinear points

CHECK YOUR UNDERSTANDING
Can two points be noncollinear? Can three?

no; yes

Nonconsecutive integers

Integers that do not follow each other in any order. For example, 4 and 6 are nonconsecutive integers, but they are consecutive even integers.

CHECK YOUR UNDERSTANDING
Are 5 and 6 nonconsecutive integers?

no

Nonterminating decimal

Also called Infinite decimal. A decimal that continues without end. It can be a repeating decimal, that is, one in which a block of digits repeats without end, such as 0.235235235 . . . . Three dots are written to indicate that the decimal continues without end. The notation $0.\overline{235}$ is also used. The bar over the digits indicates that this block of digits repeats without end. A nonterminating decimal can also be nonrepeating. For example, 0.2121121112 . . . is a nonrepeating decimal.

CHECK YOUR UNDERSTANDING
Is 0.3045454545 . . . a nonterminating repeating decimal?

yes

Normal distribution curve

Also called Normal curve. A bell-shaped curve that is a graph of a normal distribution (many measurements distributed evenly about the mean). Both low scores and high scores do not occur frequently. Measurements of heights of people, intelligence quotients, shoe sizes, and so on, are normally distributed. A normal curve is pictured below.

Normal Distribution Curve

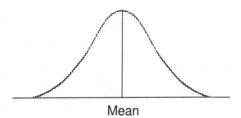

Mean

CHECK YOUR UNDERSTANDING
Would you expect the graph of the distribution of weights of people in a large population to be a a normal distribution curve?

yes

Null set

See Empty set.

N

Number

A number is an abstract mathematical entity.

EXAMPLE The number 12 is an even number.

A number can be named in these forms:

Word form: Three thousand, eighty-two

Standard form: 3,082

Expanded form: $(3 \times 1000) + (0 \times 100) + (8 \times 10) + (2 \times 1)$

CHECK YOUR UNDERSTANDING
What number is 12 ÷ 2 a name for?

6

Number line

Also called Real number line. A line on which real numbers are assigned to points. The numbers are called coordinates of the points. The point to which the number 0 is assigned is called the origin. A number line is usually drawn horizontally. The points to the right of the origin are assigned positive numbers. The points to the left of the origin are assigned negative numbers. Every point on a number line has a unique real number corresponding to it and every real number has a unique point corresponding to it. The rational number, $^-1\frac{1}{2}$, has the point midway between $^-1$ and $^-2$ corresponding to it.

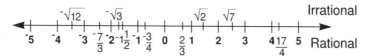
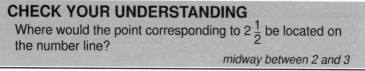

CHECK YOUR UNDERSTANDING
Where would the point corresponding to $2\frac{1}{2}$ be located on the number line?

midway between 2 and 3

Number pattern

A sequence of numbers arranged according to some formula.

EXAMPLE   1, 2, 4, 7, 11, 16, ...

In this sequence to obtain the next number, the pattern is add 1 more than was added to the preceding number.

CHECK YOUR UNDERSTANDING
What is the pattern in the following sequence of numbers?
1, 2, 4, 8, 16, 32, . . .

to obtain the next number, double the preceding number

Number theory

The study of properties of integers. It includes such topics as composite numbers, divisibility, factoring, multiples, prime numbers, and other topics.

CHECK YOUR UNDERSTANDING
Would one expect to find a definition of a prime number in number theory?

yes

Numeral

A symbol that names a number. For example, the symbol 5 is a numeral that names the number 5. Some other symbols that also name the number 5 are: $6 - 1$, $10 \div 2$, $2\frac{1}{2} \times 2$, and so on. In the base ten numeration system there are ten basic numerals, called digits: 0, 1, 2, 3, 4, 5, 6, 7, 8, 9.

CHECK YOUR UNDERSTANDING
Is the following question about a number or a numeral?
How many digits are there in 560?

numeral; there are 3 digits in the numeral

Numerator

The top number of a fraction. In $\frac{3}{4}$, the numerator is 3.

CHECK YOUR UNDERSTANDING

What is the numerator in $\frac{5}{9}$?

5

Numerical expression

A combination of numerals and operation symbols. Each of the following is a numerical expression:

$$34 \qquad 7.3 - 3.2 \qquad 3 \times 4 - 6 \qquad 12 \div 3 + 2 \times 8$$

See also Expression.

CHECK YOUR UNDERSTANDING

Is 2 x 3 + 6 x 7 a numerical expression?

yes

Obtuse angle

An angle that measures more than 90° and less than 180°.

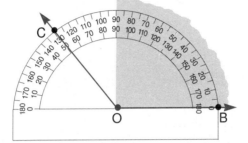

Angle COB measures 130°. It is an obtuse angle.

CHECK YOUR UNDERSTANDING
An angle measures 105°. Is it an obtuse angle?

yes

Obtuse triangle

A triangle that has one obtuse angle.

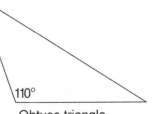

110°

Obtuse triangle
One angle greater than 90°

CHECK YOUR UNDERSTANDING
The sum of the measures of the three angles in a triangle is 180°. Can a triangle have two obtuse angles?

no

Octagon

A polygon with eight sides.

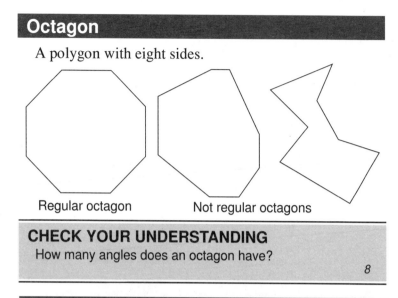

Regular octagon   Not regular octagons

CHECK YOUR UNDERSTANDING
How many angles does an octagon have?

8

Octahedron

A polyhedron
with eight faces.

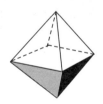

CHECK YOUR UNDERSTANDING
What kind of a geometric figure is each face of an octahedron?

triangle

Odd integer

An integer that is not divisible by 2.

EXAMPLES   3   79   ⁻15   ⁻37

CHECK YOUR UNDERSTANDING
Is 16 an odd integer?

no; 16 ÷ 2 = 8

Odds

A way of stating probabilities. Suppose that the odds in favor of a horse winning a race are 1 to 5 or $\frac{1}{5}$. This means that the horse is expected to win 1 and lose 5 out of 6 races. Thus, the probability of the horse losing is $\frac{5}{6}$ and the probability of the horse winning is $\frac{1}{6}$.

$$\text{Odds in favor} = \frac{\text{number of favorable outcomes}}{\text{number of unfavorable outcomes}}$$

$$\text{Odds against} = \frac{\text{number of unfavorable outcomes}}{\text{number of favorable outcomes}}$$

CHECK YOUR UNDERSTANDING

What are the odds in favor of a horse winning a race if the probability of winning is $\frac{2}{3}$?

2 to 1

One-to-one correspondence

A relationship between two sets in which one member of one set is matched with exactly one member of the other set. The sets are said to be matching sets.

Two finite sets in one-to-one correspondence have the same number of elements.

Two finite matching sets: $\{1, 5, 9, 10\}$
$\{4, 7, 8, 15\}$

Two infinite matching sets:

The set of all odd counting numbers, $O = \{1, 3, 5, 7, \dots\}$

The set of all even counting numbers, $E = \{2, 4, 6, 8, \dots\}$

CHECK YOUR UNDERSTANDING

Is there a one-to-one correspondence between the set of all whole numbers and the set of all counting numbers?

yes, n is matched with n + 1

Open sentence

A sentence that contains one or more variables. It can be an equation or an inequality. An open sentence is neither true nor false. It can be made into a true or false sentence by replacing a variable with a number. If x is replaced with 2 in $3x + 5 = 11$, then it becomes a true sentence, $(3 \times 2) + 5 = 11$. Any other replacement of x will result in a false sentence.

EXAMPLES Open sentences that are equations:
$$2x - 7 = 9 \text{ (one variable)}$$
$$3x + 6y = {}^-3 \text{ (two variables)}$$
Open sentences that are inequalities:
$$3x - 1 < 4 \text{ (one variable)}$$
$$2x - 5y \geq 6 \text{ (two variables)}$$

CHECK YOUR UNDERSTANDING

Is $3x - 4 > 5$ an open sentence?

yes

Operation of arithmetic

An act upon one or more numbers to produce one number for an answer. If an operation is performed on one number, then it is a unitary operation. For example, squaring is a unitary operation. It is performed on one number, $5^2 = 25$.

If an operation is performed on two numbers, then it is called a binary operation. For example, subtraction is a binary operation, $7 - 2 = 5$. The four basic operations of arithmetic are addition, subtraction, multiplication, and division.

CHECK YOUR UNDERSTANDING

Is multiplication a binary operation?

yes

Opposite of a number

Also called Additive inverse of a number. The same number but of opposite sign. The additive inverse of 0 is 0.

Number	Additive inverse
$^+7$	$^-7$
$^-4$	$^+4$
0	0

The opposite of a positive number is negative. The opposite of a negative number is positive.

When a number and its opposite are added, the result is 0.

EXAMPLES $^+7 + {}^-7 = 0$ $^-4 + {}^+4 = 0$ $0 + 0 = 0$

CHECK YOUR UNDERSTANDING
What is the opposite of $^-9$? of $^+11$?

$^+9, {}^-11$

Opposite operations

Operations that undo each other. For example, addition and subtraction are opposite operations: adding 5 to a number is undone by subtracting 5: $3 + 5 - 5 = 3$. Adding a number, then subtracting the same number gets us back to the original number. In general, for addition and subtraction, $a + n - n = a$.

CHECK YOUR UNDERSTANDING
Are multiplication and division opposite operations?

yes; example: $3 \times 2 \div 2 = 3$; in general, $a \times n \div n = a$

Opposite sides and angles

In a triangle An angle and a side are opposite if the other two sides are sides of the angle. In triangle ABC, angle A is opposite side BC.

C

A   B

In a quadrilateral Angles that have no common side and sides that have no common vertex are opposite. In quadrilateral QRST, angles R and T are one pair of opposite angles. In quadrilateral DEFG, sides DE and FG are one pair of opposite sides.

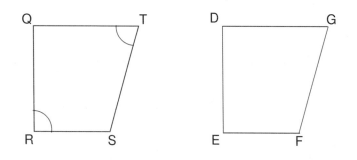

Q   T

R   S

D   G

E   F

Order of operations

The following agreed-upon order of performing several operations:

1. If grouping symbols are used, perform the operations within the grouping symbols first.
2. Perform all multiplications and divisions in order from left to right.
3. Then perform all additions and subtractions in order from left to right.

$20 - (2^3 + 3) \times (8 - 6) + 5 \times 2 - 3$ Operations in parentheses first

$20 - \quad 11 \quad \times \quad 2 \quad + 5 \times 2 - 3$ Multiplications and divisions

$20 - \qquad 22 \qquad + \quad 10 \quad - 3$ Additions and subtractions

5

CHECK YOUR UNDERSTANDING
What is $4 + 4 \times 2^3$ equal to?

36

Order property

See Commutative property.

Ordered pair

A pair in which one member is designated as the first and the other member as the second. Parentheses are used to designate ordered pairs. In the ordered pair (5,2), 5 is the first member and 2 is the second member. Coordinates of points in a plane are given as ordered pairs. Points with coordinates (3,5) and (5,3) are two different points.

See also Coordinate system.

CHECK YOUR UNDERSTANDING
What is the second member in the ordered pair (5,1)?

1

Ordinal number

A number used to designate the place in an ordered arrangement. In the sentence "I am the first in line", *first* (1st) is an ordinal number. Other ordinal numbers are second (2nd), third (3rd), fourth (4th), fifth (5th), and so on.

Ordinate

Another name for the *y*-coordinate that indicates the vertical distance of a point from the origin along the *y*-axis in a coordinate system. The ordinate is the second number in an ordered pair that gives the coordinates of a point. A point described by the coordinates (3,4) has 4 for its ordinate.

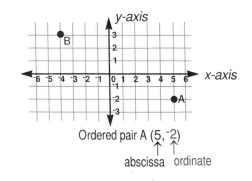

Ordered pair A (5, ¯2)
abscissa ordinate

Origin

The point assigned to zero on the number line or the point where the *x*- and *y*-axes intersect in a coordinate system.

O

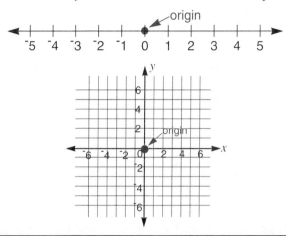

CHECK YOUR UNDERSTANDING
Does the word origin indicate beginning?

yes

Orthocenter

The point of intersection of the three altitudes of a triangle. In the triangle at the right point O is the orthocenter of triangle ABC.

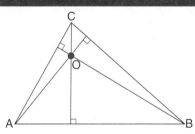

CHECK YOUR UNDERSTANDING
What is the least number of altitudes required to locate the incenter of a circle?

2, because two intersecting segments determine a unique point

Orthogonal

See Perpendicular.

Ounce (oz)

A unit of weight in the customary system. 16 ounces is equal to one pound (lb).

CHECK YOUR UNDERSTANDING
How many ounces are there in 3 pounds?

48

Outcome

In probability, a result of performing an experiment. In tossing a coin, there are two possible outcomes, heads (H) or tails (T).

CHECK YOUR UNDERSTANDING
How many possible outcomes are there in rolling a die?

six:1,2,3,4,5,6

Overlapping figures

In geometry, figures that have parts of their interiors in common. Triangles ABC and DEF are overlapping triangles. They share the shaded portion.

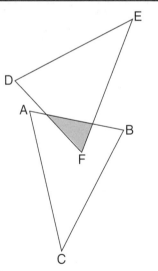

CHECK YOUR UNDERSTANDING
What shape is the overlapping part of triangles ABC and DEF?

a triangle

Palindrome

Also called Palindromic number. A number that is the same whether read from right to left or left to right, such as 1672761.

CHECK YOUR UNDERSTANDING
Use the digits 3 and 4 to make all possible three-digit palindromes.

333, 444, 343, 434

Parabola

A curve in which every point is the same distance from a fixed point, called the focus (F), as it is from a fixed line, called the directrix (*d*). The axis of the parabola is a line about which the parabola is symmetric. The vertex (V) of a parabola is the point at which the parabola intersects the axis.

CHECK YOUR UNDERSTANDING
According to the definition of a parabola, is the length of segment FP_2 equal to the length of segment TP_2 ?

yes

Paradox

A contradiction to something known to be true, reached by means of a seemingly reasonable argument. For example, suppose two different-sized circles with a common center are turned one rotation. Since the initial points on the circles align after the rotation, it appears that the circles have traveled the same distance and therefore have the same circumference. But one circle is obviously smaller than the other.

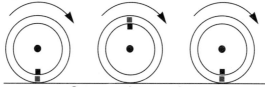

|←——— One complete rotation ———→|

See also Zeno's paradox.

CHECK YOUR UNDERSTANDING

If one would argue that every angle is a right angle by means of a seemingly reasonable argument, would that be a paradox?

yes

Parallel (II)

Lines and planes that do not intersect. They are everywhere the same distance from each other.

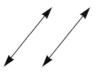   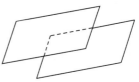

Parallel lines   Parallel planes

Rays and line segments that are parts of parallel lines are also parallel.

CHECK YOUR UNDERSTANDING

Are two lines that have one point in common parallel?

no

Parallelogram

A quadrilateral with both pairs of opposite sides parallel.

Parallelogram: $\overline{AB} \parallel \overline{DC}$, $\overline{AD} \parallel \overline{BC}$

Parentheses

Grouping symbols that indicate in what order operations should be performed.

EXAMPLE $(3 + 6) \times 8$

Parentheses indicate that addition is to be performed first: $(3 + 6) \times 8 = 9 \times 8$ or 72.

Partial product

Found in multiplication of numbers with two or more digits. It is a product of one digit in one factor and the other number.

EXAMPLE

$$
\begin{array}{r}
47 \\
\times\ 23 \\
\hline
141 \\
94 \\
\hline
1081
\end{array}
$$

141 ← partial product (3×47)
94 ← partial product (20×47)

Partial sum in an infinite series

The indicated sum of the first term and any finite number of other consecutive terms in an infinite series.

Infinite series: $1 + \dfrac{1}{2} + \dfrac{1}{4} + \dfrac{1}{8} + \dfrac{1}{16} + \dfrac{1}{32} + \ldots$

Partial sum	**Partial sum**	**Partial sum**
$1 + \dfrac{1}{2}$	$1 + \dfrac{1}{2} + \dfrac{1}{4}$	$1 + \dfrac{1}{2} + \dfrac{1}{4} + \dfrac{1}{8}$

CHECK YOUR UNDERSTANDING

For the series above, is $1 + \dfrac{1}{2} + \dfrac{1}{4} + \dfrac{1}{8} + \dfrac{1}{16}$ a partial sum?

yes

Pascal's triangle

A number pattern named after Blaise Pascal, a French mathematician of the 17th century. The numbers in each row are obtained by adding two numbers in the row above and writing a 1 at the beginning and end of the row.

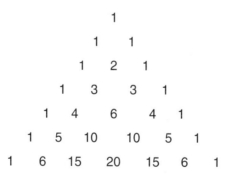

```
              1
           1     1
        1     2     1
      1     3     3     1
    1     4     6     4     1
  1     5    10    10     5     1
1    6    15    20    15     6     1
```

The pattern continues without end.

CHECK YOUR UNDERSTANDING

The number 15 in the 7th row above is obtained by adding what two numbers?

5 and 10

Pentagon

A polygon with five sides.

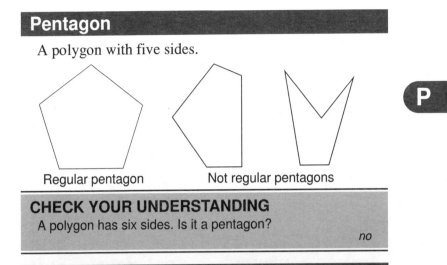

Regular pentagon   Not regular pentagons

Pentagonal number

Also called Figurate number. A number created by using pentagons as illustrated below. The general formula for obtaining the nth pentagonal number is $\frac{1}{2}n(3n - 1)$. To find the third pentagonal number, substitute 3 for n in the formula: $\frac{1}{2} \times 3 \times (3 \times 3 - 1) = 12$.

First Five Pentagonal Numbers

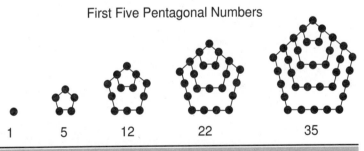

1   5   12   22   35

Percent (%)

Per hundred. Ratio of a number to 100 with a percent sign.

EXAMPLE 9% means 9 out of 100 or $\frac{9}{100}$

WRITING A DECIMAL AS A PERCENT

To write a decimal as a percent, move the decimal point to the right two places and write a percent sign.

$0.37 = 37\%$ $0.30 = 30\%$ $1.00 = 100\%$

$0.05 = 5\%$ $0.20 = 20\%$ $6.50 = 650\%$

$0.0005 = 0.05\%$ $0.007 = 0.7\%$ $0.0025 = 0.25\%$

WRITING A PERCENT AS A DECIMAL

To write a percent as a decimal, use the fact that $x\%$ means $\frac{x}{100}$. Then divide the numerator by the denominator.

$4.5\% = \frac{4.5}{100} = 0.045$ $\frac{1}{2}\% = \frac{\frac{1}{2}}{100} = \frac{1}{2} \times \frac{1}{100} = \frac{1}{200} = 0.005$

$$33\frac{1}{3}\% = \frac{33\frac{1}{3}}{100} = \frac{\frac{100}{3}}{100} = \frac{100}{3} \times \frac{1}{100} = \frac{1}{3} = 0.\overline{3}$$

A shortcut to writing a percent as a decimal is to move the decimal point two places to the left.

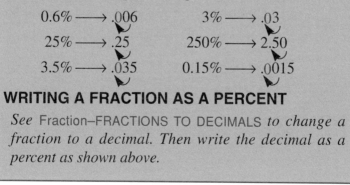

$0.6\% \longrightarrow .006$ $3\% \longrightarrow .03$

$25\% \longrightarrow .25$ $250\% \longrightarrow 2.50$

$3.5\% \longrightarrow .035$ $0.15\% \longrightarrow .0015$

WRITING A FRACTION AS A PERCENT

See Fraction–FRACTIONS TO DECIMALS *to change a fraction to a decimal. Then write the decimal as a percent as shown above.*

WRITING A PERCENT AS A FRACTION OR MIXED NUMBER

Write the percent as a fraction with the denominator of 100, then simplify the fraction whenever possible.

$$25\% = \frac{25}{100} = \frac{1}{4} \qquad\qquad 37\% = \frac{37}{100}$$

$$66\frac{2}{3}\% = \frac{66\frac{2}{3}}{100} = \frac{2}{3} \qquad\qquad \frac{3}{4}\% = \frac{\frac{3}{4}}{100} = \frac{3}{400}$$

$$250\% = \frac{250}{100} = \frac{5}{2} = 2\frac{1}{2} \qquad 600\% = \frac{600}{100} = 6$$

FINDING WHAT PERCENT ONE NUMBER IS OF ANOTHER

What percent of 120 is 60? (60 is what percent of 120?)

$$p \times 120 = 60 \qquad\qquad 60 = p \times 120$$
$$p = \frac{60}{120} = 0.5 = 50\% \qquad\qquad \frac{60}{120} = p$$
$$p = 0.5 = 50\%$$

FINDING A PERCENT OF A NUMBER

What number is 40% of 80?

Using a decimal

$$n = 40\% \times 80$$
$$n = 0.4 \times 80 = 32$$

Using a fraction

$$n = 40\% \times 80$$
$$n = \frac{40}{100} \times 80 = \frac{2}{5} \times 80 = 32$$

FINDING THE ORIGINAL NUMBER WHEN A PERCENT OF IT IS KNOWN

25% of what number is 8?

Using a decimal

$$0.25 \times n = 8$$
$$n = \frac{8}{0.25} = 32$$

Using a fraction

$$25\% = \frac{1}{4}$$
$$\frac{1}{4} \times n = 8$$
$$n = 4 \times 8 = 32$$

CHECK YOUR UNDERSTANDING

What does 7% mean?

7 out of 100 or $\frac{7}{100}$

Percent change

Also called Percent increase *or* Percent decrease. Change from a given number expressed as a percent of that number. For example, the increase in the price of an article from $20 to $30 is an increase of 50%. A decrease in the price of an article from $50 to $40 is a decrease of 20%.

FINDING PERCENT CHANGE

The price of a book changed from $5 to $8. What is the percent increase?

1. Find the difference in prices and write it as a fraction with the original price as the denominator.

   $8 - 5 \rightarrow \underline{3 \leftarrow \text{difference}}$
   $5 \leftarrow \text{original price}$

2. Write the fraction as a percent: $\frac{3}{5} = 0.6 = 60\%$
   The percent increase is 60%.

CHECK YOUR UNDERSTANDING

What percent increase is an increase from $50 to $60?

20%

Percent decrease

See Percent change.

Percent increase

See Percent change.

Percentile

A way of comparing performance, usually on a test, with others. For example, a person scoring in the 60th percentile performed better than 60% of those taking the same test. 39% of those taking the test performed better.

CHECK YOUR UNDERSTANDING

What percent of those taking the same test performed better than the person who scored in the 90th percentile?

9%

Perfect number

A number for which the sum of its proper factors (all factors except the number itself), is equal to the number. For example, 28 is a perfect number, since $28 = 1 + 2 + 4 + 7 + 14$.

See also Abundant number *and* Deficient number.

CHECK YOUR UNDERSTANDING
Is 6 a perfect number?

yes; its proper factors are 1, 2, and 3; 1 + 2 + 3 = 6

Perfect square

A whole number that can be named as a product of a number with itself.

EXAMPLE $81 = 9 \times 9 = 9^2$

CHECK YOUR UNDERSTANDING
Is 100 a perfect square?

yes; 100 = 10 × 10

Perfect square trinomial

In algebra, a trinomial that is the square of a binomial. For example, $x^2 + 6x + 9$ is a perfect square trinomial, since it is equal to $(x + 3)^2$.

HOW TO FACTOR A PERFECT SQUARE TRINOMIAL
Factor: $x^2 + 6x + 9$
Look for a pair of numbers whose product is the last term (9) and whose sum is the coefficient of the second term (6). This pair is 3, 3: $(x + 3)(x + 3)$ or $(x + 3)^2$.

CHECK YOUR UNDERSTANDING
Is $x^2 + 8x + 16$ a perfect square trinomial? If yes, what binomial is it the square of?

yes; x + 4; (x + 4)(x + 4) = (x + 4)² = x² + 8x + 16

Perimeter

The distance around the outside of a shape or figure.

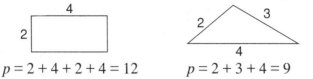

$p = 2 + 4 + 2 + 4 = 12$ $p = 2 + 3 + 4 = 9$

CHECK YOUR UNDERSTANDING
What is the perimeter of a square in which each side is
5 in. long?

20 in.

Permutation

An arrangement of objects in a particular order. Given
the letters x, y, and z, the following are the
permutations of 3 letters taken 2 at a time:
xy, yx, xz, zx, yz, zy. Thus, there are 6 permutations of
3 letters taken 2 at a time.

See also Combination.

CHECK YOUR UNDERSTANDING
Are xy and yx two different permutations?

yes

Perpendicular (⊥)

Also called Normal *or* Orthogonal. Meeting at right
angles. Two lines that intersect at right angles are
perpendicular. Two rays or segments are perpendicular
if they are parts of lines that are perpendicular. Two
planes are perpendicular if they meet at right angles.

CHECK YOUR UNDERSTANDING
Are the two legs of a right triangle perpendicular to each other?

yes

Perpendicular bisector of segment

A line, ray, or line segment that divides a segment into two congruent segments and is perpendicular to the segment. Every point on the perpendicular bisector is equidistant from the endpoints of the segment.

Line ℓ is a perpendicular bisector of segment AB. Point C is the same distance from point A as it is from point B.

CHECK YOUR UNDERSTANDING
If the distance from point D to point B is 2 cm, what is the distance from point D to point A? *2 cm*

Pi (π)

The ratio of the circumference of any circle to the length of its diameter. $\pi = 3.14159265358979\ldots$ π is a nonterminating nonrepeating decimal or an irrational number. Some commonly used rational-number approximations of π are 3.14 and $\frac{22}{7}$.

CHECK YOUR UNDERSTANDING
What is a whole number approximation of π? *3*

Pick's Formula

A formula for finding the area of a polygon on a grid of unit squares: $A = \frac{1}{2}b + i - 1$, where A is the area of the polygon, b is the number of points on the boundary of the polygon, and i is the number of points in the interior. For the polygon on the right:
$A = \frac{1}{2} \times 8 + 8 - 1 = 11$ or 11 square units.

CHECK YOUR UNDERSTANDING
A polygon on a square grid has 12 points on the boundary and 8 points in the interior. What is the area of the polygon?
$A = \frac{1}{2} \times 12 + 8 - 1 = 13$

Pictograph

Also called Pictogram. A display of information using symbols or pictures. The pictograph below displays information about the average lives of six animals. According to this pictograph, the average life of a giraffe is 18 years.

Average Number of Years Animals Live

Animals	
Mouse	☐ ☐
Kangaroo	☐ ☐
Giraffe	☐ ☐ ☐ ☐ ☐ ☐
Fox	☐ ☐ ☐ ☐
Wolf	☐ ☐ ☐ ☐ ☐
Deer	☐ ☐ ☐ ☐ ☐

Each symbol ☐ stands for 3 years.

CHECK YOUR UNDERSTANDING
According to the pictograph, what is the average life of a mouse?

6 years

Pie graph

See Circle graph.

Pint (pt)

A unit for measuring liquid capacity. 1 pint is equal to 16 ounces or 2 cups or $\frac{1}{2}$ quart.

See Table of Measures *on page 449.*

CHECK YOUR UNDERSTANDING
How many pints are there in 2 gallons?

16

Place value

In a positional system of notation the number assigned to each place that a digit occupies. For example, in the base-ten numeration system the place occupied by 5 in 5421 has the value of 1000. It is called the thousands place. The value of the digit 5 is 5000.

Whole Numbers

Billions			Millions			Thousands			Ones		
hundreds	tens	ones	hundreds	tens	ones	hundreds	tens	ones	hundreds	tens	ones
		2	4	0	6	0	7	0	8	9	5

Read: 2 billion, 4 hundred 6 million, 70 thousand, eight hundred ninety-five.

Decimals

ones		tenths	hundredths	thousandths	ten-thousandths	hundred-thousandths	millionths
8	.	0	0	0	5	6	5

Read: eight *and* five hundred sixty-five millionths.
└decimal point is read as *and*

Can also be read: eight, point, zero, zero, zero, five, six, five.

CHECK YOUR UNDERSTANDING
What is the value of the place occupied by 1 in 12,345?

10,000

Plane

A flat surface that extends
without end (infinitely) in
all directions. It has
no thickness.

CHECK YOUR UNDERSTANDING
If a plane contains one point of a line, must it contain all
the points of the line?

no

Plane figure

A geometric figure that lies entirely in one plane.

CHECK YOUR UNDERSTANDING
Is a sphere a plane figure?

no

Plane of symmetry

A plane that cuts a solid figure into two parts that are
exactly alike. For example, a plane that passes

through the center of
a sphere is a plane
of symmetry for the
sphere. The sphere
is symmetric
about the plane.

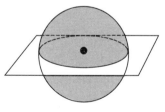

CHECK YOUR UNDERSTANDING
What geometric shape is the intersection of the plane of
symmetry with a sphere? Is there an infinite number of
planes of symmetry for a sphere?

circle; yes

Plane symmetry

A geometric figure is said to
have plane symmetry
if there is a plane
about which
the figure
is symmetric.

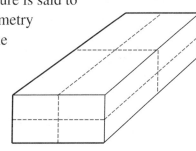

3 planes of symmetry

CHECK YOUR UNDERSTANDING
Does a square pyramid have plane symmetry?

yes

Plotting

Marking points in a coordinate system. To plot ($^-$3,2)
in a coordinate system go 3 units to the left from the
origin and up 2.

CHECK YOUR UNDERSTANDING
How would you plot (2,5) in a coordinate system?

2 units to the right from the origin, then 5 up

Plus sign

The symbol + has two different meanings in
mathematics:

In 8 + 5 = 13 it means *add*.
In $^+$4 it means *positive*.

CHECK YOUR UNDERSTANDING
What does the symbol + mean in $^+$100?

positive

Point

An undefined entity in geometry. A point has position but no dimension. Geometric figures are considered to be sets of points.

CHECK YOUR UNDERSTANDING
What number would describe the dimension of a point?

zero

Point-slope form of equation of line

An equation of a line of the form $y - y_1 = m(x - x_1)$ where (x_1, y_1) are the coordinates of a given point on the line and m is the slope of the line.

GRAPHING A LINE FROM A POINT-SLOPE EQUATION

Point slope form: $\quad y - y_1 = m(x - x_1)$
Graph the equation $y - 1 = 5(x - 2)$.

y-coordinate slope x-coordinate

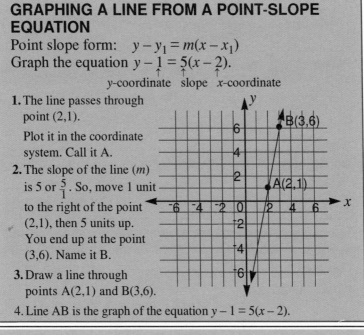

1. The line passes through point (2,1).

   Plot it in the coordinate system. Call it A.

2. The slope of the line (m) is 5 or $\frac{5}{1}$. So, move 1 unit to the right of the point (2,1), then 5 units up. You end up at the point (3,6). Name it B.

3. Draw a line through points A(2,1) and B(3,6).

4. Line AB is the graph of the equation $y - 1 = 5(x - 2)$.

CHECK YOUR UNDERSTANDING
A line passes through the point (1,6) and has the slope of ⁻2. Is its point-slope equation $y - 6 = {}^-2(x - 1)$?

yes

Point symmetry

A figure is symmetric about a point if every segment drawn from one point of the figure through the point of symmetry cuts the figure in a point that is the same distance from the point of symmetry as the first point. In a square the point of symmetry is its center (point C in the figure at the right). The length of line segment AC is the same as the length of segment BC.

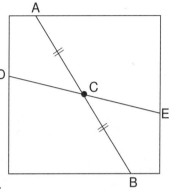

P

CHECK YOUR UNDERSTANDING

The square above has point symmetry about point C. Is the length of segment CE the same as the length of segment CD?

yes

Polygon

A simple closed curve made up of segments. Each segment in a polygon is called a side of the polygon. A polygon can have any number of sides, but it must have at least three sides. Polygons that are both equiangular and equilateral (all angles of the same measure and all sides of the same length) are called regular polygons.

See the following pages for more information about polygons.

CLASSIFICATION OF POLYGONS BY NUMBER OF SIDES

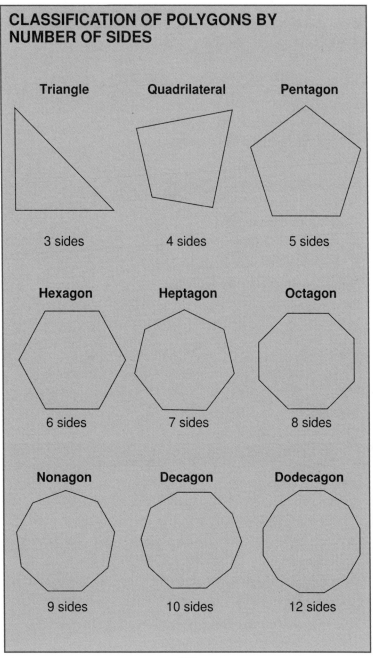

Triangle	Quadrilateral	Pentagon
3 sides	4 sides	5 sides

Hexagon	Heptagon	Octagon
6 sides	7 sides	8 sides

Nonagon	Decagon	Dodecagon
9 sides	10 sides	12 sides

EQUIANGULAR POLYGONS

A polygon in which each angle has the same measure

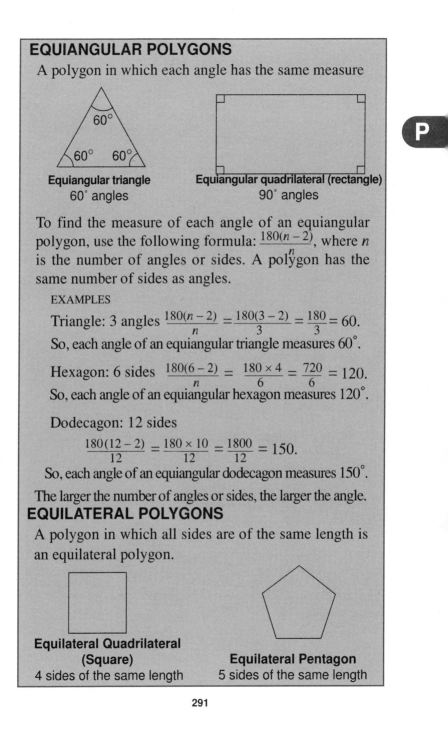

Equiangular triangle
60° angles

Equiangular quadrilateral (rectangle)
90° angles

To find the measure of each angle of an equiangular polygon, use the following formula: $\frac{180(n-2)}{n}$, where n is the number of angles or sides. A polygon has the same number of sides as angles.

EXAMPLES

Triangle: 3 angles $\frac{180(n-2)}{n} = \frac{180(3-2)}{3} = \frac{180}{3} = 60$.
So, each angle of an equiangular triangle measures 60°.

Hexagon: 6 sides $\frac{180(6-2)}{n} = \frac{180 \times 4}{6} = \frac{720}{6} = 120$.
So, each angle of an equiangular hexagon measures 120°.

Dodecagon: 12 sides
$$\frac{180(12-2)}{12} = \frac{180 \times 10}{12} = \frac{1800}{12} = 150.$$
So, each angle of an equiangular dodecagon measures 150°.

The larger the number of angles or sides, the larger the angle.

EQUILATERAL POLYGONS

A polygon in which all sides are of the same length is an equilateral polygon.

Equilateral Quadrilateral (Square)
4 sides of the same length

Equilateral Pentagon
5 sides of the same length

DRAWING REGULAR POLYGONS

You will need a ruler, a compass, and a protractor.

Drawing a regular hexagon

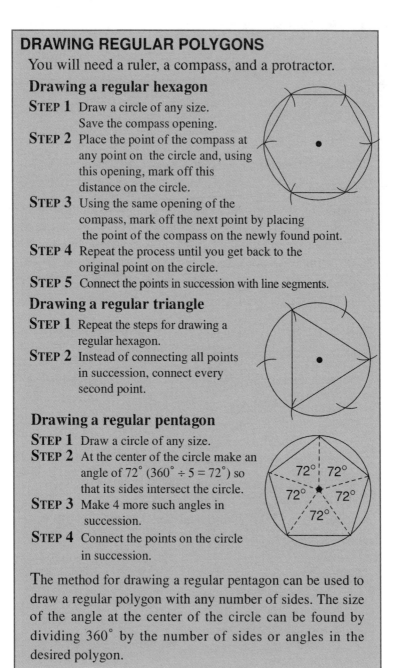

STEP 1 Draw a circle of any size.
Save the compass opening.

STEP 2 Place the point of the compass at any point on the circle and, using this opening, mark off this distance on the circle.

STEP 3 Using the same opening of the compass, mark off the next point by placing the point of the compass on the newly found point.

STEP 4 Repeat the process until you get back to the original point on the circle.

STEP 5 Connect the points in succession with line segments.

Drawing a regular triangle

STEP 1 Repeat the steps for drawing a regular hexagon.

STEP 2 Instead of connecting all points in succession, connect every second point.

Drawing a regular pentagon

STEP 1 Draw a circle of any size.

STEP 2 At the center of the circle make an angle of 72° (360° ÷ 5 = 72°) so that its sides intersect the circle.

STEP 3 Make 4 more such angles in succession.

STEP 4 Connect the points on the circle in succession.

The method for drawing a regular pentagon can be used to draw a regular polygon with any number of sides. The size of the angle at the center of the circle can be found by dividing 360° by the number of sides or angles in the desired polygon.

Polygonal numbers

See Figurate numbers.

Polyhedron   *plural* polyhedra

P

A figure in space that is made up of polygons (a simple closed curve made up of line segments) and their interiors, called faces. The intersections of faces are called edges. The points at which edges meet are called vertices (singular vertex). A special kind of a polyhedron is a regular polyhedron. All of its faces are congruent regular polygons, and all of its angles are congruent angles. There are only five regular polyhedra.

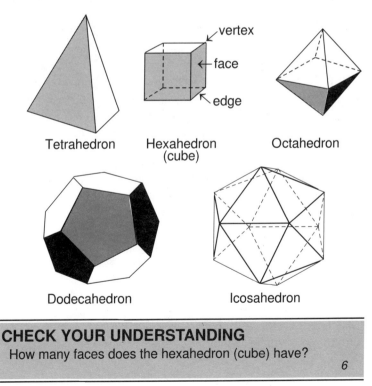

vertex

face

edge

Tetrahedron   Hexahedron   Octahedron
                    (cube)

Dodecahedron   Icosahedron

CHECK YOUR UNDERSTANDING
How many faces does the hexahedron (cube) have?

6

Polynomial

A sum and/or difference of terms.

EXAMPLES

$$\underset{\underset{\text{coefficient}}{\uparrow}\;\underset{\text{constant term}}{\uparrow}}{3x - 2} \qquad \underset{\underset{\text{constant term}}{\uparrow}}{4x^2 - 5x + 3}$$

A polynomial with two terms is called a binomial.
A polynomial with three terms is called a trinomial.

EXAMPLES   binomial   trinomial

$$3x - 2 \qquad\qquad 4x^2 - 5x + 3$$

If a polynomial has one variable, then the degree of the polynomial is the exponent of the highest power.

EXAMPLES

degree one   degree two

$2x + 5$ $3x^2 + 2x - 1$

Also called   *Also called*
linear polynomial.   quadratic polynomial.

If a polynomial has more than one variable, its degree is the highest sum of exponents among the terms. The degree of $3x^2y + 5xyz^2$ is 4, the sum of the exponents of the three variables in $5xyz^2$ $(1 + 1 + 2)$.

A polynomial with terms arranged from the smallest to the largest powers of the variable is said to be in ascending order. The polynomial $3x + 4x^2 - 7x^4 + 2x^5$ is in ascending order.

See also Factor of a polynomial – FACTORING POLYNOMIALS.

CHECK YOUR UNDERSTANDING

What is the degree of the polynomial $2x + 3xy$?

2

Polynomial equation

An equation that has a polynomial in one or both sides of the equation.

Polynomial equation: $4x^2 + 3x - 7 = 0$.

It is a polynomial equation of degree 2, since the highest exponent term has the degree of 2.

P

Polynomial function

A function (a set of ordered pairs such that no two ordered pairs have the same first member) whose values are given by a polynomial.

For example, $f(x) = x^2 + x + 3$ is a polynomial function of degree two. It can be shown as a set of ordered pairs as follows: $\{(x, x^2 + x + 3)\}$. Below are some of the ordered pairs that belong to this function:

x	$f(x)$ or $x^2 + x + 3$	Ordered pair
0	3	(0,3)
1	5	(1,5)
2	9	(2,9)
3	15	(3,15)
$^-1$	3	($^-1$,3)
$^-2$	5	($^-2$,5)
$^-3$	9	($^-3$,9)

295

Positional system of numeration

A system for writing names of numbers so that the place in which a digit is placed determines the value of the digit. In base-ten numeration system, the values of places are as follows:

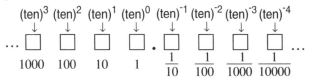

$(ten)^3$ $(ten)^2$ $(ten)^1$ $(ten)^0$ $(ten)^{-1}$ $(ten)^{-2}$ $(ten)^{-3}$ $(ten)^{-4}$

... □ □ □ □ . □ □ □ □ ...

1000   100   10   1 $\dfrac{1}{10}$ $\dfrac{1}{100}$ $\dfrac{1}{1000}$ $\dfrac{1}{10000}$

CHECK YOUR UNDERSTANDING

In base-ten numeration system, what is the value of the third place to the right of the decimal point?

$\dfrac{1}{1000}$

Positive integer

A whole number greater than 0.

EXAMPLES $^+1$ $^+9$ $^+56$

A number without a sign is also understood to be positive. 1, 9, 56 are positive integers.

CHECK YOUR UNDERSTANDING

Is $^+5$ a positive integer?

yes

Positive number

Also called Signed number. A number greater than 0. A number without a sign is also understood to be positive. Positive numbers include 0.007, 2.75, $\dfrac{5}{6}$, $3\dfrac{1}{4}$, and $6\sqrt{2}$.

CHECK YOUR UNDERSTANDING

Is $\dfrac{1}{3}$ a positive number?

yes

Positive sign

A sign that shows a number is greater than 0. For example, the positive sign in these numbers shows they are numbers greater than 0: $^+5$, $^+3\frac{1}{2}$, $^+7.25$.

P

CHECK YOUR UNDERSTANDING
Is the sign in 6 + 8 a positive sign?

no, it is a plus sign that means add

Postulate

See Axiom.

Pound (lb)

A unit of weight in the customary system. It is equal to 16 ounces (oz).

See Table of Measures *on page 449.*

CHECK YOUR UNDERSTANDING
How many ounces are there in 3 pounds?

48

Power of a number

A number raised to an exponent.

EXAMPLES 5^1 five to the first power

5^2 five to the second power or five squared

5^3 five to the third power or five cubed

5^4 five to the fourth power

and so on

Generally, a^n means $\underbrace{a \cdot a \cdot a \cdot \ldots \cdot a}$ or a to the nth power.

a used as a factor *n* times

See next page for PROPERTIES OF POWERS.

PROPERTIES OF POWERS
(LAWS OF EXPONENTS)

(x and y are real numbers, and a and b are positive integers)

Product of Powers

$$x^a x^b = x^{a+b}$$ To multiply powers with the same base, add the exponents. Keep the same base.

NOTE: $x^a y^b$ cannot be simplified because the bases are not the same.

EXAMPLE $2^3 \cdot 2^4 = (2 \cdot 2 \cdot 2)(2 \cdot 2 \cdot 2 \cdot 2) = 2^7 = 2^{3+4}$

Quotient of Powers ($x \neq 0$)

CASE 1 $a > b$ $\quad \dfrac{x^a}{x^b} = x^{a-b}$

EXAMPLE $\quad \dfrac{2^5}{2^3} = \dfrac{2 \cdot 2 \cdot 2 \cdot 2 \cdot 2}{2 \cdot 2 \cdot 2} = 2^2 = 2^{5-3}$

CASE 2 $a < b$

$$\dfrac{x^a}{x^b} = \dfrac{1}{x^{b-a}}$$

EXAMPLE $\quad \dfrac{2^3}{2^5} = \dfrac{1}{2^{5-3}} = \dfrac{1}{2^2} = \dfrac{1}{4}$

CASE 3 $a = b$

$$\dfrac{x^a}{x^b} = \dfrac{x^a}{x^a} = 1$$

EXAMPLE $\quad \dfrac{3^6}{3^6} = 1$

Power of a Power

$$(x^a)^b = x^{ab}$$ To raise a power to a power, multiply the exponents. Keep the same base.

EXAMPLE $\quad (2^3)^2 = 8^2 = 64$ and $2^{3 \times 2} = 2^6 = 64$, so $(2^3)^2 = 2^{3 \times 2}$

Power of a product

$(xy)^a = x^a \cdot y^a$ To raise a product to a power, raise each number to the power and multiply.

EXAMPLE $(2 \cdot 3)^2 = 6^2 = 36$ and $2^2 \cdot 3^2 = 4 \cdot 9 = 36$, so $(2 \cdot 3)^2 = 2^2 \cdot 3^2$

Power of a quotient ($y \neq 0$)

$\left(\dfrac{x}{y}\right)^a = \dfrac{x^a}{y^a}$ To raise a quotient to a power, raise each number to the power and divide.

EXAMPLE $\left(\dfrac{2}{3}\right)^2 = \dfrac{2}{3} \cdot \dfrac{2}{3} = \dfrac{4}{9}$ and $\dfrac{2^2}{3^2} = \dfrac{4}{9}$

so $\left(\dfrac{2}{3}\right)^2 = \dfrac{2^2}{3^2}$

Power of ten

A number obtained by raising 10 to a whole-number power. The resulting name is written as 1 followed by the number of 0's indicated by the exponent.

Any nonzero number raised to the power 0 is equal to 1. So, $10^0 = 1$.

Any number raised to the power 1 is equal to that number. So, $10^1 = 10$.

Other powers of 10 through 1 million are:

$10^2 = 100$	hundred
$10^3 = 1000$	thousand
$10^4 = 10{,}000$	ten thousand
$10^5 = 100{,}000$	hundred thousand
$10^6 = 1{,}000{,}000$	million

See also Quadrillions, etc. *on page 447.*

SHORTCUTS FOR MULTIPLYING DECIMALS BY POWERS OF TEN

Multiply:	Shift the decimal point
$49.83 \times 10 = 498.3$	1 place to the right
$49.83 \times 100 = 4,983$	2 places to the right
$49.83 \times 1,000 = 49,830$	3 places to the right
$49.83 \times 10,000 = 498,300$	4 places to the right
$58.32 \times 0.1 = 5.832$	1 place to the left
$58.32 \times 0.01 = 0.5832$	2 places to the left
$58.32 \times 0.001 = 0.05832$	3 places to the left

SHORTCUTS FOR DIVIDING DECIMALS BY POWERS OF TEN

Divide:	Shift the decimal point
$73.85 \div 10 = 7.385$	1 place to the left
$73.85 \div 100 = 0.7385$	2 places to the left
$73.85 \div 1,000 = 0.07385$	3 places to the left
$73.85 \div 10,000 = 0.007385$	4 places to the left

Write zeros to place the decimal point correctly when necessary.

CHECK YOUR UNDERSTANDING

Is 12^{10} a power of 10?

no; it is a power of 12

Precision of measurement

The smallest unit of measurement used in measuring. If a measurement is reported to be 3.23 units, then the precision of this measurement is 0.01 unit (one hundredth of a unit).

CHECK YOUR UNDERSTANDING

What is the precision of measurement reported to be 4.2 units?

one-tenth of a unit

Premise

See Axiom.

Prime factor

A factor of a number that is a prime number. For example, 3 is a prime factor of 12.

CHECK YOUR UNDERSTANDING

Is 5 a prime factor of 30?

yes

Prime factorization

Also called Complete factorization. Factoring a number into its prime factors only. Each whole number has a unique (exactly one) prime factorization, except for the order of the factors.

EXAMPLE

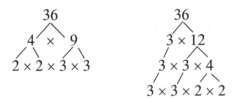

Each prime factorization gives the same prime factors.

CHECK YOUR UNDERSTANDING

What is the prime factorization of 182?

2 × 7 × 13

Prime number

A counting number that has exactly two factors, 1 and the number itself. The number 1 is neither prime nor composite. The first 10 prime numbers are: 2, 3, 5, 7, 11, 13, 17, 19, 23, 29.

CHECK YOUR UNDERSTANDING
List the next five prime numbers.

31, 37, 41, 43, 47

Prime polynomial

See Irreducible polynomial.

Principal

The amount of money on which interest is paid.

CHECK YOUR UNDERSTANDING
You invested $100 for one year at a simple interest rate of 5% computed annually. At the end of the year you have $105 in your account. What is your new principal?

$105

Principal root

See Principal square root.

Principal square root

Also called Principal root. The positive square root of a number. For example, there are two square roots of 25, 5 and ⁻5, because $5^2 = 25$ and $(^-5)^2 = 25$. Since 5 is the positive square root of 25, it is the principal square root.

CHECK YOUR UNDERSTANDING
What is the principal square root of 100?

10

Prism

A solid with two parallel congruent bases and rectangles or parallelograms for faces. The bases of a prism can be any polygon. If the faces make right angles with the bases, then the prism is called a right prism. If these angles are not right angles, then the prism is called an oblique prism. The line segments at which faces intersect are called edges, and endpoints are called vertices (singular vertex). A right prism with bases that are regular polygons is called a regular prism.

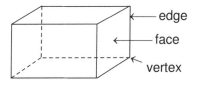

Right rectangular prism

 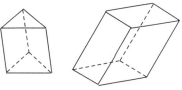

Regular pentagonal prism   Oblique prisms

See also Lateral area, Surface area, *and* Volume.

CHECK YOUR UNDERSTANDING

What kind of polygons are the bases of the triangular prism in the picture above?

triangles

Probability

The chance of an event occurring. The number of favorable outcomes divided by the total number of all possible outcomes.

EXAMPLE The theoretical or a priori probability of the spinner landing on red is the number of favorable outcomes, 2, divided by the total number of possible outcomes, 5, or $\frac{2}{5}$. $P(red) = \frac{2}{5}$.

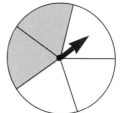

However, if you experiment by spinning the spinner 100 times, the spinner may not land on red exactly 40 times. The number of times the spinner landed on red during the experiment divided by the number of times you did the experiment is called the experimental or empirical probability. (It will be a fraction close to $\frac{2}{5}$.)

ANOTHER EXAMPLE If you toss a coin 100 times and a head lands up 52 times, the experimental probability of heads landing up is $\frac{52}{100}$ or $\frac{13}{25}$. The theoretical probability of heads landing up is 1 out of 2 or $\frac{1}{2}$. Note that $\frac{13}{25}$ is close to $\frac{1}{2}$.

The probability of an event is a number from 0 to 1. A probability of 0 means no chance of an event occurring. Probability of 1 means that an event is certain to occur.

See also Odds.

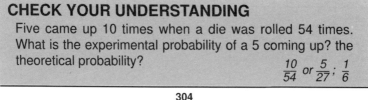

CHECK YOUR UNDERSTANDING

Five came up 10 times when a die was rolled 54 times. What is the experimental probability of a 5 coming up? the theoretical probability?

$\frac{10}{54}$ or $\frac{5}{27}$; $\frac{1}{6}$

Product

The result of multiplication.

Ways of showing a product

Using two variables: ab $a \cdot b$ $a \times b$ $(a)(b)$

Using two numbers: $^-5 \underset{\uparrow}{\cdot} 3$ $^-5 \underset{\uparrow}{\times} 3$ $(^-5\underset{\uparrow}{)}(3)$

       dot   multiplication sign   parentheses

CHECK YOUR UNDERSTANDING

The product 4 · ⁻6 can be shown in two more ways. What are they?

4 × ⁻6, (4)(⁻6)

Profit

In a transaction, what is left after all of the expenses have been covered.

CHECK YOUR UNDERSTANDING

A catering business made a sale of $4,500. The expenses were $4,000. What was the profit?

$500

Proper factors

All factors of a number excluding the number itself.

EXAMPLE The proper factors of 12 are 1, 2, 3, 4, 6.

CHECK YOUR UNDERSTANDING

What are the proper factors of 20?

1, 2, 4, 5, 10

Proper fraction

A fraction in which the numerator is less than the denominator.

EXAMPLE $\dfrac{3}{5}$ $\leftarrow$ numerator
$\leftarrow$ denominator

CHECK YOUR UNDERSTANDING

Is $\dfrac{7}{6}$ a proper fraction?

no; the numerator (7) is greater than the denominator (6)

Proper subset

See Subset.

Property

A characteristic of a number, geometric figure, mathematical operation, equation, or inequality.

Property of a number: 8 is divisible by 2.

Property of a geometric figure: Each of the four sides of a square is of the same length.

Property of an operation: Addition is commutative. For all numbers x and y, $x + y = y + x$.

Property of an equation: For all numbers a, b, and c, if $a = b$, then $a + c = b + c$.

Property of an inequality: For all numbers a, b, and c, if $a > b$, then $a - c > b - c$.

See also Addition property of equations, Addition property of inequality, Associative property, Closure property, Commutative property, Density property, Distributive property, Division property of equations, Division property of inequality, Identity property of addition, Identity property of multiplication, Inverse property of addition, Inverse property of multiplication, Multiplication property of equations, Multiplication property of inequality, Power of a number–properties of powers (Laws of exponents), Proportion property, Reflexive property of congruence, Reflexive property of equality, Reflexive property of similarity, Substitution property, Subtraction property of equality, Subtraction property of inequality, Symmetric property of congruence, Symmetric property of equality, Symmetric property of similarity, Transitive property of congruence, Transitive property of equality, Transitive property of similarity, Triangle inequality property, Zero property of addition, *and* Zero property of multiplication.

CHECK YOUR UNDERSTANDING

What properties does the number 9 have?

divisible by 3; it is a perfect square (3^2); it is an odd number

Proportion

A statement of the form, $\frac{a}{b} = \frac{c}{d}$. Each of a, b, c, d is called a term of the proportion. In a proportion, a and d (the first and fourth terms) are called the extremes and b and c (the second and third terms) are called the means. In a true proportion, the product of the means equals the product of the extremes.

HOW TO TELL WHETHER A PROPORTION IS TRUE

Use cross multiplication. (Multiply the extremes, multiply the means.) If the products (called cross-products) are equal, the proportion is true. If they are not equal, the proportion is false.

EXAMPLES

$$\frac{4}{7} \stackrel{?}{=} \frac{5}{8} \qquad\qquad \frac{5}{9} \stackrel{?}{=} \frac{15}{27}$$

$$4 \times 8 \stackrel{?}{=} 7 \times 5 \qquad\qquad 5 \times 27 \stackrel{?}{=} 9 \times 15$$

$$32 \neq 35 \qquad\qquad 135 = 135$$

The proportion is false.   The proportion is true.

SOLVING PROPORTIONS

EXAMPLE Find the value of x to obtain a true proportion:

$$\frac{4}{x} = \frac{5}{x+3}$$

For the proportion to be true, the product of the extremes must be equal to the product of the means: $4(x+3) = 5x$

$$4x + 12 = 5x$$

$$x = 12$$

Check $\dfrac{4}{x} = \dfrac{5}{x+3}$

$$\frac{4}{12} \stackrel{?}{=} \frac{5}{12+3}$$

$$\frac{4}{12} \stackrel{?}{=} \frac{5}{15}$$

$$4 \times 15 \stackrel{?}{=} 12 \times 5$$

$$60 = 60 \quad \text{So, 12 is the solution of } \frac{4}{x} = \frac{5}{x+3}$$

USING PROPORTIONS TO FIND MISSING LENGTHS OF SIDES IN SIMILAR TRIANGLES

In similar triangles, lengths of corresponding sides have equal ratios.

EXAMPLE

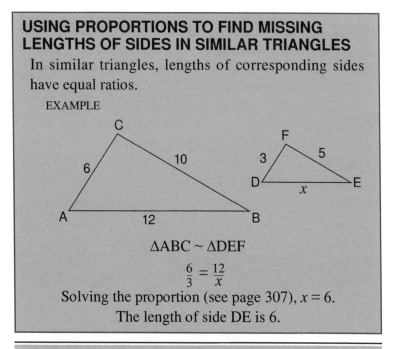

$$\triangle ABC \sim \triangle DEF$$

$$\frac{6}{3} = \frac{12}{x}$$

Solving the proportion (see page 307), $x = 6$.
The length of side DE is 6.

CHECK YOUR UNDERSTANDING

Is $\frac{3}{5} = \frac{12}{20}$ a true proportion? If yes, what is the product of the means and the extremes?

yes; 60

Proportion property

If $\frac{a}{b} = \frac{c}{d}$, then $ad = bc$ ($b \neq 0$, $d \neq 0$). a and d are the extremes; b and c are the means. The product of the extremes is equal to the product of the means.

EXAMPLE

$$\frac{4}{12} = \frac{5}{15}$$
$$4 \times 15 = 12 \times 5$$
$$60 = 60$$

CHECK YOUR UNDERSTANDING

According to the proportion property, what equation follows from the proportion $\frac{3}{7} = \frac{9}{21}$?

3 × 21 = 7 × 9

Proportional parts

In geometry, similar polygons have proportional parts. Triangles ABC and A' B' C' are similar. Their corresponding sides are proportional, that is $\frac{AB}{A'B'} = \frac{BC}{B'C'} = \frac{CA}{C'A'}$ or

$$\frac{36}{18} = \frac{20}{10} = \frac{38}{19}$$

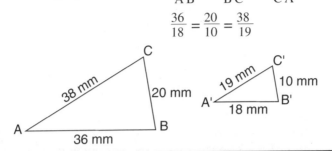

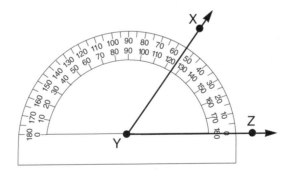

CHECK YOUR UNDERSTANDING

In the case of proportional sides in triangles ABC and A'B'C' above, what is the ratio of each pair of corresponding sides in simplest form (lowest terms)?

2 to 1 or $\frac{2}{1}$ or 2

Protractor

An instrument for measuring angles in degrees.

CHECK YOUR UNDERSTANDING

The protractor in the picture above shows that angle XYZ measures how many degrees?

55°

Pure imaginary number

See Complex number.

Pyramid

A solid figure whose base can be any polygon and whose faces are triangles. Pyramids are named by the shape of their bases. The point at which the faces meet is called the vertex of the pyramid. The segment in which the faces intersect is called an edge. The altitude of the pyramid is a segment from its vertex perpendicular to the base. A pyramid with a regular polygon for its base and one endpoint of its altitude the center of its base is called a regular pyramid.

Triangular pyramid or
Tetrahedron

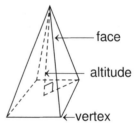

face

altitude

←vertex

Square pyramid

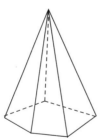

Pentagonal pyramid

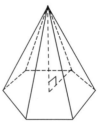

Regular hexagonal pyramid

See also Lateral area, Surface area, *and* Volume.

CHECK YOUR UNDERSTANDING

What kind of polygon is the base of the pentagonal pyramid?

pentagon

Pythagorean theorem

Also called Pythagorean relation, Pythagorean rule, *or* Pythagorean property. A relationship between the lengths of the sides in a right triangle. In a right triangle, the square of the hypotenuse is equal to the sum of the squares of its legs.

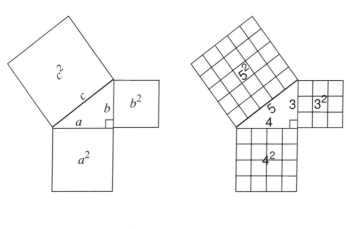

$$c^2 = a^2 + b^2$$

$$5^2 = 4^2 + 3^2$$
$$25 = 16 + 9$$
$$25 = 25$$

CHECK YOUR UNDERSTANDING

Is a triangle whose sides are 5 in., 12 in., and 13 in. long a right triangle?

yes; $5^2 + 12^2 = 25 + 144 = 169$, $13^2 = 169$

Pythagorean triple

Three numbers a, b, c, such that $c^2 = a^2 + b^2$.

EXAMPLE   3, 4, 5

$$3^2 + 4^2 = 5^2$$

$$9 + 16 = 25$$

Other examples of Pythagorean triples.

5, 12, 13	7, 24, 25	8, 15, 17
12, 35, 37	16, 63, 65	18, 80, 82
36, 77, 85	54, 72, 90	60, 91, 109

An infinite number of Pythagorean triples can be obtained from these Pythagorean triples by multiplying each of the three numbers in a Pythagorean triple by the same number.

EXAMPLE   Multiply each of the three numbers 3, 4, and 5 by 6:

$$3 \times 6 = 18 \qquad 4 \times 6 = 24 \qquad 5 \times 6 = 30$$

$$18^2 + 24^2 = 30^2 \qquad 324 + 576 = 900$$

There is a formula for generating Pythagorean triples from two numbers. Given two numbers, a and b, such that $a > b$, the following will yield Pythagorean triples:

$$a^2 - b^2 \qquad 2ab \qquad a^2 + b^2$$

EXAMPLE Let $a = 7$ and $b = 2$. Then:

$$a^2 - b^2 = 7^2 - 2^2 \qquad 2ab = 2 \times 7 \times 2$$
$$= 49 - 4 \qquad\qquad\quad = 28$$
$$= 45$$
$$a^2 + b^2 = 7^2 + 2^2 = 49 + 4 = 53$$
$$45^2 + 28^2 = 53^2 \qquad 2025 + 784 = 2809$$

CHECK YOUR UNDERSTANDING

What Pythagorean triple of numbers will be obtained by using $a = 2$ and $b = 1$ in the formula above?

3, 4, 5

Quadrant

The x-axis and the y-axis separate the plane into four parts called quadrants. The axes are not parts of the quadrants.

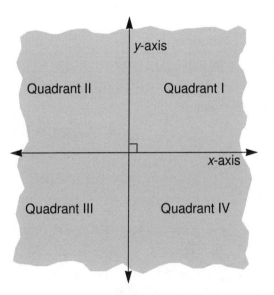

See also Coordinate system.

CHECK YOUR UNDERSTANDING

Do the quadrants have any overlapping parts?

no

Quadratic

See Quadratic equation.

Quadratic equation

Also called Quadratic. A polynomial equation containing a variable to the second degree (power 2). Its standard form is $ax^2 + bx + c = 0$. In this form, ax^2 is the quadratic (second-degree) term, bx is the linear (first-degree) term, and c is the constant. Also a is the coefficient of the quadratic term, and b is the coefficient of the linear term. A quadratic equation of the form $ax^2 + c = 0$ is called a pure quadratic equation or simply a pure quadratic.

SOLVING A PURE QUADRATIC EQUATION

It is not necessary to use the quadratic formula to solve a pure quadratic.

EXAMPLE $x^2 - 9 = 0$ Add 9 to each side
$$x^2 - 9 + 9 = 0 + 9$$ of the equation.
$$x^2 = 9 \quad x = \pm\sqrt{9} \quad x = 3 \text{ or } x = {}^-3.$$

Check: $x^2 - 9 = 0$ $x^2 - 9 = 0$
$$3^2 - 9 \overset{?}{=} 0 \qquad ({}^-3)^2 - 9 \overset{?}{=} 0$$
$$9 - 9 \overset{?}{=} 0 \qquad\quad 9 - 9 \overset{?}{=} 0$$
$$0 = 0 \qquad\qquad\quad 0 = 0$$

So, the roots (solutions) are 3 and ⁻3.

SOLVING A QUADRATIC EQUATION BY FACTORING

Quadratic equations whose roots are integers can be solved by factoring.

EXAMPLE $x^2 + 4x - 21 = 0$

To factor, find two numbers whose sum is 4 (the coefficient of the middle term) and whose product is ⁻21 (the constant term). They are 3 and ⁻7.

So, $x^2 + 4x - 21 = (x - 3)(x + 7)$

The product of two factors is 0 if one or both of the factors are 0: $x - 3 = 0$ or $x + 7 = 0$

$$x = 3 \qquad\qquad x = {}^-7$$

Check: $x^2 + 4x - 21 = 0$ $x^2 + 4x - 21 = 0$

$$3^2 + 4 \cdot 3 - 21 \overset{?}{=} 0 \qquad ({}^-7)^2 + 4 \cdot {}^-7 - 21 \overset{?}{=} 0$$

$$9 + 12 - 21 \overset{?}{=} 0 \qquad\quad 49 - 28 - 21 \overset{?}{=} 0$$

$$21 - 21 \overset{?}{=} 0 \qquad\qquad 49 - 49 \overset{?}{=} 0$$

$$0 = 0 \qquad\qquad\qquad\quad 0 = 0$$

So, the roots are 3 and $^-7$.

SOLVING EQUATIONS IN QUADRATIC FORM

An equation in quadratic form can be changed to a quadratic equation by an appropriate substitution.

EXAMPLE $x^{\underset{\uparrow}{4}} + 3x^2 - 4 = 0$

        degree 4

STEP 1   Substitute y for x^2.

To replace x^2 by y in $x^4 + 3x^2 - 4 = 0$, note that $x^4 = (x^2)^2$. So, $x^4 + 3x^2 - 4 = y^2 + 3y - 4 = 0$.

STEP 2   Solve for y by factoring: $y = {}^-4$ or $y = 1$. (The quadratic formula can also be used to solve for y.)

STEP 3   Substitute x^2 for y: $x^2 = {}^-4$ or $x^2 = 1$.

$x^2 = {}^-4$ has no real-number solutions, since any real number squared is positive or 0.

The solutions of $x^2 = 1$ are 1 and $^-1$.

Check: $x^4 + 3x^2 - 4 = 0$ $x^4 + 3x^2 - 4 = 0$

$$1^4 + 3 \cdot 1^2 - 4 \overset{?}{=} 0 \qquad ({}^-1)^4 + 3({}^-1)^2 - 4 \overset{?}{=} 0$$

$$1 + 3 - 4 \overset{?}{=} 0 \qquad\qquad 1 + 3 - 4 \overset{?}{=} 0$$

$$0 = 0 \qquad\qquad\qquad\quad 0 = 0$$

CHECK YOUR UNDERSTANDING

Is $3x^2 - 4x + 5 = 0$ a quadratic equation?

yes

Quadratic expression

In algebra, an expression in one or more variables in which the highest degree term is of degree 2.

EXAMPLE $\underbrace{3x^2}_{} - 4 + 3x$

highest degree term

If an expression has more than one variable, then the degree of a term is determined by adding the exponents of the variables.

EXAMPLE $\underbrace{5xy}_{} + x - 4y + 7$

highest degree term (of degree 1 + 1 or 2)

CHECK YOUR UNDERSTANDING

Is the expression $7xy - 5x + 3y - 9$ a quadratic expression?

yes; 7xy is of degree 2

Quadratic form

A form of an equation of degree higher than 2 that can be reduced to a quadratic equation by an appropriate substitution for the variable.

EXAMPLE The equation $x^4 + 5x^2 - 36 = 0$ is a fourth degree equation. Substituting y for x^2 results in a quadratic equation in y:

$$y^2 + 5y - 36 = 0$$

See SOLVING EQUATIONS IN QUADRATIC FORM *on page 315.*

CHECK YOUR UNDERSTANDING

What substitution should be made in the equation $3x^4 - 2x^2 - 8 = 0$ to obtain a quadratic equation with variable y?

y for x^2; quadratic equation: $3y^2 - 2y - 8 = 0$

Quadratic formula

A formula for solving quadratic equations. Given the general form of a quadratic equation, $ax^2 + bx + c = 0$, the roots (solutions) of the equation are given by the formula,

$$x_{1,2} = \frac{-b \pm \sqrt{b^2 - 4ac}}{2a}$$

To solve the equation $2x^2 + 3x - 2 = 0$ using the formula, substitute 2 for a, 3 for b and $^-2$ for c:

$$x_1 = \frac{^-3 + \sqrt{3^2 - 4 \times 2 \times {}^-2}}{2 \times 2} \qquad x_2 = \frac{^-3 - \sqrt{3^2 - 4 \times 2 \times {}^-2}}{2 \times 2}$$

$$= \frac{^-3 + \sqrt{9 - {}^-16}}{4} \qquad\qquad = \frac{^-3 - \sqrt{9 - {}^-16}}{4}$$

$$= \frac{^-3 + \sqrt{25}}{4} \qquad\qquad = \frac{^-3 - \sqrt{25}}{4}$$

$$= \frac{^-3 + 5}{4} \qquad\qquad\qquad = \frac{^-3 - 5}{4}$$

$$= \frac{2}{4} = \frac{1}{2} \qquad\qquad\qquad = \frac{^-8}{4} = {}^-2$$

CHECK YOUR UNDERSTANDING
Given the quadratic equation $2x^2 + 5x - 3 = 0$, what should be substituted for a, b, and c in the quadratic formula to solve the equation?

2 for a, 5 for b, ⁻3 for c

Quadratic function

A function whose value is given by a quadratic polynomial. It is the set of ordered pairs of the form $\{(x, ax^2 + bx + c)\}$, also written as $y = ax^2 + bx + c$. Since every function is also a relation, the above is also a quadratic relation.

EXAMPLES $y = 5x^2$ $y = 3x^2 - 5$ $y = 4x^2 + 3x - 1$

CHECK YOUR UNDERSTANDING
Does the ordered pair $(x, 2x^2 + 3x + 1)$ belong to a quadratic function?

yes

Quadratic polynomial

See Polynomial.

Quadratic relation

See Quadratic function.

Quadratic term

A term of the second degree (squared or of power 2) in an equation, inequality, or polynomial.

EXAMPLES $5x^2$ $^-3y^2$ $6cd$ $2ab$

Quadrilateral

A polygon with four sides.

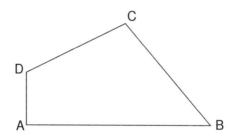

Kites, parallelograms, rectangles, rhombi, squares, and trapezoids are all quadrilaterals with special features.

Quart (qt)

A unit of liquid measure. There are 4 quarts in a gallon.

CHECK YOUR UNDERSTANDING
How many quarts are there in 3 gallons?

12

Q

Quartile

The value at the points that separate a set of data into four parts. The middle point or middle quartile is called the median. The other two points are called the upper quartile and lower quartile.

EXAMPLE Find the quartiles of these bowling scores.

Bowling scores of 11 teenagers

110 118 100 94 105 121 91 101 107 125 107

1. Arrange these data in order from least to greatest.

91 94 100 101 105 107 107 110 118 121 125

↑   ↑   ↑   ↑   ↑

extreme lower quartile   median   upper quartile extreme

2. Find the median (middle score). [107]

3. Find the median of the 5 scores above the median (upper quartile) [118] and 5 scores below the median (lower quartile). [100]

The interquartile range is the difference between the upper quartile and lower quartile. For the bowling scores, it is $118 - 100$, or 18.

CHECK YOUR UNDERSTANDING
Find the quartiles for this set of data: 70, 65, 72, 78, 66, 72, 78, 74, 76.

lower quartile: 68, median: 72, upper quartile: 77

319

Quotient

The result of division.

EXAMPLES

$$24 \div 3 = 8$$

dividend divisor quotient

$$3x^4 \div x = 3x^3$$

dividend divisor quotient

CHECK YOUR UNDERSTANDING

What is the quotient in $42 \div 7 = 6$? In $5x^3 \div x^2 = 5x$?

6; 5x

Radian

A unit for measuring angles. A central angle with sides and intercepted arcs all the same length measures 1 radian.

∠O measures 1 radian

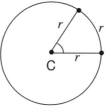

∠C measures 1 radian

Some Radian-Degree Equivalents		
Degrees	Radians	
	Exact	Approximate (4 decimal places)
1°	$\frac{\pi}{180}$	0.0175
30°	$\frac{\pi}{6}$	0.5236
45°	$\frac{\pi}{4}$	0.7854
57.3°	1	1.0000
60°	$\frac{\pi}{3}$	1.0472
90°	$\frac{\pi}{2}$	1.5708
180°	π	3.1417

CHECK YOUR UNDERSTANDING

If the sides of a central angle are 2 units long, how long should the intercepted arc be to make an angle of 1 radian?

2 units

Radical

A root of a number, such as $\sqrt{5}$ (square root of 5). The symbol $\sqrt{}$ is called the radical sign and $\sqrt{5}$ is called a radical. The number 5 under the radical sign is called the radicand. In $\sqrt[3]{7}$, 3 is called the index. $\sqrt[3]{7}$ is read cube root or third root of 7. The index is not written for square roots. If two or more radicals have the same index, then they are called like radicals. If two or more radicals have different indices, then they are called unlike radicals.

See also Cube root *and* Square root.

CHECK YOUR UNDERSTANDING
What does $\sqrt[4]{16}$ mean?

the fourth root of sixteen, which is equal to 2

Radical equation

An equation that contains one or more radicals, such as
$$\sqrt{2x + 8} + 2 = \sqrt{x} + 4$$

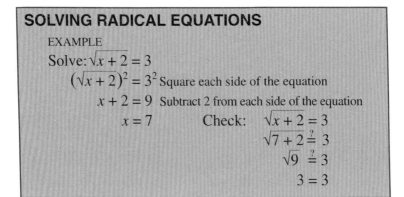

SOLVING RADICAL EQUATIONS

EXAMPLE

Solve: $\sqrt{x + 2} = 3$

$\left(\sqrt{x + 2}\right)^2 = 3^2$ Square each side of the equation

$x + 2 = 9$ Subtract 2 from each side of the equation

$x = 7$ Check: $\sqrt{x + 2} = 3$

$\sqrt{7 + 2} \overset{?}{=} 3$

$\sqrt{9} \overset{?}{=} 3$

$3 = 3$

EXAMPLE

Solve: $\sqrt{x+2} - \sqrt{x-1} = 1$

$(\sqrt{x+2} - \sqrt{x-1})^2 = 1^2$ Square each side.

$x + 2 - 2\sqrt{x+2}\sqrt{x-1} + x - 1 = 1$

$2x - 2\sqrt{x+2}\sqrt{x-1} + 1 = 1$ Combine like terms.

$^-2\sqrt{x+2}\sqrt{x-1} = ^-2x$ Get x on one side.

$\sqrt{x+2}\sqrt{x-1} = x$ Divide both sides by $^-2$.

$x^2 + x - 2 = x^2$ Square each side.

$x = 2$ Subtract x^2 from both sides, add 2 to both sides.

Check: $\sqrt{x+2} - \sqrt{x-1} = 1$

$\sqrt{2+2} - \sqrt{2-1} \overset{?}{=} 1$

$2 - 1 \overset{?}{=} 1$

$1 = 1$

R

CHECK YOUR UNDERSTANDING
Is $\sqrt{x} = 5$ a radical equation?

yes

Radical expression

An expression that contains one or more radicals, such as $\sqrt{2x-3} + \sqrt{x-5}$.

CHECK YOUR UNDERSTANDING
Is $\sqrt{a+9} - 6$ a radical expression?

yes

Radical sign
See Radical.

Radicand
See Radical.

Radius
plural radii

Of a circle: A segment connecting the center of a circle to any point on the circle. Also the length of a segment connecting the center of a circle to any point on the circle.

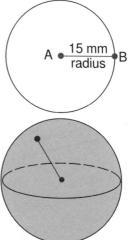

A •—15 mm—• B
radius

Of a sphere: A segment connecting the center of a sphere to any point on the sphere. Also the length of a segmentconnecting the center of a sphere to any point on the sphere.

CHECK YOUR UNDERSTANDING
How many radii does a circle have? How many radii does a sphere have?

an infinite number; an infinite number

Random

Happening by chance.

Random Event An outcome of an experiment that cannot be predicted with certainty. For example, in rolling a die there are six possible random outcomes: 1, 2, 3, 4, 5, 6.

Random Number A number selected by chance such as drawn from a hat or generated by a computer by chance.

Random Sample A collection of numbers or other items that are placed in the sample by chance. No prediction can be made whether something will be selected.

Random Selection Choosing something by chance.

CHECK YOUR UNDERSTANDING
When tossing a coin either heads (H) or tails (T) will come up. Is each of these a random outcome?

yes

Range of a distribution

Also called Range of a set of data. The difference between the largest and smallest number in a set of data. The range can be given as an interval.

EXAMPLE   3, 8, 11, 15, 20
Range: 20 – 3 = 17, or from 3 to 20.

CHECK YOUR UNDERSTANDING
What is the range of the ages of 5 children whose ages in years are the following: 2, 4, 7, 10, 14?

14 – 2 = 12, or from 2 to 14

R

Range of a function

The set of all second members (elements) of a function. Given the function {(1,5), (2,10) (3,15), (4,20), (5,25)}, the range is {5, 10, 15, 20, 25}. The domain of the function is the set of all first members, {1, 2, 3, 4, 5}.

CHECK YOUR UNDERSTANDING
What is the range of the following function?
{(1,3), (2,6), (3,9), (4,12)}

{3,6,9,12}

Rate

A comparison by a ratio of two different kinds of units.

EXAMPLES OF RATES

1. A car travels at the rate of 45 miles per hour (mph). Mile is one kind of unit; hour is another kind of unit.

2. A machine produces 100 bolts per minute. Bolt is one kind of unit; minute is another kind of unit.

CHECK YOUR UNDERSTANDING
Sound travels about 1.5 kilometers per second (km/s). Is it correct to say that the *rate* of travel of sound is about 1.5 kilometers per second?

yes, kilometer is one kind of unit, second is another kind of unit.

Rate of interest

See Interest.

Ratio

A comparison of two quantities by division.

EXAMPLES

1. The ratio of teachers to students at Washington High School is 1 to 25, or $\frac{1}{25}$, or 1:25.
2. The ratio of boys to girls at birth is 102 to 100, or $\frac{102}{100}$ or 102:100.

See also Proportion, Scale drawing, *and* Trigonometric ratios.

CHECK YOUR UNDERSTANDING

There are 17 girls and 14 boys in a 7th grade class. What is the ratio of girls to boys?

17 to 14, $\frac{17}{14}$, or 17:14

Ratio in geometric progression

See Geometric progression.

Ratio of similitude

See Similar figures.

Rational expression

A polynomial or the quotient of two polynomials, such as $\dfrac{x^2 + 3}{2x^3 - 3x^2 + 5x - 2}$. The denominator cannot be 0.

UNDEFINED VALUE OF A RATIONAL EXPRESSION

If the denominator of a rational expression is 0, the value of the expression is not defined.

EXAMPLE $\dfrac{2x + 7}{x - 5}$

The value of this expression is undefined if $x = 5$.

SIMPLIFYING RATIONAL EXPRESSIONS

$$\frac{24x^3}{8x} = \frac{2 \cdot 2 \cdot 2 \cdot 3x^3}{2 \cdot 2 \cdot 2x} = 3x^2$$

$$\frac{2a^2 - a - 3}{a^2 + 6a + 5} = \frac{(a+1)(2a-3)}{(a+1)(a+5)} = \frac{2a-3}{a+5}$$

MULTIPLYING RATIONAL EXPRESSIONS

Rule for multiplying rational expressions:

$$\frac{a}{b} \cdot \frac{c}{d} = \frac{ac}{bd}$$

EXAMPLES

$$\frac{8x^3}{3y^2} \cdot \frac{6y^5}{12x^6} = \frac{2 \cdot 2 \cdot 2 \cdot x^3}{3y^2} \cdot \frac{2 \cdot 3y^5}{2 \cdot 2 \cdot 3x^6} = \frac{2x^3}{3y^2} \cdot \frac{2y^5}{x^6} = \frac{4y^3}{3x^3}$$

$$\frac{2x^2 + 5x - 3}{4x^2 + 4x - 3} = \frac{(x+3)(2x-1)}{(2x-1)(2x+3)} = \frac{x+3}{2x+3}$$

DIVIDING RATIONAL EXPRESSIONS

Rule for dividing rational expressions:

$$\frac{a}{b} \div \frac{c}{d} = \frac{a}{b} \cdot \frac{d}{c} = \frac{ad}{bc}$$

To divide one rational expression by another, invert the second expression and multiply (*See* Multiplying rational expressions *above*).

ADDING AND SUBTRACTING RATIONAL EXPRESSIONS: LIKE DENOMINATORS

Rule for Adding and Subtracting Rational Expressions

$$\frac{a}{b} + \frac{c}{b} = \frac{a+c}{b} \qquad \frac{a}{b} - \frac{c}{b} = \frac{a-c}{b}$$

EXAMPLES

$$\frac{9x}{7} + \frac{2x}{7} = \frac{9x + 2x}{7} = \frac{11x}{7}$$

$$\frac{4x^2}{2x^3 - 3x + 5} - \frac{2x+1}{2x^3 - 3x + 5} = \frac{4x^2 - (2x+1)}{2x^3 - 3x + 5} = \frac{4x^2 - 2x - 1}{2x^3 - 3x + 5}$$

FINDING THE LEAST COMMON DENOMINATOR (LCD) OF RATIONAL EXPRESSIONS

EXAMPLE Find the LCD for $\dfrac{7}{12x^2}$ and $\dfrac{5}{8x^3}$.

Factor each denominator into prime factors:

$$12x^2 = 2 \cdot 2 \cdot 3 \cdot x \cdot x \qquad 8x^3 = 2 \cdot 2 \cdot 2 \cdot x \cdot x \cdot x$$

There are three 2's in the second denominator, so the first denominator needs one more 2. There is one 3 in the first denominator, so the second denominator needs one 3. There are 3 x's in the second denominator, so the first denominator needs one more x.

The LCD is $2 \cdot 2 \cdot 2 \cdot 3 \cdot x \cdot x \cdot x$ or $24x^3$.

ADDING AND SUBTRACTING RATIONAL EXPRESSIONS: UNLIKE DENOMINATORS

EXAMPLE $\dfrac{7}{12x^2} + \dfrac{5}{8x^3}$ The LCD is $24x^3$ (*See above*).

$$\frac{7}{12x^2} + \frac{5}{8x^3} = \frac{7 \cdot 2x}{24x^3} + \frac{5 \cdot 3}{24x^3} = \frac{14x + 15}{24x^3}$$

COMPLEX RATIONAL EXPRESSIONS

EXAMPLES

1. Rational expression in the numerator only:

$$\frac{\dfrac{2x + 3}{x - 1}}{x^2 + 4}$$

2. Rational expression in the denominator only:

$$\frac{a + 1}{\dfrac{a^2 + 2 - 3}{2a - 5}}$$

3. Rational expressions in both the numerator and denominator: $\dfrac{\dfrac{n^2 + n + 3}{n - 1}}{\dfrac{n^3 + n - 4}{n - 6}}$

328

SIMPLIFYING RATIONAL EXPRESSIONS

1. Rational expression in the numerator only:

$$\text{Use } \frac{a}{b} \div \frac{c}{d} = \frac{a}{b} \cdot \frac{d}{c} = \frac{ad}{bc}$$

$$\frac{\dfrac{2x+3}{x-1}}{x^2+4} = \frac{2x+3}{x-1} \div \frac{x^2+4}{1} = \frac{2x+3}{x-1} \cdot \frac{1}{x^2+4}$$

$$= \frac{2x+3}{(x-1)(x^2+4)} = \frac{2x+3}{x^3-x^2+4x-4}$$

2. Rational expression in the denominator only:

$$\frac{a+1}{\dfrac{a^2+a-3}{2a-5}} = \frac{a+1}{1} \div \frac{a^2+a-3}{2a-5}$$

$$= \frac{a+1}{1} \cdot \frac{2a-5}{a^2+a-3}$$

$$= \frac{(a+1)(2a-5)}{a^2+a-3} = \frac{2a^2-3a-5}{a^2+a-3}$$

3. Rational expressions in both the numerator and denominator:

$$\frac{\dfrac{n^2+n+3}{n-1}}{\dfrac{n^3+n-4}{n-6}} = \frac{n^2+n+3}{n-1} \div \frac{n^3+n-4}{n-6}$$

$$= \frac{n^2+n+3}{n-1} \cdot \frac{n-6}{n^3+n-4}$$

$$= \frac{(n^2+n+3)(n-6)}{(n-1)(n^3+n-4)}$$

$$= \frac{n^3-5n^2-3n-18}{n^4-n^3+n^2-5n+4}$$

SOLVING EQUATIONS WITH RATIONAL EXPRESSIONS

EXAMPLES

1. Solve: $\dfrac{3}{a} + \dfrac{2}{3a} = \dfrac{1}{3}$

   $\dfrac{3 \cdot 3}{3a} + \dfrac{2}{3a} = \dfrac{1}{3}$ LCD is $3a$.

   $\dfrac{9+2}{3a} = \dfrac{1}{3}$

   $\dfrac{11}{3a} = \dfrac{1}{3}$ Use: If $\dfrac{a}{b} = \dfrac{c}{d}$ then $ad = bc$.

   $11 \cdot 3 = 3a$

   $3a = 33$

   $a = 11$ Check: $\dfrac{3}{a} + \dfrac{2}{3a} = \dfrac{1}{3}$

   $\dfrac{3}{11} + \dfrac{2}{3 \cdot 11} \overset{?}{=} \dfrac{1}{3}$

   $\dfrac{3 \cdot 3}{11 \cdot 3} + \dfrac{2}{3 \cdot 11} \overset{?}{=} \dfrac{1}{3}$

   $\dfrac{9+2}{33} \overset{?}{=} \dfrac{1}{3}$

   $\dfrac{11}{33} \overset{?}{=} \dfrac{1}{3}$

   $\dfrac{1}{3} = \dfrac{1}{3}$

2. Solve: $\dfrac{x+2}{x-3} = \dfrac{4x+8}{3x-8}$

   $(x+2)(3x-8) = (x-3)(4x+8)$ Use: If $\dfrac{a}{b} = \dfrac{c}{d}$, then $ad = bc$.

   $(x+2)(3x-8) = (x-3) \cdot 4(x+2)$ Divide each side by $x+2$ $(x \neq {}^{-}2)$

   $3x - 8 = 4(x-3)$

   $3x - 8 = 4x - 12$

   $x = 4$ Check: $\dfrac{x+2}{x-3} = \dfrac{4x+8}{3x-8}$

   $\dfrac{4+2}{4-3} \overset{?}{=} \dfrac{4 \cdot 4 + 8}{3 \cdot 4 - 8}$

   $\dfrac{6}{1} \overset{?}{=} \dfrac{24}{4}$

   $6 = 6$

CHECK YOUR UNDERSTANDING

Is $\dfrac{x}{2x-3}$ a rational expression?

yes

330

Rational number

A number that can be expressed in the form $\frac{a}{b}$, where a and b are integers and $b \neq 0$.

EXAMPLES

$\frac{4}{^-9} \begin{matrix}\leftarrow a \\ \leftarrow b\end{matrix}$ 0.23 or $\frac{23}{100}$ $\sqrt{4}$ or 2 or $\frac{2}{1}$ $3\frac{3}{4}$ or $\frac{15}{4}$

Every integer is a rational number, since it can be expressed in the form $\frac{a}{b}$. For example $5 = \frac{5}{1}$.

Every rational number has a unique (exactly one) point on the number line corresponding to it.

Some rational numbers on a number line:

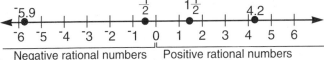

Negative rational numbers   Positive rational numbers

COMPARING RATIONAL NUMBERS

A number line can be used to compare rational numbers.

EXAMPLES

$\frac{^-1}{2} < 1$ The point corresponding to $\frac{^-1}{2}$ is to the left of the point corresponding to 1.

$4.2 > 1$ The point corresponding to 4.2 is to the right of the point corresponding to 1.

$1\frac{1}{2} > \frac{^-1}{2}$ The point corresponding to $1\frac{1}{2}$ is to the right of the point corresponding to $\frac{^-1}{2}$.

ADDING, SUBTRACTING, MULTIPLYING, AND DIVIDING RATIONAL NUMBERS

The rules for operating with fractions apply to rational numbers. The rules of signs for operating with integers apply to rational numbers.

See Fraction *and* Integers.

CHECK YOUR UNDERSTANDING

Is 0.27 a rational number? If yes, express it in the form $\frac{a}{b}$.

yes; $\frac{27}{100}$

Rational zero

A rational number that, when substituted for the variable in a polynomial, makes the polynomial equal to 0. For example, $\frac{-1}{2}$ is a rational zero of the polynomial $2x + 1$, because $\frac{-1}{2}$ is a rational number and $2\left(\frac{-1}{2}\right) + 1 = 0$.

CHECK YOUR UNDERSTANDING
Is $\frac{2}{3}$ a rational zero of $3x - 2$?

yes

Rationalizing the denominator

Multiplying a denominator, that is an irrational number and the numerator by a number so that the resulting product in the denominator is a rational number. To rationalize $\frac{\sqrt{3}}{\sqrt{5}}$, multiply the denominator and the numerator by $\sqrt{5}$. The resulting fraction is equal to the original fraction and has a rational number in the denominator:

$$\frac{\sqrt{3}}{\sqrt{5}} = \frac{\sqrt{3} \times \sqrt{5}}{\sqrt{5} \times \sqrt{5}} = \frac{\sqrt{15}}{5}$$

See also Radical *and* Radical expression.

CHECK YOUR UNDERSTANDING
What should the denominator and the numerator of $\frac{\sqrt{5}}{\sqrt{7}}$ be multiplied by to obtain a fraction equal to $\frac{\sqrt{5}}{\sqrt{7}}$ with a rational number in the denominator?

$\sqrt{7}$

Ray

A set of points that is a subset of a line. It has one endpoint and extends infinitely in one direction.

A   B

$\overrightarrow{AB}$ Read: Ray AB
The endpoint comes first.

Endpoint, A

See also Parallel *and* Perpendicular.

CHECK YOUR UNDERSTANDING
How far to the right does ray AB continue?

without end

R

Real numbers

Rational and irrational numbers.

EXAMPLES   rational numbers   irrational number

$$25 \quad \frac{5}{3} \quad 0.\underset{\uparrow}{6}7 \quad 0.3\underset{\uparrow}{4}3434... \text{ or } \overline{34} \quad \underset{\downarrow}{\sqrt{5}}$$

terminating decimal   repeating decimal

CHECK YOUR UNDERSTANDING
Is $\sqrt{7}$ a real number? Is it an irrational number?

yes; yes

Reciprocal

Also called Multiplicative inverse. For any nonzero number x, the reciprocal is $\frac{1}{x}$. The number 0 has no reciprocal. The reciprocal of a fraction $\frac{a}{b}$ is the fraction $\frac{b}{a}$.

Number	Reciprocal	Number	Reciprocal
6	$\frac{1}{6}$	$\frac{3}{-7}$	$\frac{-7}{3}$
$^-4$	$\frac{1}{-4}$	$\frac{3}{5}$	$\frac{5}{3}$
1	1	$\sqrt{2}$	$\frac{1}{\sqrt{2}}$ or $\frac{\sqrt{2}}{2}$

CHECK YOUR UNDERSTANDING
What is the reciprocal of $\frac{5}{7}$?

$\frac{7}{5}$

Rectangle

A quadrilateral with four right angles. The opposite sides of a rectangle are congruent (of the same length) and are parallel. Thus, a rectangle is a special parallelogram. If all four sides of a rectangle are congruent, then it is a square.

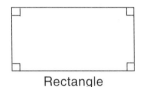

Rectangle

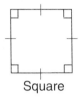

Square

See also Area *and* Perimeter.

Rectangular coordinate system

See Coordinate system.

Redundant number

See Abundant number.

Reflection

Also called Flip. One of the three basic rigid motions, which are: reflection (flip), rotation (turn), and translation (slide).

In a line Line segment A'B' is a reflection of segment AB in line ℓ. Each point on line segment A'B' is the same distance from line ℓ as its corresponding point on line segment AB.

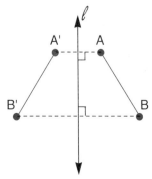

In a plane Point A' is
the reflection of point A
in plane p.

Points A' and A are the
same distance from
point O.

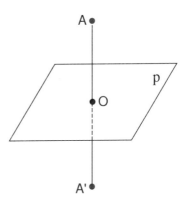

In a point Curve A'B' is a reflection of curve AB in point O. Every point of the curve is the same distance from point O as its corresponding point of the reflection of the curve.

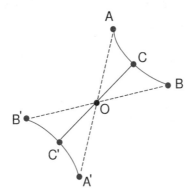

CHECK YOUR UNDERSTANDING

Is the figure obtained by reflection exactly the same as the original figure?

yes

Reflectional symmetry

A figure has reflectional symmetry if it can be folded
along a line and the two parts will coincide.

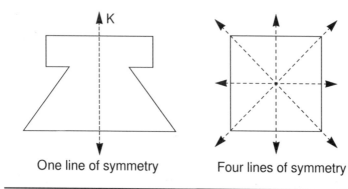

One line of symmetry   Four lines of symmetry

CHECK YOUR UNDERSTANDING
Does a circle have reflectional symmetry?

yes

Reflex angle

An angle whose measure
is between 180° and 360°.

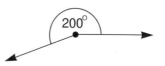

CHECK YOUR UNDERSTANDING
Is an angle whose measure is 189° a reflex angle?

yes

Reflexive property of congruence

Any geometric figure is congruent to itself: for every
figure F, F ≅ F.

CHECK YOUR UNDERSTANDING
According to the reflexive property of congruence, is a
given triangle ABC congruent to itself?

yes

Reflexive property of equality

Any number is equal to itself: for every number x, $x = x$.

CHECK YOUR UNDERSTANDING
Is 5 = 5 an example of the reflexive property of equality?

yes

Reflexive property of similarity

Any geometric figure is similar to itself: for every figure F, F ~ F.

CHECK YOUR UNDERSTANDING
Is the statement square ABCD is similar to square ABCD an example of the reflexive property of similarity ?

yes

Reflexive relation

A relation in which each member of the relation has that relation to itself. For example, the relation *is as tall as* is a reflexive relation in a set of people, because every person is as tall as himself or herself.

CHECK YOUR UNDERSTANDING
Is the relation *is as smart as* a reflexive relation in a set of people?

yes

Region

A closed curve together with its interior. For example, the triangular region ABC consists of triangle ABC together with its interior. The shading inside the triangle is used to indicate that the interior of the triangle is included in the triangular region.

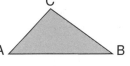

CHECK YOUR UNDERSTANDING
Describe the rectangular region of a rectangle ABCD.

the rectangle ABCD together with its interior

Regroup

See Borrow *and* Carry.

Related sentences/facts

Sentences that follow from each other, such as
$7 + 3 = 10$, so $10 - 3 = 7$ or $4 \times 6 = 24$, so $24 \div 6 = 4$.

CHECK YOUR UNDERSTANDING
What addition sentences are related to the subtraction sentence $9 - 3 = 6$?

$6 + 3 = 9, 3 + 6 = 9$

Relation

A set of ordered pairs, such as $\{(1,5),(2,10),(3,15),(4,20),\ldots\}$. The three dots indicate that this particular relation has an infinite number of members. Its general member would be shown as $(n,5n)$ (the second member of each ordered pair is obtained by multiplying the first member by 5).

A relation can have a finite or an infinite number of members. The members of a relation do not have to be numbers. For example, a relation may have ordered pairs in which the first member is a person and the second member is the person's weight in pounds, such as $\{(\text{Jennifer}, 112), (\text{Brian}, 110), (\text{Meg}, 99), (\text{Gregory}, 101)\}$.

WAYS OF DESCRIBING RELATIONS
In Words

a is a child of b	(Nick is a child of Kate)
a is a factor of b	(2 is a factor of 12)
a is three times b	(15 is 3 times 5, $15 = 3 \times 5$)
a is a multiple of b	(27 is a multiple of 3)
a is greater than b	(7 is greater than 3, $7 > 3$)
a is equal to b	($2 + 3$ is equal to 5, $2 + 3 = 5$)

By a Diagram

⁻2	↔	⁻4
⁻1	↔	⁻2
0	↔	0
1	↔	2
2	↔	4
3	↔	6

The diagram shows these ordered pairs:
$(⁻2,⁻4),(⁻1,⁻2),(0,0),(1,2),(2,4),(3,6)$

R

By an Equation $y = 2x + 3$ or $f(x) = 2x + 3$

Some of the pairs that belong to this relation:
$(⁻2,⁻1),(⁻1,1),(0,3),(1,5),(2,7),(3,9)$

By a Graph

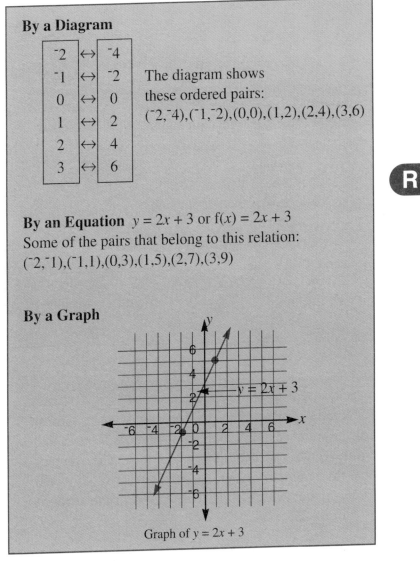

$y = 2x + 3$

Graph of $y = 2x + 3$

See also Function.

CHECK YOUR UNDERSTANDING

Is {(2,3),(3,4),(4,5)} a relation?

yes

Relation diagram

See Relation.

Relation signs

There are five basic relation signs used in elementary mathematics:

$=$ is equal to	$3 + 2 = 5$
$>$ is greater than	$8 > 6$
$\geq$ is greater than or equal to	$7 \geq 7$
$<$ is less than	$9 < 2 + 15$
$\leq$ is less than or equal to	$0 \leq 1$

CHECK YOUR UNDERSTANDING

Is there one of the basic relation signs used in the statement $3 < 5$?

yes; < (is less than)

Relative error

The ratio of the accuracy of an approximate number to the number. For example, a segment is measured with accuracy to 1 in. to be 20 in. long. The accuracy of this measurement is half the unit used for measuring, which is 0.5 in. The relative error is $\frac{0.5}{20}$ or 0.025.

See also Greatest possible error.

CHECK YOUR UNDERSTANDING

What is the relative error of a measurement of 10 in. made with accuracy to 1 in.?

$\frac{0.5}{10}$ *or 0.05*

Relative frequency

The ratio of frequency in a given category to the total number, usually expressed as a decimal. For a given set of data, the sum of relative frequencies is equal to 1.

EXAMPLE   In a class of 20 students, 5 students got A's, 6 students got B's, 4 students got C's, and 5 students got D's. These are the frequencies in the four categories.

The relative frequencies are:

A's: $\frac{5}{20}$ or 0.25

B's: $\frac{6}{20}$ or 0.3

C's: $\frac{4}{20}$ or 0.2

D's: $\frac{5}{20}$ or 0.25

The sum of the relative frequencies is $0.25 + 0.3 + 0.2 + 0.25$ or 1.

CHECK YOUR UNDERSTANDING

In a class of 50 students, 10 students got A's. What is the relative frequency of A's?

$$\frac{10}{50} = \frac{1}{5} = 0.2$$

Relatively prime numbers

Numbers whose only common factor is 1.

EXAMPLES   5 and 8 are relatively prime.
9 and 32 are relatively prime.
8 and 14 are **not** relatively prime, since they have a common factor of 2.

CHECK YOUR UNDERSTANDING

Are 4 and 12 relatively prime?

no; they have common factors of 2 and 4

Remainder

A whole number that is left after one whole number is divided by another.

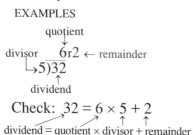

EXAMPLES

quotient
↓
divisor   6r2 ← remainder
    ↳5)32
        ↑
    dividend

Check: $32 = 6 \times 5 + 2$

dividend = quotient × divisor + remainder

General Form

quotient
↓
$a \div b = q, r$
↑   ↑   ↑
dividend divisor remainder

Check: $a = b \cdot q + r$

CHECK YOUR UNDERSTANDING
What is the remainder when 43 is divided by 8?

3

Rename

See Borrow *and* Carry.

Repeating decimal

Also called Infinite repeating decimal. A decimal with one or more digits repeating without end.

EXAMPLES 0.33 ... Three dots indicate that 3 continues to repeat without end.
Also written as $0.\overline{3}$ The bar over 3 indicates that 3 repeats without end.

$3.0\overline{57}$ 057 repeats without end.

$2.0\overline{56}$ 56 repeats without end.

See also Decimal-REPEATING DECIMAL AS A FRACTION.

CHECK YOUR UNDERSTANDING
What digits repeat without end in $5.7\overline{46}$?

46

Replacement set

A set of numbers to be used as a set for potential solutions of equations or inequalities.

EXAMPLES

Solve: $x^2 - 1 = 0$

Replacement set: the set of all real numbers.
The solutions of the equation are the real numbers 1 and $^-1$.

Solve: $x + 2 = 0$

Replacement set: the set of positive integers.
The solution of $x + 2 = 0$ is $^-2$.
Since $^-2$ is not in the replacement set (positive integers), the solution set of $x + 2 = 0$ is the empty set (there is no solution).

CHECK YOUR UNDERSTANDING
Does the equation $x + 1 = 0$ have a solution if the replacement set for potential solutions is the set of all positive integers?

no; $^-1$ is not a positive integer

Reversal primes

Given a prime number, say 37, its reversal is 73. 37 and 73 are reversal primes, since both are prime numbers.

CHECK YOUR UNDERSTANDING
Are 17 and 71 reversal primes?

yes; their digits are reversed and both are prime numbers

343

Rhombus
plural rhombi

A parallelogram with all four sides the same length (congruent).

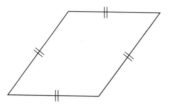

In addition to four congruent sides, a rhombus has the following properties: opposite sides parallel, opposite angles the same measure (congruent), diagonals bisect each other at right angles, and diagonals bisect the angles of the rhombus.

CHECK YOUR UNDERSTANDING
Is a square a rhombus?

yes

Right angle (⌐)

An angle that measures 90°.

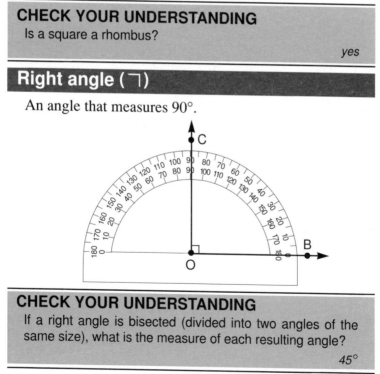

CHECK YOUR UNDERSTANDING
If a right angle is bisected (divided into two angles of the same size), what is the measure of each resulting angle?

45°

Right triangle

A triangle with one right angle. The side opposite the right angle is called a hypotenuse. The two sides forming the right angle are called legs.

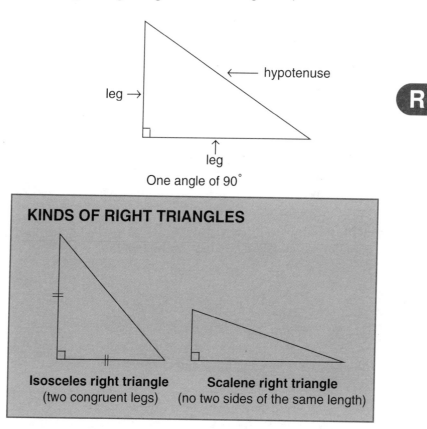

One angle of 90°

KINDS OF RIGHT TRIANGLES

Isosceles right triangle
(two congruent legs)

Scalene right triangle
(no two sides of the same length)

See Pythagorean theorem *for finding the length of a missing side.*

CHECK YOUR UNDERSTANDING

Can a right triangle have three congruent sides?

no; to be congruent each angle would have to be 60°

Rigid motion

See Reflection, Rotation, *and* Translation.

Roman numerals

The ancient numerals that originated in the Roman Empire. They are in use today for such things as displaying the years of construction of buildings and copyright years on films.

Basic Roman Numerals

Roman	I	V	X	L	C	D	M
Base ten	1	5	10	50	100	500	1000

NAMING NUMBERS WITH ROMAN NUMERALS

The Roman system of naming numbers is additive and subtractive. The values of single numerals are added or subtracted.

Rule: When a letter is followed by a letter with a smaller value, add the values of the letters .

EXAMPLES $DCC = 500 + 100 + 100 = 700$

$MCCCXX = 1000 + 100 + 100 + 100 + 10 + 10 = 1320$

Rule: When a letter is before a letter with a larger value, subtract the smaller-value letter from the larger-value letter. I, X, and C are used in this way.

EXAMPLES $IX = 10 - 1 = 9$

$XL = 50 - 10 = 40$

$XC = 100 - 10 = 90$

$MCD = 1000 + 500 - 100 = 1400$

CHECK YOUR UNDERSTANDING

What are the base-ten equivalents for the following Roman numerals: MCC, CXXX, CIX, CD?

1200, 130, 109, 400

Root of a number

Square Root: The square root of a number n is a number whose square is equal to n.

5 and ⁻5 are square roots of 25, because $5 \times 5 = 25$ and $⁻5 \times ⁻5 = 25$. The two square roots of 25, $\sqrt{25}$ and $⁻\sqrt{25}$, are the two real-number solutions of the equation $x^2 = 25$.

Cube Root: A cube root of a number n is a number whose cube is equal to n. 2 is a cube root of 8, because $2^3 = 8$. Cube root of 8, $\sqrt[3]{8}$, is the only real-number solution of the equation $x^3 = 8$.

Nth Root: In general, the nth root of a number x, $\sqrt[n]{x}$, is a number r such that the product in which r is used n times is equal to x: $\underbrace{r \cdot r \cdot r \cdot \ldots \cdot r}_{n \text{ times}} = x$

See also Radical.

R

CHECK YOUR UNDERSTANDING
What are the two square roots of 36?

6 and ⁻6

Root of an equation

Also called Solution. A number or numbers such that, when substituted for a variable or variables, the result is a true statement. For example, the root of the equation $x - 5 = 0$ is 5, since $5 - 5 = 0$.

See also Solution of an equation, Solution of an inequality, Solution of a system of equations, Solution of a system of inequalities, Solution set, Solving, *and* Solving an equation by inspection.

CHECK YOUR UNDERSTANDING
What is the root of the equation $x - 3 = 0$?

3

Rotation

Also called Turn. Turning a figure about a point, which serves as the center of rotation a given number of degrees. It is one of the three basic rigid motions of geometry, along with reflection (flip), and translation (slide).

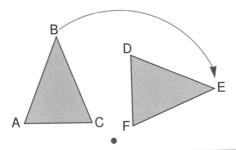

CHECK YOUR UNDERSTANDING

In the rotation above, point B is "rotated" into which point?

point E

Rotational symmetry

A shape (figure) has rotational symmetry if, after a finite number of rotations of the figure about a point, the figure returns to its original position.

ROTATIONAL SYMMETRY OF AN EQUILATERAL TRIANGLE

Equilateral triangle ABC can be rotated 120° clockwise about the center of rotation, O, so that point A moves onto point B, B onto C, and C onto A. An equilateral triangle is said to have a 120° rotational symmetry. After three such 120° rotations, the three vertices return to their original positions.

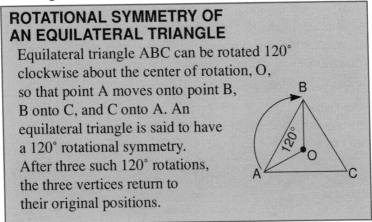

348

ROTATIONAL SYMMETRY OF A SQUARE

Square ABCD can be rotated 90° clockwise about the center of rotation, O, so that point A moves onto point B, B onto C, C onto D, and D onto A. A square is said to have a 90° rotational symmetry. After four such 90° rotations, the four vertices return to their original positions.

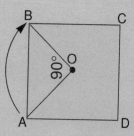

ROTATIONAL SYMMETRY OF A REGULAR PENTAGON

Regular pentagon ABCDE can be rotated 72° clockwise about the center of rotation, O, so that point A moves onto point B, B onto C, C onto D, D onto E, and E onto A. A regular pentagon is said to have a 72° rotational symmetry. After five such 72° rotations, the five vertices return to their original positions.

R

CHECK YOUR UNDERSTANDING

A regular hexagon has a 60° rotational symmetry. After how many 60° rotations will the six vertices return to their original positions?

six

Rounding whole numbers

Round 6879 to the nearest hundred.

Find the place to which you are rounding.	Look at the digit one place to the right. Is it 5 or greater than 5?	If yes, add 1 to the place you are rounding. If no, keep it the same. 7 > 5. Add 1

6879
↑
hundreds

6879

6900

OTHER EXAMPLES

Number	Nearest ten	Nearest hundred	Nearest thousand
475	480	500	0
6093	6090	6100	6000
77,852	77,850	77,900	78,000
247,388	247,390	247,400	247,000

See also Decimal - ROUNDING DECIMALS.

Sales tax rate

Tax specified as a percent of the price of an item. It is added to the price of the item. The rate of sales tax varies from state to state.

EXAMPLE Sales tax rate is 7%.
The price of an item is $10 before tax.
Amount of sales tax: $0.07 \times \$10 = \$0.70$.
$\$10 + \$0.70 = \$10.70$
The customer will pay $10.70.

S

CHECK YOUR UNDERSTANDING
If the price of an item is $100 before tax and the sales tax is 6%, what is the cost of the item with the sales tax?

$106

Sample

In statistics, a subset taken from a set of people or things.

EXAMPLES A subset is chosen from the numbers 1 through 100. Every fourth number will be chosen. The sample contains all numbers divisible by 4 starting with 4 and ending with 100.

A subset is chosen from names in a telephone directory to call about buying interest in oil drilling. Names are chosen by chance. This makes it a 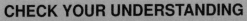random sample.

CHECK YOUR UNDERSTANDING
From a population of 25,000 people, 200 people are chosen to receive questionnaires. Is that a sample of that population?

yes

Sample space

In probability, the set of all possible outcomes of an experiment.

> EXAMPLES The sample space for the experiment of rolling a die is {1, 2, 3, 4, 5, 6}.
>
> The sample space for an experiment of rolling a die and spinning a spinner on a circle that is $\frac{1}{3}$ red, $\frac{1}{3}$ blue, and $\frac{1}{3}$ yellow is: {(1,red), (2,red), (3,red), (4,red), (5,red), (6,red), (1,blue), (2,blue), (3,blue), (4,blue), (5,blue), (6,blue), (1,yellow), (2,yellow), (3,yellow), (4,yellow), (5,yellow), (6,yellow)}.

CHECK YOUR UNDERSTANDING
How many members does the sample space for the experiment of tossing a coin have? What are they?

2; {Heads,Tails} or {H,T}

Sampling

A process used to select a sample.

CHECK YOUR UNDERSTANDING
One hundred people are selected randomly from a telephone book. Is that sampling?

yes

Satisfy

A solution of an equation or an inequality is said to satisfy the equation or inequality.

> EXAMPLE 5 satisfies the equation $x - 5 = 0$, because $5 - 5 = 0$.

CHECK YOUR UNDERSTANDING
Does 3 satisfy the equation $x - 3 = 0$?

yes

Scale

An arrangement of numbers in some order at uniform intervals.

EXAMPLES

Marks arranged in a line at 1 cm intervals.

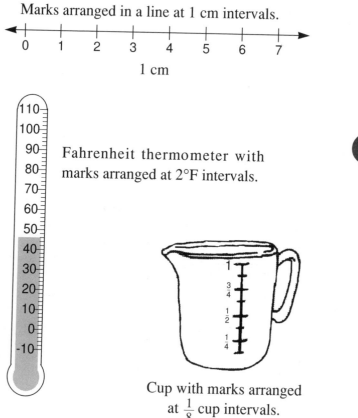

1 cm

Fahrenheit thermometer with marks arranged at 2°F intervals.

Cup with marks arranged at $\frac{1}{8}$ cup intervals.

S

See also Map scale *and* Scale factor.

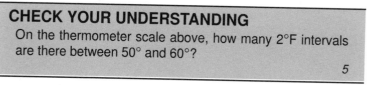

CHECK YOUR UNDERSTANDING

On the thermometer scale above, how many 2°F intervals are there between 50° and 60°?

5

Scale drawing

A drawing that is of the same shape as the actual object but of a different size.

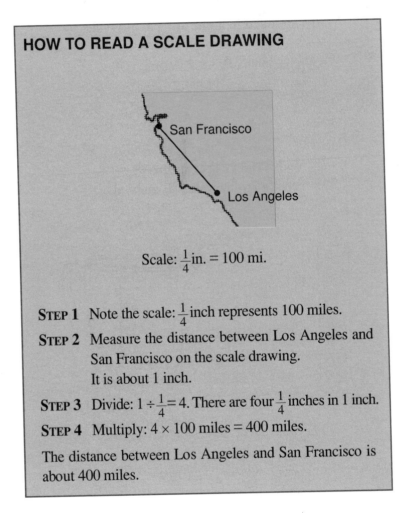

HOW TO READ A SCALE DRAWING

Scale: $\frac{1}{4}$in. = 100 mi.

STEP 1 Note the scale: $\frac{1}{4}$ inch represents 100 miles.

STEP 2 Measure the distance between Los Angeles and San Francisco on the scale drawing. It is about 1 inch.

STEP 3 Divide: $1 \div \frac{1}{4} = 4$. There are four $\frac{1}{4}$ inches in 1 inch.

STEP 4 Multiply: 4×100 miles = 400 miles.

The distance between Los Angeles and San Francisco is about 400 miles.

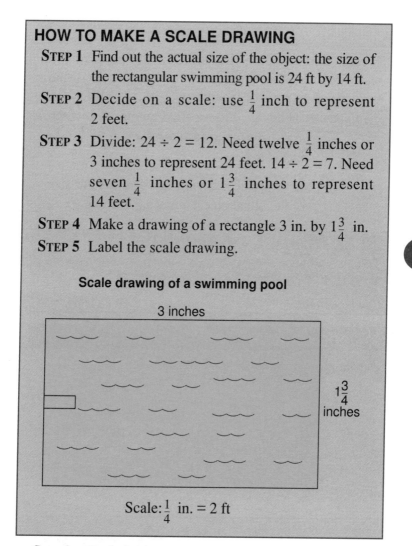

HOW TO MAKE A SCALE DRAWING

STEP 1 Find out the actual size of the object: the size of the rectangular swimming pool is 24 ft by 14 ft.

STEP 2 Decide on a scale: use $\frac{1}{4}$ inch to represent 2 feet.

STEP 3 Divide: $24 \div 2 = 12$. Need twelve $\frac{1}{4}$ inches or 3 inches to represent 24 feet. $14 \div 2 = 7$. Need seven $\frac{1}{4}$ inches or $1\frac{3}{4}$ inches to represent 14 feet.

STEP 4 Make a drawing of a rectangle 3 in. by $1\frac{3}{4}$ in.

STEP 5 Label the scale drawing.

Scale drawing of a swimming pool

3 inches

$1\frac{3}{4}$ inches

Scale: $\frac{1}{4}$ in. = 2 ft

See also Scale factor.

CHECK YOUR UNDERSTANDING

A scale drawing of an office building is made on a sheet of $8\frac{1}{2}$-by-11-inch paper. Is the scale drawing larger or smaller than the actual building?

smaller

Scale factor

A ratio that compares the sizes of the parts of the scale drawing of an object with the actual sizes of the corresponding parts of the object.

EXAMPLES The size of the scale drawing is $\frac{1}{5}$ of the size of the actual object. The scale factor is $\frac{1}{5}$.

If the scale drawing is 10 times the size of the actual object, the scale factor is 10.

CHECK YOUR UNDERSTANDING

The size of a scale drawing is 100 times smaller than the size of the actual object. What is the scale factor?

$\frac{1}{100}$

Scalene triangle

A triangle with no two sides the same length.

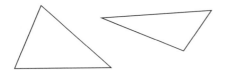

no two sides in any one triangle congruent

CHECK YOUR UNDERSTANDING

The sides of a triangle are 3 cm, 4 cm, and 3 cm long. Is this a scalene triangle?

no; 2 sides are the same length

Scatter diagram

See Scattergram.

Scatter plot

See Scattergram.

Scattergram

Also called Scatter diagram *or* Scatter plot. A graph that shows the relationship between two quantities. The following scattergram shows the relationship between the times students studied and test scores.

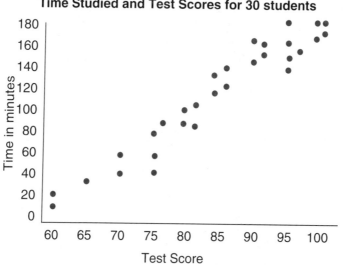

Time Studied and Test Scores for 30 students

The scattergram shows that the more time spent studying, the higher the test score.

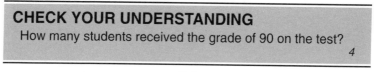

CHECK YOUR UNDERSTANDING
How many students received the grade of 90 on the test?

4

S

Scientific notation

A number expressed as a product of two factors. The first factor is 1 or a number between 1 and 10 and the second factor is a power of 10 in exponential form. Scientific notation is particularly helpful when working with very large or very small numbers.

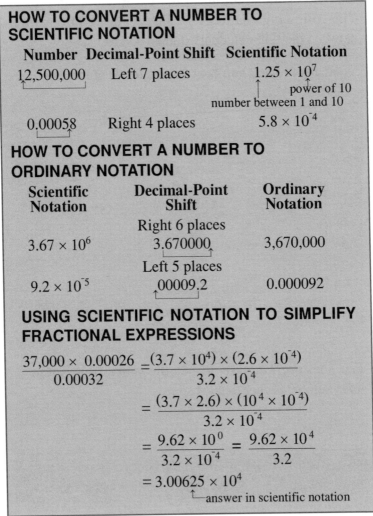

HOW TO CONVERT A NUMBER TO SCIENTIFIC NOTATION

Number	Decimal-Point Shift	Scientific Notation
12,500,000	Left 7 places	1.25×10^7
0.00058	Right 4 places	5.8×10^{-4}

power of 10
number between 1 and 10

HOW TO CONVERT A NUMBER TO ORDINARY NOTATION

Scientific Notation	Decimal-Point Shift	Ordinary Notation
3.67×10^6	Right 6 places 3.670000	3,670,000
9.2×10^{-5}	Left 5 places 00009.2	0.000092

USING SCIENTIFIC NOTATION TO SIMPLIFY FRACTIONAL EXPRESSIONS

$$\frac{37{,}000 \times 0.00026}{0.00032} = \frac{(3.7 \times 10^4) \times (2.6 \times 10^{-4})}{3.2 \times 10^{-4}}$$

$$= \frac{(3.7 \times 2.6) \times (10^4 \times 10^{-4})}{3.2 \times 10^{-4}}$$

$$= \frac{9.62 \times 10^0}{3.2 \times 10^{-4}} = \frac{9.62 \times 10^4}{3.2}$$

$$= 3.00625 \times 10^4$$

answer in scientific notation

USING A SCIENTIFIC CALCULATOR TO SIMPLIFY FRACTIONAL EXPRESSIONS

A scientific calculator with an exponential shift key (EE) or (EXP) can be used to simplify fractional expressions. First write the expression in scientific notation.

$$\frac{37,000 \times 0.00026}{0.00032} = \frac{(3.7 \times 10^4) \times (2.6 \times 10^{-4})}{3.2 \times 10^{-4}}$$

3.7 (EE) 4 (×) 2.6 (EE) (+/-) 4 (÷) 3.2 (EE) (+/-) 4 (=) 30062.5

S

Secant

See Trigonometric ratios.

Second degree equation

See Quadratic equation.

Sector of a circle

A part of the interior of the circle whose boundary consists of two radii and the arc intercepted by the radii. A sector is shaded in the picture at the right. It is enclosed by radii OA and OB and the arc AB.

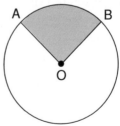

Segment

A part of a line or curve that has two endpoints. Every segment has a definite length.

EXAMPLES

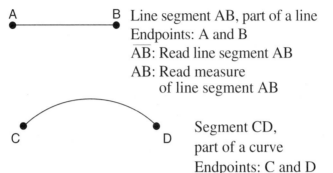

Line segment AB, part of a line
Endpoints: A and B
$\overline{AB}$: Read line segment AB
AB: Read measure
of line segment AB

Segment CD,
part of a curve
Endpoints: C and D

CHECK YOUR UNDERSTANDING

Is line segment AB the same as line segment BA?

yes

Segment of a circle

A part of the interior of the circle enclosed by an arc of the circle and the chord that cuts it off.

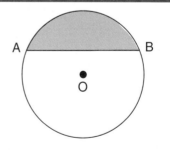

CHECK YOUR UNDERSTANDING

Is the area of the segment in the picture above less than the area enclosed by a semicircle and a diameter?

yes

Semicircle

Half of a circle. It consists of the endpoints of a diameter and all the points on the circle between these endpoints. When naming a particular semicircle, it is necessary to use a third point, such as semicircle ACB. The degree measure of a semicircle is 180.

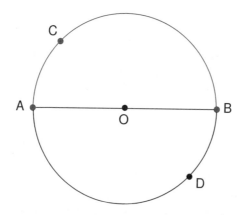

CHECK YOUR UNDERSTANDING
Is ADB a semicircle?

yes

Sense of inequality

The type of relationship indicated for two inequalities. Two or more inequalities can have the same sense or opposite senses. For example, $a > b$ and $c > d$ have the same sense, whereas $a < b$ and $c > d$ have opposite senses.

CHECK YOUR UNDERSTANDING
Do the inequalities $x > y$ and $a < b$ have the same sense?

no; opposite senses

Sentence

An equation or inequality.

TYPES OF SENTENCES

True Sentence

EXAMPLES

$$3 + 6 = 9$$
$$4 \times 6 + 9 = 33$$
$$7 > 2$$

False Sentence

EXAMPLES

$$9 - 2 = 6$$
$$6 \div 3 = 3$$
$$9 < 6$$

Open Sentence An equation or inequality that contains at least one variable. It is neither true nor false. When the variable is replaced by a number, it becomes a true or a false sentence.

EXAMPLE
$$x + 6 = 9$$
When x is replaced by 3, a true sentence is obtained:
$$3 + 6 = 9$$
Any other replacement of x gives a false sentence.

EXAMPLE
$$x - 2 > 5$$
Replacing x by any number greater than 7 will give a true sentence: $8 - 2 > 5$ is a true sentence.

CHECK YOUR UNDERSTANDING

A sentence contains a variable. Is it a true sentence?

no; it is neither true nor false; it is an open sentence

362

Sequence

Numbers usually arranged according to some pattern. Each member of the sequence is called a term of the sequence.

EXAMPLES

An infinite sequence

The sequence of natural numbers:
1, 2, 3, 4, 5, . . .
Three dots show that the sequence continues in the same pattern without end.

A finite sequence
1, 0, 1, 0, 1, 0.

See also Arithmetic progression *and* Geometric progression.

S

CHECK YOUR UNDERSTANDING

Is 2, 4, 8, 16, 32, . . . an infinite sequence? What is the pattern in this sequence?

yes; each number is double the preceding number

Series

An indicated sum of a finite sequence.

EXAMPLE

For the finite sequence 1, 2, 4, 8, 16, the series is $1 + 2 + 4 + 8 + 16$.

See also Partial sum of an infinite series.

CHECK YOUR UNDERSTANDING

What is the series for the sequence 1, 3, 9, 27?

1 + 3 + 9 + 27

Set

A collection of things. Each thing in a set is said to be a member or element of the set. Sets can have a finite or an infinite number of members. A member is said to belong to the set. To say that 5 belongs to set S, the symbol ∈ is used: 5 ∈ S, which is read, five belongs to set S. To indicate that a set is intended, names of members are listed within braces. The set of all counting numbers is shown as {1, 2, 3, 4, 5, . . .}. The three dots indicate that the sequence continues in the same pattern without end.

EXAMPLES A set of letters: {a, b, c, d}

A set of shapes: {○, △, ⬜, △, ☐}

A set of people: {Sarah, Tamara, Carlos}

See also Disjoint sets, Empty set, Finite set, Infinite, Intersection of sets, Member of a set, Replacement set, Solution set, *and* Union of sets.

CHECK YOUR UNDERSTANDING

How many members are in this set? {△, ○, ☐, ⧄, ⬜}

5

Sexagesimal system

A system of numeration based on the number 60. It was in use in ancient Babylonia. Some measures in use today are based on 60. For example, the unit for measuring angles, degree, is divided into 60 parts, with each part called a minute. A minute is divided into 60 parts, with each part called a second. Similarly, units for measuring time are based on 60. An hour is divided into 60 minutes, and a minute is divided into 60 seconds.

See also Babylonian system of numeration.

CHECK YOUR UNDERSTANDING

Is a system that uses the number ten for its base a sexagesimal system?

no

Of a triangle Segments AB, BC, and CA are sides of △ABC. The symbol $\overline{AB}$ is used to denote segment AB. The symbol AB means the length of segment AB, which is a number.

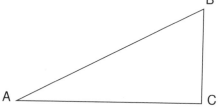

Of an angle Ray DE is one side of ∠ D. The symbol $\overrightarrow{DE}$ is used to denote ray DE.

S

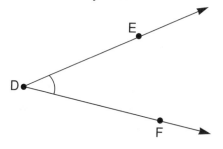

Of an equation   An equation has two sides. In the equation $x + 5 = 7$, $x + 5$ is the left side, and 7 is the right side of the equation.

Of an inequality   An inequality has two sides. In the inequality $x + 3 > y - 1$, $x + 3$ is the left side, and $y - 1$ is the right side.

CHECK YOUR UNDERSTANDING
What is the other side of ∠ D above?

ray DF

Sieve of Eratosthenes

A method for finding prime numbers among numbers from 2 to any number. The method consists of writing down all numbers from 2 to any desired number, crossing out all multiples of 2 after 2, then multiples of 3 after 3, then 5 after 5, and continuing until all multiples of primes have been crossed out. This method leaves only primes. The method is illustrated for finding prime numbers among numbers from 1 through 50.

STEP 1 Write down the numbers 1 through 50

STEP 2 Circle 2, since it is a prime number

STEP 3 Cross out all multiples of 2 greater than 2

STEP 4 Circle 3, since it is a prime number

STEP 5 Cross out all multiples of 3 greater than 3 that have not been crossed out previously

STEP 6 Circle 5, since it is a prime number

STEP 7 Cross out all multiples of 5 greater than 5 that have not been crossed out previously

STEP 8 Circle 7, since it is a prime number

STEP 9 Cross out all multiples of 7 greater than 7 that have not been crossed out previously

The remaining numbers that are not crossed out are prime: 11, 13, 17, 19, 23, 29, 31, 37, 41, 43, and 47. They are circled.

1	②	③	4	⑤	6	⑦	8
9	10	⑪	12	⑬	14	15	16
⑰	18	⑲	20	21	22	㉓	24
25	26	27	28	㉙	30	㉛	32
33	34	35	36	㊲	38	39	40
㊶	42	㊸	44	45	46	㊼	48
49	50						

Sign

See Minus sign *and* Plus sign.

Sign of a fraction

The fraction is:
positive, if the numerator and the denominator are both positive or both negative

$$\frac{^+2}{^+3} = {}^+\!\left(\frac{2}{3}\right) \text{or} \frac{2}{3} \qquad\qquad \frac{^-2}{^-3} = {}^+\!\left(\frac{2}{3}\right) \text{or} \frac{2}{3}$$

negative, if the numerator is positive and the denominator is negative, or vice versa

$$\frac{^+2}{^-3} = {}^-\!\left(\frac{2}{3}\right) \qquad\qquad\qquad \frac{^-2}{^+3} = {}^-\!\left(\frac{2}{3}\right)$$

S

CHECK YOUR UNDERSTANDING
Is the fraction $\frac{^-6}{^+5}$ positive or negative?

negative

Sign rules for addition

Rules that specify the sign of the sums when two directed (signed) numbers are added. These rules apply to all real numbers.

The sum of **two positive numbers** is **positive.**
$^+2 + {}^+7$ or $2 + 7 = 9$ (positive signs can be omitted).
The sum of **two negative numbers** is **negative.**
$^-2 + {}^-7 = {}^-9$.

The sum of a **positive and a negative** number is:
positive, if the positive number has a greater absolute value. $^-2 + {}^+7 = {}^+5$ or $^-2 + 7 = 5$.
negative, if the negative number has a greater absolute value. $^+2 + {}^-7 = {}^-5$ or $2 + {}^-7 = {}^-5$.
zero, if the numbers have the same absolute value. $^+7 + {}^-7 = 0$ or $7 + {}^-7 = 0$.

CHECK YOUR UNDERSTANDING
What is $10 + {}^-4$ equal to?

6

367

Sign rules for division

The quotient of two numbers is:

positive, if both numbers are positive or both numbers are negative.

$^+8 \div {}^+2 = {}^+4$ or $8 \div 2 = 4$ (positive signs can be omitted)

$^-8 \div {}^-2 = {}^+4$ or $^-8 \div {}^-2 = 4$

negative, if one number is positive and one negative.

$^+8 \div {}^-2 = {}^-4$ or $8 \div {}^-2 = {}^-4$

$^-8 \div {}^+2 = {}^-4$ or $^-8 \div 2 = {}^-4$

CHECK YOUR UNDERSTANDING

Is the answer positive or negative?

$^+6 \div {}^+2$; $^-6 \div {}^-3$; $^+4 \div {}^-2$; $^-9 \div {}^+8$

positive, postive, negative, negative

Sign rules for multiplication

The product of two numbers is:

positive, if both numbers are positive or both numbers are negative.

$^+8 \times {}^+2 = {}^+16$ or $8 \times 2 = 16$ (positive signs can be omitted)

$^-8 \times {}^-2 = {}^+16$ or $^-8 \times {}^-2 = 16$

negative, if one number is positive and one negative.

$^+8 \times {}^-2 = {}^-16$ or $8 \times {}^-2 = {}^-16$

$^-8 \times {}^+2 = {}^-16$ or $^-8 \times 2 = {}^-16$

CHECK YOUR UNDERSTANDING

Is the answer positive or negative?

$^+3 \times {}^+4$; $^-2 \times {}^-6$; $^+4 \times {}^-3$; $^-6 \times {}^+3$

positive, postive, negative, negative

Sign rules for subtraction

Subtraction is the opposite of addition. To subtract $a - b$, replace the subtraction problem with the corresponding addition problem: $a + (-b)$ (add the opposite of b to a). Then use sign rules for addition.

EXAMPLE $^+2 - {}^+7 = {}^+2 + {}^-7 = {}^-5$

CHECK YOUR UNDERSTANDING
What addition problem would $^-3 - {}^-9$ be replaced by?

$^-3 + {}^+9$

Signed number

Also called Directed number. Either a positive or negative number. $^-6$, $^+\sqrt{2}$, and $\frac{-3}{4}$ are examples of signed numbers.

CHECK YOUR UNDERSTANDING
Is $^-378$ a signed number?

yes

Significant digit

Also called Significant figure. The digits 1 through 9 are always significant in reporting measures. The digit 0 is significant if it is used to indicate that a measurement is found to be 0.

EXAMPLES 0.075 m   105 ft   150 ft to
                                nearest 10 ft

2 significant digits	3 significant digits	2 significant digits
The 0's are not significant. They are used merely to place the decimal point.	0 is significant because it indicates that there are 0 tens of feet.	0 at end is not significant since measure is to nearest 10 ft.

CHECK YOUR UNDERSTANDING
How many significant digits are there when reporting the weight of a boy to be 109 pounds?

3

Significant figure

See Significant digit.

Similar decimals

Decimals that have the same number of decimal places.

EXAMPLES 4.7835 and 23.9216   0.34 and 32.07

CHECK YOUR UNDERSTANDING
Are 3.5 and 5.76 similar decimals?

no; 3.5 has one decimal place, 5.76 has two decimal places

Similar figures (~)

Objects or figures that are the same shape. They are not necessarily the same size. If two polygons are similar, then their corresponding angles are congruent and the lengths of their corresponding sides have the same ratio. We say that there is similarity between similar figures.

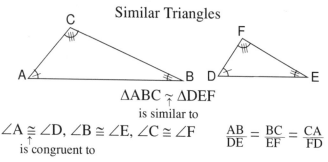

Similar Triangles

$$\triangle ABC \underset{\uparrow}{\sim} \triangle DEF$$
is similar to

$$\angle A \underset{\uparrow}{\cong} \angle D, \angle B \cong \angle E, \angle C \cong \angle F \qquad \frac{AB}{DE} = \frac{BC}{EF} = \frac{CA}{FD}$$
is congruent to

Every figure is similar to itself. If each part of a figure is twice the size of the corresponding part of another figure and they are similar, then it is said that the ratio of similitude of the larger figure to the smaller is 2:1 or simply 2.

CHECK YOUR UNDERSTANDING
Two triangles are similar. The length of each side of the smaller triangle is one-third the length of the corresponding side of the larger triangle. What is the ratio of similitude of the smaller triangle to the larger triangle?

1 : 3 or $\frac{1}{3}$

Similar fractions

See Like fractions.

Similar terms

See Like terms.

Similarity

See Similar figures.

Simple closed curve

See Closed curve.

S

Simple curve

A curve that does not intersect itself. It may not be a closed curve.

EXAMPLE

Simple curve. It is not a closed curve.

See also Closed curve.

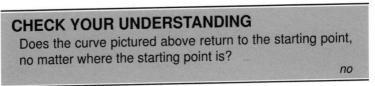

CHECK YOUR UNDERSTANDING
Does the curve pictured above return to the starting point, no matter where the starting point is?

no

Simple interest

Interest paid only on the principal (the amount invested).

EXAMPLE If the annual interest rate is 6% and $100 is invested for one year, then the amount of simple interest at the end of one year will be $6.00: $0.06 \times \$100 = \$6.00$.

CHECK YOUR UNDERSTANDING

What will be the amount earned in one year on $200 invested at an annual rate of 7% simple interest?

$14

Simplest form

Of a fraction A fraction is in simplest form if its numerator and denominator are relatively prime; that is, the only common factor they have is 1.

EXAMPLE $\frac{6}{12}$ can be simplified by dividing both the numerator and denominator by 6, the greatest common factor of 6 and 12: $\frac{6}{12} = \frac{1}{2}$. $\frac{1}{2}$ is in simplest form, because the only common factor of 1 and 2 is 1.

Of an algebraic expression An algebraic expression is in simplest form if no terms can be combined. Algebraic expressions are simplified by combining like terms.

EXAMPLE $3x^2 - 5 + 4x - 2x^2 + 4 = x^2 + 4x - 1$
$3x^2$ and $^-2x^2$ can be combined since they are similar terms. $^-5$ and 4 can be added. $x^2 + 4x - 1$ is in simplest form, because no terms can be combined.

CHECK YOUR UNDERSTANDING

Simplify the expression $4x^2 + 2 - 2x^2 - 7$. Is $\frac{6}{9}$ in simplest form?

$2x^2 - 5$; no, 6 and 9 have a common factor of 3

Simplify

See Simplest form.

Simultaneous equations

See System of equations.

Simultaneous inequalities

See System of inequalities.

Sine

See Trigonometric ratios.

Singulary operation

See Operation.

Skew lines

Two lines in space that cannot lie in the same plane. Skew lines do not intersect and are not parallel.

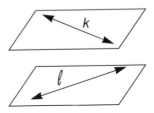

Lines k and ℓ are skew lines. They are in separate planes, are not parallel, and will not intersect, because the planes are parallel.

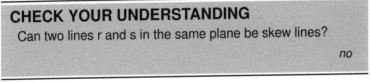

CHECK YOUR UNDERSTANDING

Can two lines r and s in the same plane be skew lines?

no

Slant height

An altitude of a face of a cone or pyramid.

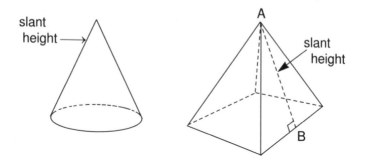

slant height

A

slant height

B

CHECK YOUR UNDERSTANDING
How many faces does the pyramid pictured above have?
How many slant heights does it have?

4; 4

Slide

Also called Translation.
A move of a figure
along a line. The size
and shape of the
figure stay the same.

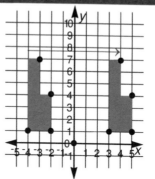

The following points correspond: (⁻2,1) and (5,1),
(⁻2,4) and (5,4), (⁻3,7) and (4,7).

See also Flip *and* Turn.

CHECK YOUR UNDERSTANDING
What point corresponds to (⁻4,1)?

(3,1)

Slope of a line

The ratio $\frac{y_2 - y_1}{x_2 - x_1}$ where (x_1, y_1) and (x_2, y_2) are the coordinates of two points on the line. The ratio is called rise-over-run. Rise is the difference of the y-coordinates; run is the difference of the x-coordinates. The slope of a line determines the steepness or the slant of the line.

SOME FACTS ABOUT THE SLOPE OF A LINE

The slope of a horizontal line, that is, a line parallel to the x-axis in a coordinate system, is equal to 0, since every point on the horizontal line has the same y-coordinate, thus giving 0 in the numerator of $\frac{y_2 - y_1}{x_2 - x_1}$.

The slope of a vertical line (a line parallel to the y-axis in a coordinate system) is not defined, since every point on the vertical line has the same x-coordinate, thus giving 0 in the denominator of $\frac{y_2 - y_1}{x_2 - x_1}$.

If a line is slanting to the right from the vertical, then its slope is positive.

If a line is slanting to the left from the vertical, its slope is negative.

See also Slope-intercept form of an equation of a line.

S

CHECK YOUR UNDERSTANDING
When is the slope of a line negative?

when the line is slanting to the left from the vertical

Slope-intercept form of an equation of a line

An equation of a line of the form $y = mx + b$, where m is the slope of the line and b is the y-intercept.

HOW TO WRITE A SLOPE-INTERCEPT EQUATION OF A LINE FROM ITS GRAPH

STEP 1 Find the x-intercept (x-coordinate of the point at which the line intersects the x-axis) of the line: $x = ^-4$.

STEP 2 Find the y-intercept (y-coordinate of the point at which the line intersects the y-axis) of the line: $y = 2$.

STEP 3 Find the slope of the line: move from point ($^-4,0$) 4 units to the right (positive distance) and up 2 units (positive distance). The slope is rise over run or $\frac{2}{4} = \frac{1}{2}$.

STEP 4 Make the substitutions in the equation $y = mx + b$: $m = \frac{1}{2}$, $b = 2$, so $y = \frac{1}{2}x + 2$

The equation of the line is $y = \frac{1}{2}x + 2$.

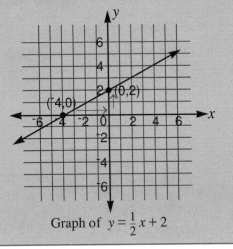

Graph of $y = \frac{1}{2}x + 2$

HOW TO GRAPH A LINE FROM ITS SLOPE-INTERCEPT EQUATION

STEP 1 Given the equation $y = \frac{-2}{3}x + 4$: the y-intercept is 4 (the line intersects the y-axis at the point (0,4)). The slope is $\frac{-2}{3}$.

STEP 2 Plot point (0,4).

STEP 3 Move from point (0,4) 3 units to the right, then 2 units down (slope is $\frac{-2}{3}$).

STEP 4 Plot point (3,2).

STEP 5 Draw a line through point (3,2) and (0,4).

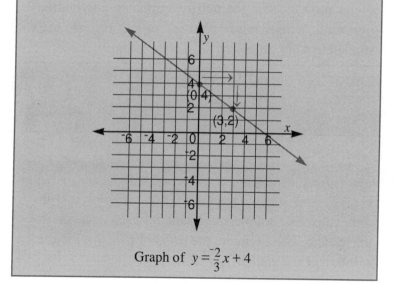

Graph of $y = \frac{-2}{3}x + 4$

CHECK YOUR UNDERSTANDING

An equation of a line is given as $y = 4x + 5$. Is it in the slope-intercept form? What is the slope of this line? What is its y-intercept?

yes; 4; 5

Solid

A three-dimensional figure in space. A cube and a sphere are examples of solids.

Solid geometry

The study of geometric figures in space (three dimensions). Such geometric figures as polyhedra, pyramids, cones, and spheres, among others, are studied in solid geometry.

Solution of a system of equations

For a system of two equations in two variables, it is an ordered pair of numbers that satisfies each equation in the system. For example, the ordered pair (4,3) is the solution of the system

$$4x - 3y = 7$$
$$3x - y = 9$$

When 4 is substituted for x and 3 for y, the following statements are obtained:

$$4x - 3y = 7 \qquad\qquad 3x - y = 9$$
$$4(4) - 3(3) = 16 - 9 = 7 \qquad 3(4) - 3 = 12 - 3 = 9$$

Thus, the ordered pair (4,3) satisfies both equations.

SOLVING SYSTEMS OF TWO EQUATIONS BY GRAPHING

Solve: $2x + y = 8$
            $3x + 4y = 17$

STEP 1   Graph each equation.

STEP 2   Read the coordinates of the point of intersection (where the lines meet). They are (3,2).

Check: $2x + y = 2 \times 3 + 2 = 6 + 2 = 8$
            $3x + 4y = 3 \times 3 + 4 \times 2 = 9 + 8 = 17$
            The solution is the ordered pair (3,2).

SOLVING SYSTEMS OF TWO EQUATIONS BY SUBSTITUTION

Solve: $2x + y = 11$
$4x - 3y = 7$

STEP 1 Solve the first equation for y: $y = 11 - 2x$

STEP 2 Substitute $11 - 2x$ for y in the second equation: $4x - 3(11 - 2x) = 7$

STEP 3 Solve the last equation for x:
$$4x - 33 + 6x = 7$$
$$10x = 40$$
$$x = 4$$

STEP 4 Substitute 4 for x in the first equation and solve it for y:
$$2 \times 4 + y = 11$$
$$8 + y = 11$$
$$y = 3$$

Check: $2x + y = 2 \times 4 + 3 = 8 + 3 = 11$
$4x - 3y = 4 \times 4 - 3 \times 3 = 16 - 9 = 7$
The solution is the ordered pair (4,3).

SOLVING SYSTEMS OF TWO EQUATIONS BY THE ADDITION METHOD

Solve: $2x - y = 16$
$x + y = 5$

STEP 1 Add using the property: if $a = b$
and $c = d$,
then $a + c = b + d$

$$2x - y = 16$$
$$x + y = 5$$
$$\overline{2x + x - y + y = 16 + 5}$$
$$3x = 21$$
$$x = 7$$

STEP 2   Substitute 7 for x in the second equation:
$$x + y = 5$$
$$7 + y = 5$$

STEP 3   Solve the last equation for y:
$$7 + y = 5$$
$$y = 5 - 7 \text{ or } {}^-2$$

Check: $2x - y = 2 \times 7 - {}^-2 = 14 + 2 = 16$
$$x + y = 7 + {}^-2 = 5$$
The solution is $(7, {}^-2)$.

SOLVING SYSTEMS OF TWO EQUATIONS BY THE ADDITION METHOD WITH MULTIPLICATION

Solve $x - y = 3$
$$2x + 3y = {}^-19$$

STEP 1   Multiply each side of the first equation by 3:
$$3x - 3y = 9$$

STEP 2   Add the last equation and the second original equation:
$$3x - 3y = 9$$
$$\underline{2x + 3y = {}^-19}$$
$$5x = {}^-10$$

STEP 3   Solve the last equation for x:
$$5x = {}^-10$$
$$x = \frac{{}^-10}{5} \text{ or } {}^-2$$

STEP 4   Substitute ${}^-2$ for x in the first equation and solve it for y:
$${}^-2 - y = 3$$
$$y = {}^-2 - 3 \text{ or } {}^-5$$

Check: $x - y = {}^-2 - {}^-5 = 3$
$$2x + 3y = 2 \times {}^-2 + 3 \times {}^-5 = {}^-4 + {}^-15 = {}^-19$$
The solution is the ordered pair $({}^-2, {}^-5)$.

Solution of a system of inequalities

Given a system of two inequalities in two variables, the solutions are all ordered pairs of numbers that satisfy both inequalities.

SOLVING SYSTEMS OF TWO INEQUALITIES BY GRAPHING

Solve: $2x + y > 4$
           $^-2x + 5y > 8$

Step 1   Graph, on the same coordinate system, the equations $2x + y = 4$ and $^-2x + 5y = 8$.

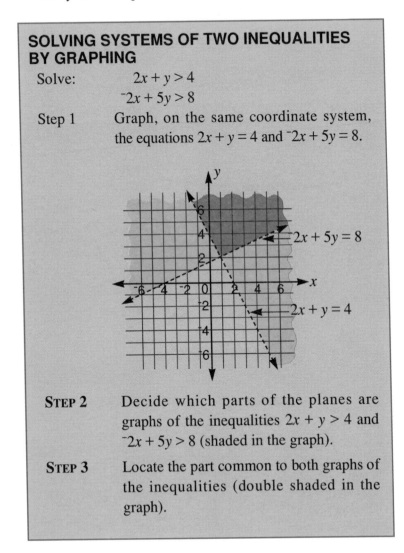

STEP 2   Decide which parts of the planes are graphs of the inequalities $2x + y > 4$ and $^-2x + 5y > 8$ (shaded in the graph).

STEP 3   Locate the part common to both graphs of the inequalities (double shaded in the graph).

STEP 4   The doubly shaded part contains the points whose coordinates are the solutions of the system of the inequalities.

$$2x + y > 4$$
$$^-2x + 5y > 8$$

STEP 5   Choose a point in the doubly shaded area and check whether its coordinates satisfy both inequalities. (1,6) $x = 1$, $y = 6$

$$2x + y = 2 \times 1 + 6 = 2 + 6 = 8 \text{ and } 8 > 4$$
$$^-2x + 5y = ^-2 \times 1 + 5 \times 6 = ^-2 + 30 = 28$$
and $28 > 8$.

The correct part of the plane is marked as the solution.

S

CHECK YOUR UNDERSTANDING

Can there be an infinite number of ordered pairs that satisfy both inequalities in a system of inequalities?

yes

Solution of an equation

Also called Root. A number or numbers that, when substituted for the variable in the equation, result in a true statement.

EXAMPLES

5 is the solution of the equation $x - 5 = 0$, because $5 - 5 = 0$.

The equation $x^2 = 25$ has two solutions, 5 and $^-5$, because $5^2 = 25$ and $(^-5)^2 = 25$.

The equation $x + x = 2x$ has an infinite number of solutions. Every number is a solution of this equation.

CHECK YOUR UNDERSTANDING

What is the solution of the equation $x - 7 = 0$?

7

Solution of an inequality

A number or numbers that, when substituted for the variable in the inequality, result in a true statement.

EXAMPLE   All numbers greater than 5 are the solutions of the inequality $x - 5 > 0$ (7 > 5, 9 > 5, and so on).

CHECK YOUR UNDERSTANDING
What are the solutions of the inequality $x - 7 > 0$?

all numbers greater than 7

Solution set

The set of all numbers that satisfy a given equation or inequality.

CHECK YOUR UNDERSTANDING
Can the solution set of an equation consist of one member?

yes

Solving

Finding all solutions of equations or inequalities.

See also Solution of a system of equations, Solution of a system of inequalities, Solution of an equation, *and* Solution of an inequality.

CHECK YOUR UNDERSTANDING
Solving the equation $x - 3 = 3$ may be shown as follows: $x - 3 + 3 = 3 + 3 \to x - 0 = 6 \to x = 6$. What solution was found?

6

Solving a triangle

Finding the lengths of all sides and measures of all angles when sufficient data are given.

CHECK YOUR UNDERSTANDING

The lengths of three sides of a triangle are given. From the lengths, one computes the measures of the three angles. Is the triangle solved?

yes

Solving an equation by inspection

Solving an equation by looking at it and solving it in one's head without writing anything down. For example, to solve the equation $x - 5 = 0$, think: 5 subtracted from what number will result in 0? Answer: 5 ($5 - 5 = 0$). The solution was found by inspection.

S

CHECK YOUR UNDERSTANDING

Can one find the solution of the equation $x - 3 = 0$ by inspection?

yes; ask: 3 subtracted from what number is 0? answer: 3

Space

In geometry, the set of all points. This is the universal set for the study of all geometric figures. Each figure is a set of points that is a subset of space.

CHECK YOUR UNDERSTANDING

There are two given parallel planes. Are they part of space?

yes

Space figure

Also called Solid figure. A set of points that is a subset of space. In geometry, every figure is a subset (part) of space.

See also Cone, Cube, Cylinder, Prism, Pyramid, *and* Sphere.

Special angles

In trigonometry, the angles measuring 30°, 45°, and 60° are considered to be special. It may be helpful to memorize the exact values of sine(sin) and cosine(cos) of these three special angles:

$$\sin 30° = \frac{1}{2} \qquad \cos 30° = \frac{\sqrt{3}}{2}$$
$$\sin 45° = \cos 45° = \frac{\sqrt{2}}{2}$$
$$\sin 60° = \frac{\sqrt{3}}{2} \qquad \cos 60° = \frac{1}{2}$$

CHECK YOUR UNDERSTANDING
How do sin 30° and cos 60° compare?

they are equal

Speed

The distance covered per unit of time by an object in motion. For example, a car may travel at 45 miles per hour (mph). Other units used to describe speed are feet per second, centimeters per second, meters per second, and so on.

CHECK YOUR UNDERSTANDING
Is feet per minute a unit of speed?

yes

Sphere

The set of all points in space that are a given distance from a fixed point. The fixed point is the center of the sphere. The distance from a point of the sphere to the center is a radius of the sphere. The term radius is also used to refer to any segment connecting a point on the sphere with the center of the sphere.

See also Hemisphere, Volume, *and* Surface area.

CHECK YOUR UNDERSTANDING
$\overline{OA}$ and $\overline{OB}$ are two radii of the sphere O. If $\overline{OA}$ is 2 cm long, how long is $\overline{OB}$?

2 cm

Square

In geometry A four-sided polygon (quadrilateral) with all sides of the same length and with all right angles.

Square
All sides of the same length.
Each angle 90°.

Of a number The product of a number and itself.

EXAMPLES $4^2 = 4 \times 4 = 16$
Read: four squared

$(^-5)^2 = ^-5 \times ^-5 = 25$
Read: negative five squared

See also Perfect square.

CHECK YOUR UNDERSTANDING
What is the perimeter of a square if one side is 4 in. long?
What is 9^2 equal to?

16 in., 81

Square centimeter

A unit of measure of area. It is equal to the area of a square in which each side is 1 cm long.

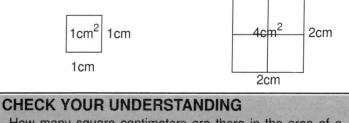

CHECK YOUR UNDERSTANDING
How many square centimeters are there in the area of a square in which each side is 2 cm long?

4

Square meter

A unit of measure of area in the metric system. It is equal to the area of a square in which each side is 1 m long.

Square numbers

Numbers that are squares of counting numbers:
$$1 = 1^2, 4 = 2^2, 9 = 3^2, 16 = 4^2, 25 = 5^2, \ldots$$

They can be represented by dots forming squares:

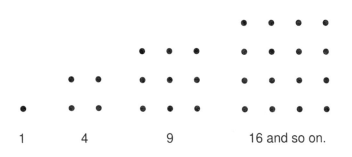

1   4   9   16 and so on.

Square root ($\sqrt{}$)

The square root of a number n is a number such that its square is equal to n.

EXAMPLE 5 and ⁻5 are square roots of 25, because $5 \times 5 = 25$ and $⁻5 \times ⁻5 = 25$. The two square roots of 25, $\sqrt{25}$ and $⁻\sqrt{25}$, are the two real-number solutions of the equation $x^2 = 25$.

PRODUCT PROPERTY OF SQUARE ROOTS

$\sqrt{x} \cdot \sqrt{y} = \sqrt{x \cdot y}$ for all non-negative numbers x and y.

EXAMPLE $\sqrt{3} \cdot \sqrt{11} = \sqrt{3 \cdot 11} = \sqrt{33}$

ADDING AND SUBTRACTING SQUARE ROOTS

EXAMPLE $5\sqrt{3} + 7\sqrt{3} - 2\sqrt{3} - \sqrt{3}$
$= (5\sqrt{3} + 7\sqrt{3}) - (2\sqrt{3} + 1 \cdot \sqrt{3})$
$= 12\sqrt{3} - 3\sqrt{3} = 9\sqrt{3}$

SIMPLIFYING SQUARE ROOTS

A square root of a number can be simplified if the number under the radical sign has a factor that is a square of a positive integer.

EXAMPLE $\sqrt{48} = \sqrt{16 \cdot 3} = \sqrt{16} \cdot \sqrt{3} = 4\sqrt{3}$

SQUARE ROOT PROPERTY OF EVEN POWERS

$\sqrt{x^{2a}} = \sqrt{x^{a+a}} = \sqrt{x^a \cdot x^a} = x^a$ for all even numbers $2a$ ($a > 0$)

EXAMPLE $\sqrt{36x^4y^{16}} = \sqrt{36} \cdot \sqrt{x^4} \cdot \sqrt{y^{16}} = 6 \cdot x^2 \cdot y^8$

SQUARE ROOT PROPERTY OF ODD POWERS

$\sqrt{x^{2a+1}} = \sqrt{x^{2a} \cdot x^1} = x^a\sqrt{x}$

EXAMPLE $\sqrt{49x^5y^9} = \sqrt{49} \cdot \sqrt{x^4 \cdot x^1 \cdot y^8 \cdot y^1} = 7 \cdot x^2 \sqrt{x} \cdot y^4 \sqrt{y}$

QUOTIENT PROPERTY OF SQUARE ROOTS

$\dfrac{\sqrt{x}}{\sqrt{y}} = \sqrt{\dfrac{x}{y}}$ for all positive numbers x and y.

EXAMPLE $\dfrac{\sqrt{48}}{\sqrt{3}} = \sqrt{\dfrac{48}{3}} = \sqrt{16} = 4$

See also Interpolation *on page 212.*

S

CHECK YOUR UNDERSTANDING

What numbers are the two square roots of 36?

6 and ⁻6

Square unit

A unit for measuring areas, such as square foot (ft^2), square meter (m^2), and so on.

See also Converting Measures *on page 451.*

CHECK YOUR UNDERSTANDING
Is a square kilometer a square unit?

yes

Standard form of a linear equation

A linear equation in two variables is in standard form if it is written as $ax + by = c$, where a, b, and c are real numbers and a and b are not both 0.

CHECK YOUR UNDERSTANDING
Is the equation $3x + 5y = 8$ in standard form?

yes

Standard form of quadratic equation

A quadratic equation in one variable is in standard form if it is written as $ax^2 + bx + c = 0$, where a, b, and c are real numbers and $a \neq 0$.

CHECK YOUR UNDERSTANDING
Is $4x^2 - 3x - 1 = 0$ in standard form?

yes

Standard numeral

Also called Standard form. A name of a whole number written in the customary form.

EXAMPLES   34,847   107,256

CHECK YOUR UNDERSTANDING
Is $30 + 5$ a standard numeral?

no

Statistics

The use of mathematics to analyze data collected on samples from various populations of people, animals, or products. Statistics is used in many fields, such as biology, education, physics, psychology, and sociology.

CHECK YOUR UNDERSTANDING

A class of students collected data on movie preferences of 15-year olds. They analyzed the data to answer the question, "What movies do the 15-year olds like most?" Did they use statistics?

yes

S

Stem and leaf plot

A frequency distribution made by arranging the data. For example, these leading batting averages can be arranged in a stem and leaf plot by making all digits except the last digit stems, the last digits leaves, and arranging both stems and leaves in order from least to greatest.

Leading Batting Averages			Stems	Leaves
.323	.321	.316	.30	1
.326	.301	.332	.31	6,8
.328	.337	.318	.32	1,3,6,8
.350	.364	.359	.33	2,2,3,6,7
.333	.388	.370	.34	
.336	.332	.361	.35	0,7,9
.368	.357		.36	1,4,8
			.37	0
			.38	8

CHECK YOUR UNDERSTANDING

What is the highest average? How many batters hit between .340 and .360? How many batters hit .332? Did any batter hit .340?

.388; 3; 2; no

391

Straight angle

An angle whose measure is 180°.

CHECK YOUR UNDERSTANDING
How many degrees are there in one-half of a straight angle?

90°

Straightedge

A ruler without markings on it. A straightedge can be used for drawing straight segments but not for measuring anything.

CHECK YOUR UNDERSTANDING
A ruler has centimeters marked on it. Is it a straightedge?

no

Subset (⊆ or ⊂)

Set A is a subset of set B if every element of set A is also an element of set B. It is symbolized by A ⊆ B. Every set is a subset of itself, that is, for every set A, A ⊆ A. Set A is a proper subset of set B if every element of set A is also an element of set B, but A ≠ B. This means that set B has at least one element that is not an element of set A. It is denoted by A⊂B (read: set A is a proper subset of set B). The empty set (null set) is a subset of every set.

EXAMPLE Given set {*a,b,c*}, the following are all of its subsets: { }, {*a*}, {*b*}, {*c*}, {*a,b*}, {*a,c*}, {*b,c*}, {*a, b, c*}.

All of the above, except the last set, are also proper subsets of {*a, b, c*}.

CHECK YOUR UNDERSTANDING
Is the set of all even numbers a subset of all counting numbers? Is it a proper subset?

yes; yes

Substitution

Replacing one symbol by another. For example, 5 can be substituted for x in the equation $3x - 6 = 9$ to obtain the true statement $(3 \times 5) - 6 = 9$ or $15 - 6 = 9$.

CHECK YOUR UNDERSTANDING
What number will be obtained by substituting 3 for x in $5x - 2$?

13

Substitution method for systems of equations

See Solution of a system of equations - SOLVING SYSTEMS OF TWO EQUATIONS BY SUBSTITUTION.

S

Substitution property

One name of a number can be substituted for another name of the same number in any expression. In general, if $x = y$, then x can be substituted for y and y for x.

EXAMPLE   Given $7 = 2 + 5$.

Then 7 can be substituted for $2 + 5$
in the statement $2 + 5$ is an odd number
to get the statement 7 is an odd number.

CHECK YOUR UNDERSTANDING
It is known that $6 = 2 + 4$. According to the substitution property, can 6 be substituted for $2 + 4$ in any statement about $2 + 4$?

yes

Subtraction

A mathematical operation that tells "how many" or "how much" is left when one number is "taken away" from another. Subtraction is one of the four basic operations of arithmetic, along with addition, multiplication, and division. Subtraction is the inverse of addition: $5 + 2 - 2 = 5$. In general: $a + b - b = a$, and if $a - b = c$, then $c + b = a$. In $17 - 9 = 8$, 17 is the minuend, 9 is the subtrahend, and 8 is the difference. Subtraction is a binary operation because it is performed on two numbers.

SUBTRACTING WHEN BORROWING IS NEEDED

Step 1 Subtract ones	Step 2 Subtract tens 9 > 4. Borrow 1 from hundreds.	Step 3 Subtract hundreds
$$\begin{array}{r} 546 \\ -\ 193 \\ \hline 3 \end{array}$$	$$\begin{array}{r} ^{4\,14} \\ \cancel{5}46 \\ -\ 193 \\ \hline 53 \end{array}$$	$$\begin{array}{r} ^{4\,14} \\ \cancel{5}46 \\ -\ 193 \\ \hline 353 \end{array}$$

Another way to think of borrowing is a regrouping or renaming of places to subtract. In the example above, rename or regroup 5 hundreds 4 tens as 4 hundreds 14 tens to subtract tens.

CHECKING SUBTRACTION BY ADDING

Subtract	Check by adding
$$\begin{array}{r} 12{,}546 \\ -\ \ \ \ 827 \\ \hline 11{,}719 \end{array}$$	$$\begin{array}{r} ^{1\ \ \ 1} \\ 11{,}719 \\ +\ \ \ \ 827 \\ \hline 12{,}546 \end{array}$$

See also Casting out nines.

RELATED FACTS

Here are two examples of related subtraction facts:

$$15 - 7 = 8 \qquad 11 - 4 = 7$$
$$15 - 8 = 7 \qquad 11 - 7 = 4$$

For each addition fact of two unequal numbers, there are two related subtraction facts:

$$7 + 9 = 16 \qquad 16 - 9 = 7 \qquad 16 - 7 = 9$$

When a number is added to itself, there is one related subtraction fact: $\quad 7 + 7 = 14 \qquad 14 - 7 = 7$

See also Basic facts.

COMPLEMENTARY METHOD OF SUBTRACTION

A method of subtracting whole numbers by adding the complement of the subtrahend and subtracting the appropriate power of ten. A complement of a number is the number that can be added to a number to get the closest power of ten. For example, the complement of 564 is 436 ($564 + 436 = 1,000$).

Here's how to use the complementary method to subtract 4768 from 9825.

Add the complement of 4768.
($4768 + 5232 = 10,000$)
Then subtract the appropriate
power of ten (10,000).

$$
\begin{array}{r}
9825 \\
- 4768 \\
\end{array}
\qquad
\begin{array}{r}
9825 \\
+15232 \\
\hline
5057 \\
\end{array}
$$

It is convenient just to write the signed digit 1, as a reminder to subtract 10,000.

So, $9825 - 4768 = 5057$

DECOMPOSITION METHOD OF SUBTRACTION

The common names for this method are borrowing, regrouping, or renaming to subtract. See SUBTRACTION WHEN BORROWING IS NEEDED on page 394.

See also Equal additions method of subtraction.

Subtraction property of equality

Also called Subtraction property for equations. The same number may be subtracted from each side of an equation to form an equivalent equation. If $a = b$, then $a - c = b - c$.

CHECK YOUR UNDERSTANDING
Does the following illustrate the use of the subtraction property of equality? If $7 = 3 + 4$, then does $7 - 4 = 3 + 4 - 4$?

yes

Subtraction property of inequality

The same number may be subtracted from each side of an inequality to form an equivalent inequality. If $a > b$, then $a - c > b - c$. Also, if $a < b$, then $a - c < b - c$.

CHECK YOUR UNDERSTANDING
Does the following illustrate the use of the subtraction property of inequality? Are both statements true?

If $8 > 6$, then $8 - 2 > 6 - 2$

yes; yes

Subtrahend

The number in a subtraction statement that is being subtracted.

EXAMPLE $9 - 3 = 6$

minuend subtrahend difference

CHECK YOUR UNDERSTANDING
What is the subtrahend in $12 - 7 = 5$?

7

Sufficient

The condition C_1 is sufficient for condition C_2 if whenever C_1 holds so does C_2. For example, whenever a triangle has three congruent sides (C_1), then it is an equilateral triangle (C_2). So, the condition of having three congruent sides (C_1) is sufficient for a triangle to be equilateral (C_2). In order for a quadrilateral to be a rhombus (C_2), it is necessary that the opposite sides be parallel (C_1). C_1 is **not** a sufficient condition for C_2. The sides must also be of equal length.

CHECK YOUR UNDERSTANDING
Is having one right angle (C_1) a sufficient condition for a triangle to be a right triangle (C_2)?

yes

Sum

The result of addition.

EXAMPLE $3 + 6 = 9$

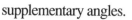
addends   sum

CHECK YOUR UNDERSTANDING
What is the sum in $4 + 7 = 11$?

11

Supplementary angles

Two angles are supplementary if the sum of their measures is 180° (a straight angle).

Angles a and b are supplementary angles.

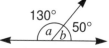

130°   50°

CHECK YOUR UNDERSTANDING
Are two angles whose measures are 40° and 140° supplementary?

yes

Surface

A portion of space that is flat like a plane or curved like the surface of the sphere.

CHECK YOUR UNDERSTANDING
Is a face of a cube a surface?

yes

Surface area

The total area of the surface of a solid. Unlike lateral area it includes the area of the base(s) of the figure.

FORMULAS FOR FINDING SURFACE AREAS OF SPACE FIGURES

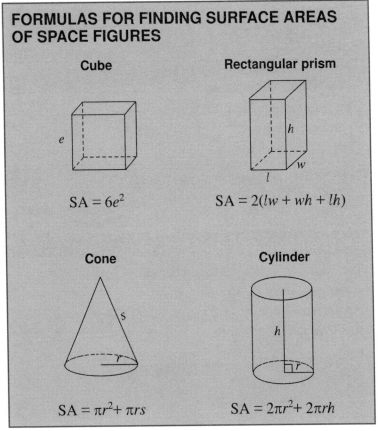

Cube

$SA = 6e^2$

Rectangular prism

$SA = 2(lw + wh + lh)$

Cone

$SA = \pi r^2 + \pi rs$

Cylinder

$SA = 2\pi r^2 + 2\pi rh$

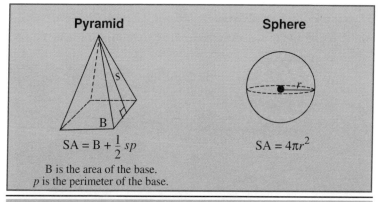

Pyramid

$$SA = B + \frac{1}{2} sp$$

B is the area of the base.
p is the perimeter of the base.

Sphere

$$SA = 4\pi r^2$$

CHECK YOUR UNDERSTANDING

The surface area of a pyramid consists of two parts. What are they?

area of the base plus the area of all faces

Syllogism

See Inference.

Symbol

Letters and marks used in mathematics to name numbers, operations, sets, relations, and so on.

EXAMPLES

Symbols for numbers: 27, XIV

Symbols for operations: $+, -, \times, \div, \sqrt{\ }$

Symbol for a set: { }

Symbols for set operations: ∪ (union), ∩ (intersection)

Variables as symbols: x, n

Symbols for relations for numbers: $=, >, <, \geq, \leq, \neq$

Symbols for relations for sets: ⊆ (is a subset of),
⊂ (is a proper subset of), ∈ (is a member of)

See Symbol list *on page 458.*

CHECK YOUR UNDERSTANDING

Is = a mathematical symbol? What does it mean?

yes; is equal to

Symmetric property of congruence

The following statement is true for all geometric figures A and B:

If figure A ≅ figure B, then figure B ≅ figure A.

CHECK YOUR UNDERSTANDING

Is it true that if triangle ABC is congruent to triangle DEF, then triangle DEF is congruent to triangle ABC?

yes

Symmetric property of equality

If $x = y$, then $y = x$ is true for all numbers x and y.

CHECK YOUR UNDERSTANDING

Is the following statement true?
If $7 = 3 + 4$, then $3 + 4 = 7$.

yes

Symmetric property of similarity

The following is true for all geometric figures A and B:
If figure A ~ figure B, then figure B ~ figure A.

CHECK YOUR UNDERSTANDING

Is it true that if triangle ABC is similar to triangle DEF, then triangle DEF is similar to triangle ABC?

yes

Symmetric relation

A relation, say R, that has the following property:

If x R y, then y R x.

Read: If x has a relation to y, then y has the same relation to x.

EXAMPLES OF SYMMETRIC RELATIONS

Is equal to (=)   If $13 = 4 + 9$ then $4 + 9 = 13$

In general: For all numbers x and y, if $x = y$, then $y = x$.

Is congruent to ($\cong$) If figure A $\cong$ figure B, then figure B $\cong$ figure A.

Is not equal to ($\neq$)   If $4 \neq 7$, then $7 \neq 4$.

S

If there is one instance for which a relation is not true, then the relation is not symmetric.

EXAMPLE   Relation: Is a brother of

John is a brother of Mary.

It is not true that Mary is a brother of John.

The relation is a brother of is not symmetric.

CHECK YOUR UNDERSTANDING

Is the relation is greater than (>) a symmetric relation; that is, is the following statement true: If $x > y$, then $y > x$?

no; 5 > 3, but it is not true that 3 > 5

Symmetry

There are three kinds of symmetries.

Line Symmetry or Reflectional Symmetry

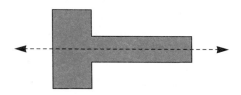

The figure has line symmetry. When folded along the line of symmetry, the two parts of the figure will coincide.

Plane Symmetry

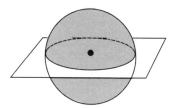

The sphere has plane symmetry. The two halves of the sphere are reflections of each other in the plane of symmetry.

Point Symmetry

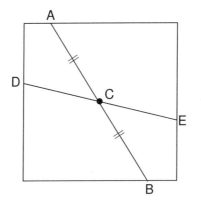

The square has point symmetry. AC = CB, DC = CE. This is true for every segment that passes through the point of symmetry, C, and has endpoints on the square.

CHECK YOUR UNDERSTANDING

Does a rectangle have line symmetry? Does a cylinder have plane symmetry? Does a circle have point symmetry?

yes; yes; yes

403

System of equations

Also called Simultaneous equations. Two or more equations in two or more variables considered together or simultaneously. The equations in the system may or may not have a common solution. A system of equations may have no common solution, one common solution, or an infinite number of common solutions. A system of equations that has at least one common solution is called a consistent system. A system that has no common solution is called an inconsistent system.

Consistent system	Inconsistent system
$3x + y = 7$	$3x + y = 7$
$2x + y = 5$	$3x + y = 2$
Common solution: (2,1)	No common solution.

A system of equations with exactly one common solution is called an independent system of equations.

Independent system of equations

$$x - 3y = 2 \quad \text{and} \quad x + y = 6$$

The equations have exactly one common solution of (5,1).The first equation also has a solution of (8,2) which is not a solution of the second equation.

A system of equations with all solutions in common is called a dependent system of equations.

Dependent system of equations

$$x - 3y = 2 \text{ and } 2x - 6y = 4$$

All solutions of the first equation are solutions of the second equation. Some common solutions are (5,1), (8,2), and (11,3).

See also Solution of a system of equations.

S

System of inequalities

Also called Simultaneous inequalities. Two or more inequalities in two or more variables that are considered together or simultaneously. The system may or may not have common solutions.

See also Solution of a system of inequalities.

Table of values

The data used to make a graph in the coordinate system. For example, the values for x and y in the table below are used as ordered pairs to graph the equation $y = 2x + 1$.

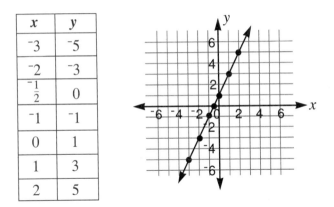

x	y
$^-3$	$^-5$
$^-2$	$^-3$
$^-\frac{1}{2}$	0
$^-1$	$^-1$
0	1
1	3
2	5

CHECK YOUR UNDERSTANDING

What is the value of y when x is 0 in y = 2x + 1?

1

Tangent

See Trigonometric ratios.

Tangent circles

Circles that touch each other at one point. Circles can be either externally tangent or internally tangent.

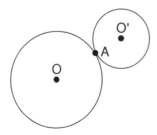

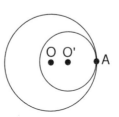

Circles O and O' are externally tangent at point A.

Circles O and O' are internally tangent at point A.

CHECK YOUR UNDERSTANDING

How many points do two tangent circles have in common?

one

Tangent to a curve

A line that touches a curve at one point. The point of contact is called the point of tangency. Line ℓ is a tangent to curve *c*. Point P is the point of tangency.

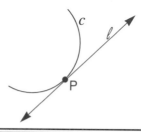

CHECK YOUR UNDERSTANDING

Does tangent ℓ have more than one point in common with curve *c*?

no

Tangram

A Chinese mathematical puzzle. The pieces of the puzzle are called tans. The finished arrangements made from the pieces are called tangrams. To try the puzzle, make a large copy of the square below and cut out the seven tans.

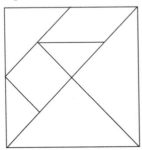

The object is to make designs using all seven pieces without overlapping. Tangrams of animal shapes, rectangles, triangles, parallelograms, trapezoids, hexagons, quadrilaterals, pentagons, and other designs can be made using the seven tans.

Temperature

See Celsius scale, Fahrenheit scale, *and* Kelvin scale.

Term

See Expression, Proportion, *and* Sequence.

Terminating decimal

A decimal that has a finite number of decimal places.

EXAMPLES   0.25   5.875   45.902854

CHECK YOUR UNDERSTANDING
Is 3.12 a terminating decimal?

yes

Ternary numeration system

A numeration system with three as the base. It uses three digits, 0, 1, 2. The value of places in the ternary system are powers of three:

$$3^3 \quad 3^2 \quad 3^1 \quad 3^0 \quad 3^{-1} \quad 3^{-2} \quad 3^{-3}$$

... $\square$ $\square$ $\square$ $\square$. $\square$ $\square$ $\square$ ...

The value of the numeral 201 in base three is:
$$(2 \times 3^2) + (0 \times 3^1) + (1 \times 3^0) \text{ or } 19.$$

CHECK YOUR UNDERSTANDING
What is the value of the numeral 211 in base three?

twenty-two

Tessellation

An arrangement of polygonal regions covering the plane without overlapping or leaving any gaps.

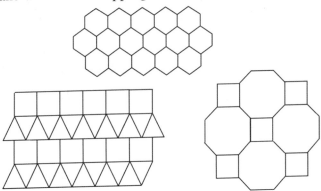

The degree measures around the common point of the angles of the figures must total 360 degrees to tessellate a plane.

CHECK YOUR UNDERSTANDING
Can the tessellations shown in the pictures above be continued in all directions?

yes

Tetrahedron

See Pyramid.

Theory of numbers

See Number theory.

Thousand

10 hundreds (1000). As a power of 10: 10^3.

CHECK YOUR UNDERSTANDING
What does 10^3 mean in terms of multiplication?

$10 \times 10 \times 10$

Three-dimensional figure

Also called Space figure *or* Solid figure. A geometric figure in space that has volume. The figure occupies part of space.

CHECK YOUR UNDERSTANDING
Is a sphere a three-dimensional figure?

yes

Time line

A line that shows some events in history arranged from left to right.

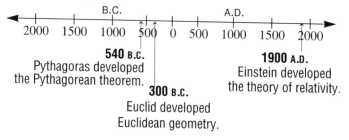

CHECK YOUR UNDERSTANDING
Between what two periods marked on the time line would an event that took place in 1150 A.D. be shown?

between 1000 and 1500 A.D.

Time zones

The United States is divided into four time zones: Eastern, Central, Mountain, and Pacific. As we move east from one zone to the next, the time advances 1 hour.

EXAMPLE It is 8 A.M. in San Francisco. Then it is 9 A.M in Salt Lake City, 10 A.M in St. Louis, and 11 A.M in New York City.

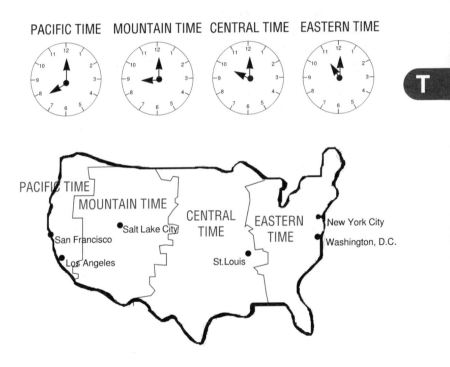

PACIFIC TIME   MOUNTAIN TIME   CENTRAL TIME   EASTERN TIME

PACIFIC TIME

MOUNTAIN TIME

CENTRAL TIME

EASTERN TIME

Salt Lake City

San Francisco

Los Angeles

St. Louis

New York City

Washington, D.C.

T

CHECK YOUR UNDERSTANDING

It is 7 P.M. in Washington, D.C. What time is it in Los Angeles?

4 P.M.

Ton (t)

A unit for measuring weight in the U.S. Customary System. It is equal to 2000 pounds (lb). A fully grown African elephant weighs about 8 tons.

CHECK YOUR UNDERSTANDING
How many pounds are there in 5 tons?

10,000

Transformations

See Reflection, Rotation, *and* Translation.

Transitive property of congruence

The following statement is true for all geometric figures A, B, and C: If figure A $\cong$ figure B and figure B $\cong$ figure C, then figure A $\cong$ figure C.

CHECK YOUR UNDERSTANDING
If $\triangle F \cong \triangle G$ and $\triangle G \cong \triangle H$, what do you know about $\triangle F$ and $\triangle H$?

$\triangle F \cong \triangle H$

Transitive property of equality

If $x = y$ and $y = z$, then $x = z$.

CHECK YOUR UNDERSTANDING
If $a = b$ and $b = c$, what do you know about a and c?

$a = c$

Transitive property of similarity

The following is true for all geometric figures C, D, and E: If figure C $\sim$ figure D and figure D $\sim$ figure E, then figure C $\sim$ figure E. ($\sim$ $\leftarrow$ is similar to)

CHECK YOUR UNDERSTANDING
If figure $X \sim$ figure Y and figure $Y \sim$ figure Z, what do you know about figure X and figure Z?

figure x $\sim$ *figure* z

Transitive Relation

A relation, say R, that has the following property:

> If a R b and b R c, then a R c.

Read: If a has a relation to b and b has the same relation to c, then a has the same relation to c.

EXAMPLES

Is greater than (>)
If $7 > 3$ and $3 > 1$, then $7 > 1$.
In general: If $x > y$ and $y > z$, then $x > z$.

Is less than (<)
If $3 < 4$ and $4 < 8$, then $3 < 8$.
In general: If $x < y$ and $y < z$, then $x < z$.

Is equal to (=)
If $7 = 2 + 5$ and $2 + 5 = 1 + 6$, then $7 = 1 + 6$.
In general: if $x = y$ and $y = z$, then $x = z$.

Is congruent to ($\cong$)
If $\triangle ABC \cong \triangle DEF$ and $\triangle DEF \cong \triangle GHI$, then $\triangle ABC \cong \triangle GHI$

Some relations are not transitive.

EXAMPLE OF A RELATION THAT IS **NOT** TRANSITIVE
Is not equal to ($\neq$): $5 \neq 3$ and $3 \neq 5$, but $5 = 5$.

T

CHECK YOUR UNDERSTANDING
Complete the following statement: If $9 > 5$ and $5 > 1$, then ___.

$9 > 1$

Translating expressions

See Expression - WRITING ALGEBRAIC EXPRESSIONS FOR WORD PHRASES.

Translation

Also called Slide. Moving a geometric figure by sliding. Each of the points of the geometric figure moves the same distance in the same direction. The new points are images of the original points.

EXAMPLE

Translation of triangle ABC into triangle A'B'C':

$$A(^-5,^-2) \longrightarrow A'(1,3)$$
$$B(^-3,1) \longrightarrow B'(3,6)$$
$$C(^-2,^-4) \longrightarrow C'(4,1)$$

To move from a point to its image:

add 6 to the *x*-coordinate

add 5 to the *y*-coordinate

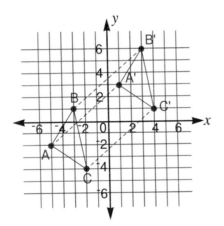

A translation is one of the three basic rigid motions of geometry, along with reflection (flip) and rotation (turn).

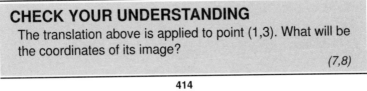

CHECK YOUR UNDERSTANDING

The translation above is applied to point (1,3). What will be the coordinates of its image?

(7,8)

Transversal

In geometry, a line (*k*) that intersects two or more lines (*m* and *n*) at different points.

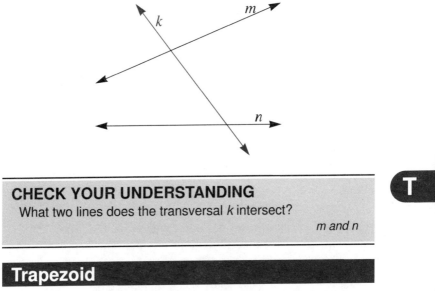

CHECK YOUR UNDERSTANDING
What two lines does the transversal *k* intersect?

m and n

Trapezoid

A quadrilateral with exactly one pair of parallel sides.

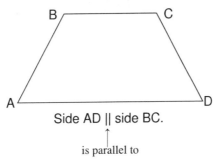

Side AD || side BC.

↑
is parallel to

See also Area.

CHECK YOUR UNDERSTANDING
No two sides in a quadrilateral are parallel. Is it a trapezoid?

no

Tree diagram

A pictorial way of representing combinations of things. There are 2 choices for a vegetable: peas or carrots. There are 3 choices for the main course: chicken, veal, or beef. How many different combinations of vegetables and main courses are there?

Tree diagram

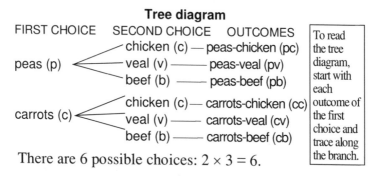

There are 6 possible choices: $2 \times 3 = 6$.

A spinner can land on any one of the regions: A, B, C, or D. How many different combinations are there for 2 spins?

Tree diagram

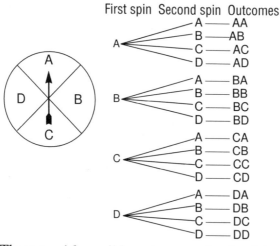

There are 16 possible outcomes: $4 \times 4 = 16$.

See also Factor tree *and* Fundamental counting principle.

Triangle

A polygon with three sides. The sum of the measures of the three angles of any triangle is 180°. Triangles can be classified according to their angles or sides.

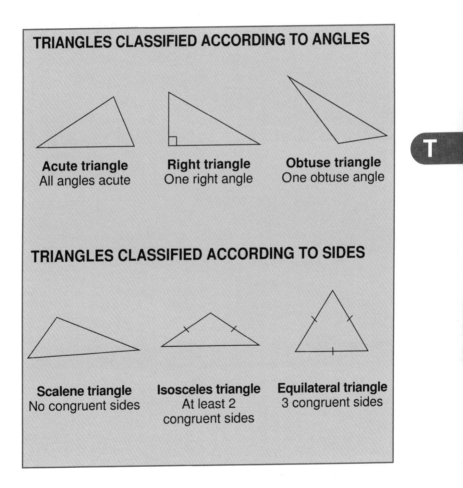

TRIANGLES CLASSIFIED ACCORDING TO ANGLES

Acute triangle
All angles acute

Right triangle
One right angle

Obtuse triangle
One obtuse angle

TRIANGLES CLASSIFIED ACCORDING TO SIDES

Scalene triangle
No congruent sides

Isosceles triangle
At least 2
congruent sides

Equilateral triangle
3 congruent sides

T

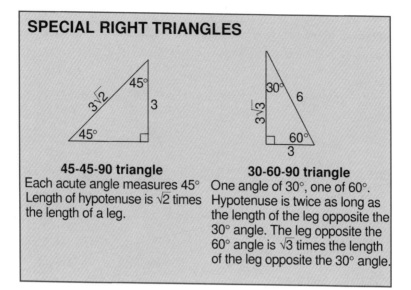

SPECIAL RIGHT TRIANGLES

45-45-90 triangle
Each acute angle measures 45°
Length of hypotenuse is √2 times
the length of a leg.

30-60-90 triangle
One angle of 30°, one of 60°.
Hypotenuse is twice as long as
the length of the leg opposite the
30° angle. The leg opposite the
60° angle is √3 times the length
of the leg opposite the 30° angle.

See also Area.

CHECK YOUR UNDERSTANDING
Which part of the word *triangle* suggests how many angles
there are?

tri (3)

Triangle inequality property

In a triangle, the sum of the lengths of two sides is
greater than the length of the third side.

CHECK YOUR UNDERSTANDING
Is it possible to make a triangle of 3 segments with lengths
5 cm, 2 cm, and 1 cm?

no; 2 + 1 < 5

Triangular number

A number created by using triangles as shown below.
The first four triangular numbers are shown.

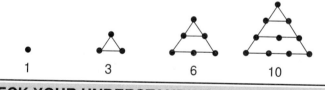

1   3   6   10

CHECK YOUR UNDERSTANDING

What is the fifth triangular number?

15

Trigonometric ratios

The ratios of the lengths of pairs of sides in a right
triangle. There are six basic trigonometric ratios used
in trigonometry: sine (sin), cosine (cos), tangent (tan),
secant (sec), cosecant (csc), and cotangent (cot).

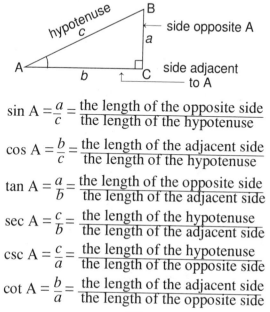

$$\sin A = \frac{a}{c} = \frac{\text{the length of the opposite side}}{\text{the length of the hypotenuse}}$$

$$\cos A = \frac{b}{c} = \frac{\text{the length of the adjacent side}}{\text{the length of the hypotenuse}}$$

$$\tan A = \frac{a}{b} = \frac{\text{the length of the opposite side}}{\text{the length of the adjacent side}}$$

$$\sec A = \frac{c}{b} = \frac{\text{the length of the hypotenuse}}{\text{the length of the adjacent side}}$$

$$\csc A = \frac{c}{a} = \frac{\text{the length of the hypotenuse}}{\text{the length of the opposite side}}$$

$$\cot A = \frac{b}{a} = \frac{\text{the length of the adjacent side}}{\text{the length of the opposite side}}$$

USING TRIGONOMETRIC RATIOS TO FIND LENGTHS OF SIDES OF RIGHT TRIANGLES

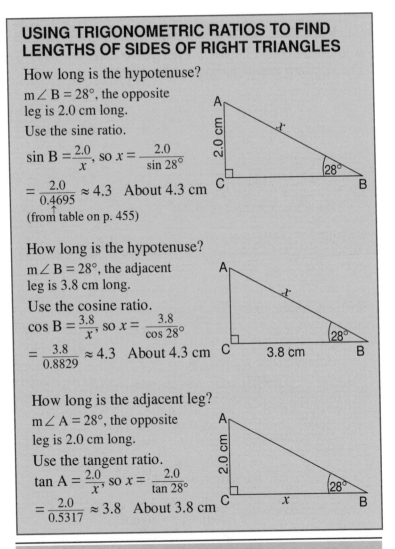

How long is the hypotenuse?

m∠B = 28°, the opposite leg is 2.0 cm long.

Use the sine ratio.

$\sin B = \dfrac{2.0}{x}$, so $x = \dfrac{2.0}{\sin 28°}$

$= \dfrac{2.0}{0.4695} \approx 4.3$ About 4.3 cm

(from table on p. 455)

How long is the hypotenuse?

m∠B = 28°, the adjacent leg is 3.8 cm long.

Use the cosine ratio.

$\cos B = \dfrac{3.8}{x}$, so $x = \dfrac{3.8}{\cos 28°}$

$= \dfrac{3.8}{0.8829} \approx 4.3$ About 4.3 cm

How long is the adjacent leg?

m∠A = 28°, the opposite leg is 2.0 cm long.

Use the tangent ratio.

$\tan A = \dfrac{2.0}{x}$, so $x = \dfrac{2.0}{\tan 28°}$

$= \dfrac{2.0}{0.5317} \approx 3.8$ About 3.8 cm

CHECK YOUR UNDERSTANDING

If the length of the leg opposite an angle in a right triangle is 1 cm and the length of the hypotenuse is 2 cm, what is the sine of the angle? Use the table on page 455 to find the degree measure of the angle.

$\dfrac{1}{2}$ or 0.5; the angle with a sine of 0.5 is 30°

Trigonometry

A branch of mathematics that combines arithmetic, algebra, and geometry. The right triangle is the basis of trigonometry. Trigonometry deals with the study of properties of trigonometric functions such as sine, cosine, and tangent and their uses in solving various mathematical, technical, and scientific problems. Trigonometric functions are used in surveying, navigation, and various sciences, such as physics.

CHECK YOUR UNDERSTANDING
Are trigonometric functions used in physics?

yes

T

Trinomial

A polynomial with three terms, such as $3x + 5y - 6$.

CHECK YOUR UNDERSTANDING
Is $4a + 6 - 3b$ a trinomial?

yes

Trisect

To divide into three parts of the same size. For example, to trisect an angle means to divide it into three parts of the same measure.

CHECK YOUR UNDERSTANDING
An angle of $90°$ is trisected. What is the measure of each part?

30°

Turn

Also called Rotation. A move of a figure about a point. The size and shape of the figure stays the same.

Point R is the point of rotation.

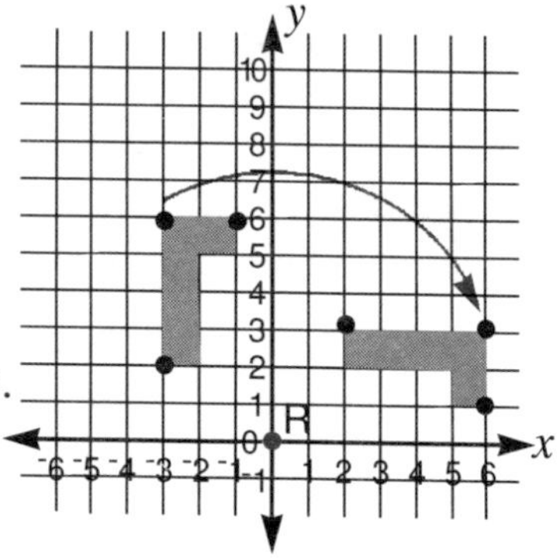

The following points correspond:.(⁻1,6) and (6,1), (⁻3,2) and (2,3), (⁻3,6) and (6,3).

CHECK YOUR UNDERSTANDING
What point corresponds to (⁻2,2)?

(2,2)

Twin primes

A pair of prime numbers whose difference is 2.

EXAMPLES
| 5, 7 | 11, 13 | 17, 19 |
| 29, 31 | 41, 43 | 59, 61 |

CHECK YOUR UNDERSTANDING
Are 71 and 73 twin primes?

yes

Two-dimensional figure

See Plane figure.

Two-point form of an equation of a line

See Equation of a line.

Undoing operation

See Inverse operation.

Union of sets (U)

An operation on sets. The union of sets A and B is the set consisting of those members (elements) that are in A, in B, and in both A and B.

EXAMPLE

$$A = \{1, 3, 5, 7\}, B = \{1, 2, 3, 4, 5\}$$
$$A \cup B = \{1, 2, 3, 4, 5, 7\}$$

Venn diagram

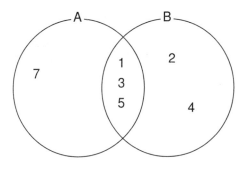

$$A \cup B = \{1, 2, 3, 4, 5, 7\}$$

CHECK YOUR UNDERSTANDING

X = {2, 4, 6} and Y = {1, 2, 3}. What is X U Y equal to?

X U Y = {1, 2, 3, 4, 6}

Unique

Only one or exactly one. For example, the equation $x - 2 = 0$ has a unique (exactly one) solution, which is the number 2.

CHECK YOUR UNDERSTANDING
Does $x - 5 = 0$ have a unique solution? If yes, what is it?

yes; 5

Unique factorization theorem

See Fundamental theorem of arithmetic.

Unit circle

A circle whose radius is 1 unit in length.

CHECK YOUR UNDERSTANDING
What is the circumference of a unit circle?

2π or about 6.28 units

Unit fraction

A fraction whose numerator is 1, such as $\frac{1}{4}$.

CHECK YOUR UNDERSTANDING
Is $\frac{2}{3}$ a unit fraction?

no; its numerator is not 1

Unit number

The number 1.

CHECK YOUR UNDERSTANDING
Is $\frac{13}{13}$ another name for the unit number?

yes

Unit of measurement

A scale used to measure. For example, degree, foot, inch, and pound are units of measurement.

CHECK YOUR UNDERSTANDING
A person is 145 cm tall. What is the unit of mesurement?

centimeter

Unit price

Also called Unit cost. The cost of one thing, such as the cost of 1 orange is $0.60.

CHECK YOUR UNDERSTANDING
The cost of 2 cucumbers is $1.10. Is this a unit cost?

no; it is not a cost of 1 thing

Unit rate

A ratio in which the denominator is 1 unit.

EXAMPLES

$$\frac{45 \text{ miles}}{1 \text{ hour}} \qquad \frac{25 \text{ students}}{1 \text{ teacher}} \qquad \frac{85 \text{ points}}{1 \text{ game}}$$

See also Ratio.

CHECK YOUR UNDERSTANDING
Is $\frac{\$1.35}{8 \text{ ounces}}$ a unit rate?

no; it does not have 1 unit in the denominator

Unit square

A square whose area (as well as each side) is equal to 1.

CHECK YOUR UNDERSTANDING
A square has a perimeter of 4 in. Is it a unit square?

yes

Unitary operation

See Operation.

U.S. customary units

See Measurement.

Units place

See Place value.

Universal set

Also called Universe. A set of all things (numbers, points) that can be used for the subject under consideration.

EXAMPLES

For the four basic operations (addition, subtraction, multiplication, and division) in first-year high school algebra, the universal set is the set of real numbers.

For plane geometry, the universal set is the set of points in the plane.

CHECK YOUR UNDERSTANDING

In solving equations, students are told that they can use only integers. Is the set of integers the universal set in this case?

yes

Universe

See Universal set.

Unknown

A number that is not known. It is usually represented by a letter or symbol in an equation or inequality. For example, in the equation $3x + 7 = 10$, x is the unknown. The value of the unknown that gives a true statement is the solution of the equation.

CHECK YOUR UNDERSTANDING
What is the unknown in the equation $4y - 3 = 5$?

y

Unlike fractions

Two or more fractions that have denominators that are not the same.

$$\frac{1}{6}, \frac{2}{5}, \text{ and } \frac{3}{4}$$

See also Like fractions.

CHECK YOUR UNDERSTANDING
Are $\frac{4}{7}$ and $\frac{2}{7}$ unlike fractions?

no; they have the same denominator

Value of a function

For any ordered pair (x,y) of a function, the value of the function at x is y.

Function: $\{(1,1),(2,4),(3,9),(4,16)\}$

The value of the function at 3 is 9.

CHECK YOUR UNDERSTANDING

What is the value of the function above at 2?

4

Value of an expression

The number obtained by substituting a specific number or numbers for a variable or variables in an expression. For example, the value of the expression $3x + 5$, when 2 is substituted for x, is 11.

CHECK YOUR UNDERSTANDING

What is the value of the expression $2x + 1$ when 3 is substituted for x?

7

Variable

A letter or other symbol that represents a number or other mathematical thing. If it represents a number, then it is also called a numerical variable. In the equation $2x + y = 9$, x and y are numerical variables.

CHECK YOUR UNDERSTANDING

What are the variables in $x + y + z = 12$?

x, y, and z

Variation

See Direct variation *and* Inverse variation.

Vector

An entity that can be represented by a directed line segment (a line segment that has magnitude and direction). The movement of a car 5 miles North can be represented by the vector at the right.

N
↑
5 miles

CHECK YOUR UNDERSTANDING

What does the vector at the right represent?

2 miles
⊢—+—▸E

the movement of something 2 miles East

Velocity

Speed in a specific direction. To describe velocity both the direction and speed are needed. For example, a car traveling east at 30 mph has a velocity of 30 mph E. Velocity is usually represented by a directed line segment called a vector.

CHECK YOUR UNDERSTANDING

A car is traveling 55 mph south. Another car is traveling 55 mph west. Do they have the same velocity?

no

Venn diagram

V

A pictorial way of representing relationships between sets.

   EXAMPLE   N is the set of counting numbers.

   A = the set of all counting numbers from 10 through 20
   B = the set of all counting numbers from 5 through 15

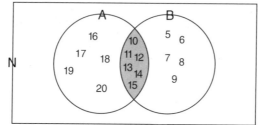

The shaded area shows the intersection of sets A and B, the set of members that the sets have in common is call the intersection of sets A and B.

EXAMPLE   N is the set of counting numbers.

C = the set of counting numbers from 1 through 10

D = the set of counting numbers from 20 through 25

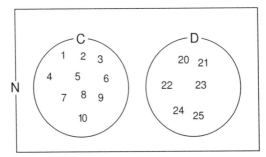

The two circles do not intersect. The sets have no members in common. The sets are called disjoint sets.

EXAMPLE   N is the set of counting numbers.

E = the set of counting numbers from 1 through 10

F = the set of counting numbers from 4 through 8

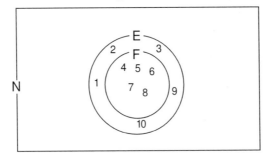

The circle representing set F is contained within the circle representing set E, since every member of set F is also a member of set E. Set F is a called a subset of set E.

CHECK YOUR UNDERSTANDING

In a Venn diagram where set X is the set of counting numbers from 1 through 10 and set Y is the set of counting numbers from 20 through 30, will the circles intersect?

no; the sets have no members in common

Of an angle A point common to the two sides of the angle.

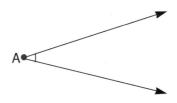

Point A is the vertex of ∠A

Of a polygon A point common to two sides of the polygon.

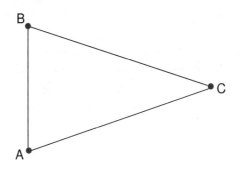

Points A, B, and C are the vertices of △ ABC.

See next page for Vertex of a polyhedron .

Of a polyhedron A point common to the edges of a polyhedron.

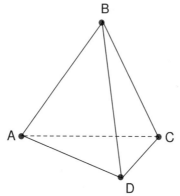

Points A, B, C, and D are the vertices of the tetrahedron.

Vertex angle of an isosceles triangle

An angle formed by the two congruent sides.

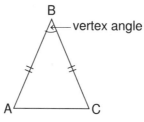

Isosceles △ABC. Sides AB and BC are congruent.

Vertical angles

Pairs of angles formed by intersecting lines. Angles AOB and COD are a pair of vertical angles. Vertical angles have the same measure.

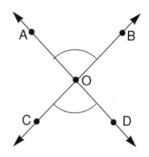

CHECK YOUR UNDERSTANDING

What is the other pair of vertical angles in the figure above?

angles AOC and BOD

Vertical axis

The *y*-axis in the coordinate system.

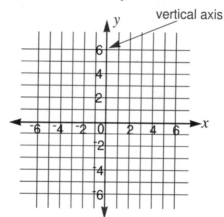

See also Coordinate system.

CHECK YOUR UNDERSTANDING

If the *y*-axis is the vertical axis, then what is the *x*-axis?

horizontal

Vertical-line test for function

A test for a graph of a relation to establish whether it is a graph of a function. A graph is a graph of a function if there exists no vertical line that intersects the graph in more than one point.

Graph of a relation that is not a function

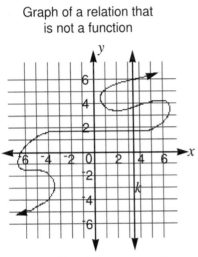

Graph of a function

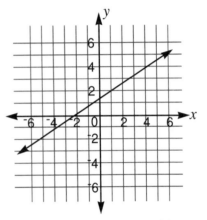

Vertical line *k* intersects the graph in more than one point

No vertical line would intersect graph in more than one point

See also Function *and* Relation.

CHECK YOUR UNDERSTANDING
In how many points does the vertical line *k* (above) intersect the graph of the relation that is not a function?

3

Volume

The measure of the interior of
a space (three-dimensional)
figure. A unit for measuring
volume is the cubic unit.

Each edge is 1 unit long.

FORMULAS FOR FINDING VOLUMES OF SPACE FIGURES

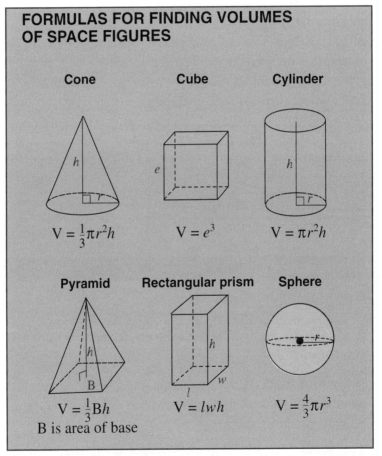

Cone

$V = \frac{1}{3}\pi r^2 h$

Cube

$V = e^3$

Cylinder

$V = \pi r^2 h$

Pyramid

$V = \frac{1}{3}Bh$
B is area of base

Rectangular prism

$V = lwh$

Sphere

$V = \frac{4}{3}\pi r^3$

V

CHECK YOUR UNDERSTANDING

Does a plane figure (two-dimensional) have volume?

no

Weight

The gravitational force exerted by the Earth or other celestial body on an object. It is equal to the product of the object's mass and the local gravity. For example, the gravity on Jupiter is 2.64 times the gravity on Earth. A person that weighs 150 lb on Earth would weigh 396 lb on Jupiter.

CHECK YOUR UNDERSTANDING

The weight of an object on the moon is 0.17 of the object's weight on Earth. If a teenager weighs 100 lb on Earth, what is the teenager's weight on the moon?

17 lb

Whole number

A number that belongs to the set
$$\{0, 1, 2, 3, 4, \ldots\}$$
It is an infinite set. There is no largest whole number.

See also Addition, Counting numbers, Division, Even number, Multiplication, Odd number, Place value, Rounding, *and* Subtraction.

CHECK YOUR UNDERSTANDING

Is 0.4 a whole number?

no; it is a decimal between the whole numbers 0 and 1

Width

The measure of the shorter of two congruent sides in a rectangle that is not a square. In the rectangle ABCD below, the width is 1.7 cm.

CHECK YOUR UNDERSTANDING
What is the width of a rectangle with dimensions 4 cm by 7 cm?

4 cm

Word expression

See Expression.

W

Word name for number

Also called Word form. A number named by a word, such as fifty-six.

CHECK YOUR UNDERSTANDING
What is the word name for 45?

forty-five

X-axis

The horizontal axis in a coordinate system.

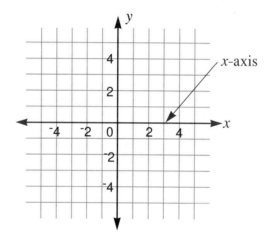

See also Coordinate system.

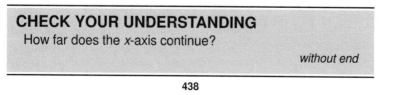

CHECK YOUR UNDERSTANDING

How far does the *x*-axis continue?

without end

X-coordinate

The first number of an ordered pair of numbers that corresponds to a point in a coordinate system. The second number is called the *y*-coordinate.

EXAMPLE Ordered pair (4, 6).

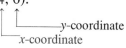

y-coordinate
x-coordinate

See also Coordinate system.

X-intercept

The point at which a graph intersects the *x*-axis.

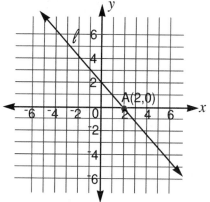

The point (2,0) is the *x*-intercept for line ℓ.

See also Coordinate system.

Yard (yd)

A unit for measuring length (distance). A yard is equal to 3 feet.

Y-axis

The vertical axis in a coordinate system.

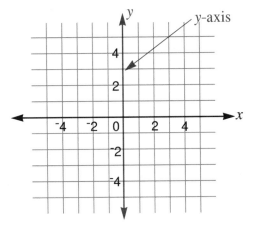

See also Coordinate system.

Y-coordinate

The second number of an ordered pair of numbers that corresponds to a point in a coordinate system. The first number is called the x-coordinate.

EXAMPLE Ordered pair (6, 8).

```
    (6, 8).
     ↑  ↑
     |  └────── y-coordinate
     └───────── x-coordinate
```

See also Coordinate system.

CHECK YOUR UNDERSTANDING

What is the y-coordinate of the point corresponding to the ordered pair (5,12)?

12

Y-intercept

The point at which a graph intersects the y-axis.

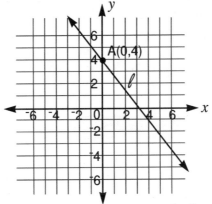

The point (0,4) is the y-intercept for line ℓ.

See also Coordinate system.

CHECK YOUR UNDERSTANDING

What is the x-coordinate of the y-intercept A?

0

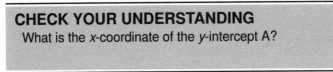

Z

Zeno's paradox

One of the famous paradoxes of antiquity. Its argument is as follows. Suppose a gun is discharged at an object 10 feet away. In order to reach the object, the bullet must travel half the distance, or 5 feet. Then it must travel half of the remaining distance, or 2.5 feet. Then half of the remaining distance, or 1.25 feet. The argument continues without end and the bullet supposedly never reaches the object, since there will always remain half the distance to be covered. Of course, it is known that the bullet will strike the object.

CHECK YOUR UNDERSTANDING
Suppose a frog is jumping out of a well that is 10 ft. high. The frog jumps a distance and falls back half the distance. Will the frog ever get out of the well?

yes

Zero (0)

A whole number, the first number among the whole numbers. It is used to denote the number of members (elements) in the empty set.

See also Identity for addition.

CHECK YOUR UNDERSTANDING
Would zero be used to indicate the absence of any members in a set?

yes

Zero exponent

The expression n^0 ($n \neq 0$) has the zero exponent. $n^0 = 1$.

CHECK YOUR UNDERSTANDING
What is 6^0 equal to?

1

Zero in division

See Division - ZERO IN DIVISION.

Zero of a function

For the function $\{x, f(x)\}$, the zero of the function is the value of x for which $f(x) = 0$.

> EXAMPLE For the function $\{(x, x - 1)\}$ the zero of the function is 1, since $x - 1 = 0$ when 1 is substituted for x.

CHECK YOUR UNDERSTANDING
What is the zero of the function $\{(x, x - 2)\}$?

2

Zero of a polynomial

The value of the variable for which the value of the polynomial is zero.

> EXAMPLE 5 is the zero of the polynomial $x - 5$, since the value of the polynomial $x - 5$ is 0 when 5 is substituted for x.

Z

CHECK YOUR UNDERSTANDING
What is the zero of the polynomial $x - 8$?

8

Zero product property

See Zero property of multiplication.

Zero property of addition

Also called Identity property of addition. The sum of zero and any number is equal to that number.

EXAMPLES $9 + 0 = 0 + 9 = 9$ $0 + {}^-16 = {}^-16$

In general, for every number n, $n + 0 = 0 + n = n$.

CHECK YOUR UNDERSTANDING

What is $0 + {}^-12$ equal to?

$^-12$

Zero property of multiplication

Also called Zero product property. Any number multiplied by 0 is equal to 0.

EXAMPLES $8 \times 0 = 0$ $0 \times {}^-13 = 0$

In general, for every number n, $n \times 0 = 0 \times n = 0$.

CHECK YOUR UNDERSTANDING

What is 37×0 equal to?

0

444

TABLE OF
PERCENT, DECIMAL, AND FRACTION EQUIVALENTS

PERCENT	DECIMAL	FRACTION
5%	.05	$\frac{1}{20}$
$6\frac{1}{4}\%$	.0625	$\frac{1}{16}$
$8\frac{1}{3}\%$	$.08\overline{3}$	$\frac{1}{12}$
10%	.10	$\frac{1}{10}$
$12\frac{1}{2}\%$	.125	$\frac{1}{8}$
$16\frac{2}{3}\%$	$.1\overline{6}$	$\frac{1}{6}$
20%	.20	$\frac{1}{5}$
25%	.25	$\frac{1}{4}$
30%	.30	$\frac{3}{10}$
$33\frac{1}{3}\%$	$.\overline{3}$	$\frac{1}{3}$
$37\frac{1}{2}\%$	.375	$\frac{3}{8}$
40%	.40	$\frac{2}{5}$

PERCENT	DECIMAL	FRACTION
50%	.50	$\frac{1}{2}$
60%	.60	$\frac{3}{5}$
$62\frac{1}{2}\%$	.625	$\frac{5}{8}$
$66\frac{2}{3}\%$	$.\overline{6}$	$\frac{2}{3}$
70%	.70	$\frac{7}{10}$
75%	.75	$\frac{3}{4}$
80%	.80	$\frac{4}{5}$
$83\frac{1}{3}\%$	$.8\overline{3}$	$\frac{5}{6}$
$87\frac{1}{2}\%$	.875	$\frac{7}{8}$
90%	.90	$\frac{9}{10}$
100%	1.00	$\frac{10}{10}$

TABLE OF PERCENT, DECIMAL, AND FRACTION EQUIVALENTS

LAWS OF EXPONENTS
(PROPERTIES OF POWERS)

Exponents (Powers)
$$a^0 = 1, a \neq 0$$
$$a^1 = a$$
$$a^2 = a \cdot a$$
$$a^3 = a \cdot a \cdot a$$
.
.
.
$$\overset{n \text{ factors}}{a^n = \overbrace{a \cdot a \cdot a \cdot \ldots \cdot a}}$$
$$a^{-m} = \frac{1}{a^m}$$

Product of Powers
$$a^m \cdot a^n = a^{(m+n)}$$

Quotient of Powers
$$a^m \div a^n = a^{(m-n)}$$

Power of a Power
$$(a^m)^n = a^{(mn)}$$

Power of a Product
$$(ab)^n = a^n \, b^n$$

Power of a Quotient
$$\left(\frac{a}{b}\right)^n = \frac{a^n}{b^n}$$

OTHER PROPERTIES AND LAWS

Factorials
$$1! = 1$$
$$2! = 2 \cdot 1$$
$$3! = 3 \cdot 2 \cdot 1$$
$$4! = 4 \cdot 3 \cdot 2 \cdot 1$$
.
.
$$n! = n(n-1)(n-2) \ldots 1$$

Trichotomy Law
For all real numbers a and b, there are exactly three possibilities:
$$a < b \qquad a > b \qquad a = b$$

Properties of Equality
For all real numbers a, b, and c:

Reflexive: $a = a$

Symmetric: If $a = b$, then $b = a$

Transitive: If $a = b$ and $b = c$, then $a = c$

QUADRILLIONS, ETC.

Some higher powers of 10 and their word names are the following:

10^9	billion	10^{39}	duodecillion
10^{12}	trillion	10^{42}	tredecillion
10^{15}	quadrillion	10^{45}	quattuordecillion
10^{18}	quintillion	10^{48}	quindecillion
10^{21}	sextillion	10^{51}	sexdecillion
10^{24}	septillion	10^{54}	septendecillion
10^{27}	octillion	10^{57}	octadecillion
10^{30}	nonillion	10^{60}	novemdecillion
10^{33}	decillion	10^{63}	vigintillion
10^{36}	undecillion	10^{100}	googol

TIME

1 minute (min) = 60 seconds (s)
1 hour (h) = 60 minutes
1 day (d) = 24 hours
1 week (wk) = 7 days

1 year (yr) = $\begin{cases} 12 \text{ months (mo)} \\ 52 \text{ weeks} \\ 365 \text{ days} \end{cases}$

1 decade = 10 years
1 century (c) = 100 years
1 millennium = 1000 years

TABLE OF MEASURES
METRIC

Length	
	1 millimeter (mm) = 0.001 meter (m)
	1 centimeter (cm) = 0.01 meter
	1 decimeter (dm) = 0.1 meter
	1 dekameter (dam) = 10 meters
	1 hectometer (hm) = 100 meters
	1 kilometer = 1000 meters

Mass/Weight	
	1 milligram (mg) = 0.001 gram (g)
	1 centigram (cg) = 0.01 gram
	1 decigram (dg) = 0.1 gram
	1 dekagram (dag) = 10 grams
	1 hectogram (hg) = 100 grams
	1 kilogram (kg) = 1000 grams
	1 metric ton (t) = 1000 kilograms

Capacity	
	1 milliliter (mL) = 0.001 liter (L)
	1 centiliter (cL) = 0.01 liter
	1 deciliter (dL) = 0.1 liter
	1 dekaliter (daL) = 10 liters
	1 hectoliter (hL) = 100 liters
	1 kiloliter (kL) = 1000 liters

In the metric system there is also a relationship between the units of capacity and the cubic units:

$$1 \text{ liter} = 1000 \text{ cubic centimeters (cm}^3\text{)}$$
$$1 \text{ milliliter} = 1 \text{ cubic centimeter}$$

Volume	
	1 cubic centimeter (cm^3) = 1000 cubic millimeters (mm^3)
	1 cubic decimeter (dm^3) = 1000 cubic centimeters
	1 cubic meter (m^3) = 1,000,000 cubic centimeters

Area	
	1 square centimeter (cm^2) = 100 square millimeters (mm^2)
	1 square meter (m^2) = 10,000 square centimeters
	1 hectare (ha) = 10,000 square meters
	1 square kilometer (km^2) = 1,000,000 square meters

TABLE OF MEASURES
CUSTOMARY

Length	1 foot (ft) = 12 inches (in.)
	1 yard (yd) = $\begin{cases} 36 \text{ inches} \\ 3 \text{ feet} \end{cases}$
	1 mile (mi) = $\begin{cases} 5280 \text{ feet} \\ 1760 \text{ yards} \\ 320 \text{ rods} \end{cases}$
	1 rod = $\begin{cases} 16.5 \text{ feet} \\ 5.5 \text{ yards} \end{cases}$
Mass/Weight	1 pound (lb) = 16 ounces (oz)
	1 ton (T) = 2000 pounds
Capacity	1 cup (c) = 8 fluid ounces (fl oz)
	1 pint (pt) = 2 cups
	1 quart (qt) = 2 pints
	1 gallon (gal) = 4 quarts
	1 peck (pk) = 8 quarts
	1 bushel (bu) = 4 pecks
Volume	1 cubic foot (ft^3) = $\begin{cases} 1728 \text{ cubic inches (in.}^3\text{)} \\ 7.5 \text{ gallons} \\ 0.8 \text{ bushels} \end{cases}$
	1 cubic yard (yd^3) = 27 cubic feet
	1 gallon = 230.4 cubic inches
Area	1 square foot (ft^2) = 144 square inches (in.^{2})
	1 square yard (yd^2) = 9 square feet
	1 acre = 43,560 square feet
	1 square mile (mi^2) = 640 acres

CONVERTING MEASURES
LENGTH AND DISTANCE

TO CONVERT FROM:	MULTIPLY BY:
centimeters to feet	0.0328
to inches	0.393
to meters	0.01
to yards	0.0109
feet to centimeters	30.48
to inches	12
to kilometers	0.0003
to meters	0.3048
to miles	0.0002
to yards	0.3333
inches to centimeters	2.54
to feet	0.083
to meters	0.0254
to millimeters	25
to yards	0.028
kilometers to miles	0.6

TO CONVERT FROM:	MULTIPLY BY:
meters to centimeters	100
to feet	3.28
to inches	39.37
to kilometers	0.001
to miles	0.0006
to millimeters	1000
to yards	1.093
miles to centimeters	160934.4
to feet	5280
to inches	63360
to kilometers	1.609
to meters	1609
to yards	1760
millimeters to inches	0.04
yards to centimeters	91.44
to feet	3
to inches	36
to meters	0.914

CONVERTING MEASURES
AREA

TO CONVERT FROM:	MULTIPLY BY:
acres to hectares	0.4
to square feet	43560
to square meters	4046.8564
to square miles	0.0016
to square yards	4840
hectares to acres	2.5
square centimeters	
to square feet	0.0011
to square inches	0.155
to square meters	0.0001
to square yards	0.00012
square feet to acres	0.00002
to square centimeters	929.0304
to square inches	144
to square meters	0.093
to square yards	0.1111

TO CONVERT FROM:	MULTIPLY BY:
square inches	
to square centimeters	6.4516
to square feet	0.007
to square meters	0.0006
to square yards	0.0007
square kilometers	
to square miles	0.4
square meters to acres	0.0002
to square centimeters	10000
to square feet	10.764
to square inches	1550.003
to square yards	1.196
square miles to acres	640
to square feet	27878400
to square kilometers	2.6
to square meters	2589988.1103
to square yards	3097600
square yards to acres	0.0002
to square centimeters	8361.2736
to square feet	9
to square inches	1296
to square meters	0.8361
to square miles	0.0000003

CONVERTING MEASURES
VOLUME AND CAPACITY

TO CONVERT FROM:	MULTIPLY BY:	TO CONVERT FROM:	MULTIPLY BY:
cubic feet to cubic inches	1728	**gallons** to cubic feet	0.1337
to cubic meters	0.0283	to cubic inches	231
to cubic yards	0.0370	to cubic meters	0.0038
to liters	28.3168	to cubic yards	0.005
cubic inches to cubic feet	0.0006	to ounces (liquid)	128
to cubic meters	0.000016	to pints (liquid)	8
to cubic yards	0.000021	to quarts (liquid)	4
to liters	0.0164	to milliliters	3785.4118
to milliliters	16.3871	to liters	3.7854
cubic meters to cubic feet	35.3147	**ounces(liquid)** to gallons	0.0078
to cubic inches	61023.74	to pints (liquid)	0.0625
to cubic yards	1.308	to quarts (liquid)	0.0313
to gallons	264.1721	to milliliters	30
to liters	1000	**pints (liquid)** to gallons	0.125
cubic yards to cubic feet	27	to quarts (liquid)	0.5
to cubic inches	46656	to liters	0.4732
to cubic meters	0.7646	to milliliters	473.1765
to liters	764.5549		

CONVERTING MEASURES

VOLUME AND CAPACITY

TO CONVERT FROM:	MULTIPLY BY:
quarts (liquid) to cubic feet	0.0334
to cubic inches	57.75
to gallons	0.25
to ounces(liquid)	32
to pints (liquid)	2
to liters	0.9464
to milliliters	946.3523
liters to cubic feet	0.0353
to cubic inches	61.0237
to cubic meters	0.001
to cubic yards	0.0013
to gallons	0.2642
to ounces (liquid)	33.8140
to pints (liquid)	2.1133
to quarts (liquid)	1.0567
to milliliters	1000
milliliters to ounces (liquid)	0.034

WEIGHT AND MASS

TO CONVERT FROM:	MULTIPLY BY:
grams to ounces	0.035
kilograms to grams	1000
to long tons	0.0009
to metric tons	0.001
to pounds	2.2
to short tons	0.0011
long tons to kilograms	1016.0469
to metric tons	1.0160
to short tons	1.12
metric tons to kilograms	1000
to long tons	0.9842
to short tons	1.1023
ounces to grams	28
pounds to kilograms	0.45
short tons to metric tons	0.9078
to kilograms	907.1847
to long tons	.8929

TABLE OF ROOTS AND POWERS

N No.	N² Sq.	√N Sq. Root	N³ Cube	∛N Cu. Root	N No.	N² Sq.	√N Sq. Root	N³ Cube	∛N Cu. Root
1	1	1.000	1	1.000	51	2,601	7.141	132,651	3.708
2	4	1.414	8	1.260	52	2,704	7.211	140,608	3.733
3	9	1.732	27	1.442	53	2,809	7.280	148,877	3.756
4	16	2.000	64	1.587	54	2,916	7.348	157,564	3.780
5	25	2.236	125	1.710	55	3,025	7.416	166,375	3.803
6	36	2.449	216	1.817	56	3,136	7.483	175,616	3.826
7	49	2.646	343	1.913	57	3,249	7.550	185,193	3.849
8	64	2.828	512	2.000	58	3,364	7.616	195,112	3.871
9	81	3.000	729	2.080	59	3,481	7.681	205,379	3.893
10	100	3.162	1,000	2.154	60	3,600	7.746	216,000	3.915
11	121	3.317	1,331	2.224	61	3,721	7.810	226,981	3.936
12	144	3.464	1,728	2.289	62	3,844	7.874	238,328	3.958
13	169	3.606	2,197	2.351	63	3,969	7.937	250,047	3.979
14	196	3.742	2,744	2.410	64	4,096	8.000	262,144	4.000
15	225	3.873	3,375	2.466	65	4,225	8.062	274,625	4.021
16	256	4.000	4,096	2.520	66	4,356	8.124	287,496	4.041
17	289	4.123	4,913	2.571	67	4,489	8.185	300,763	4.062
18	324	4.243	5,832	2.621	68	4,624	8.246	314,432	4.082
19	361	4.359	6,859	2.668	69	4,761	8.307	328,509	4.102
20	400	4.472	8,000	2.714	70	4,900	8.357	343,000	4.121
21	441	4.583	9,261	2.759	71	5,041	8.426	357,911	4.141
22	484	4.690	10,648	2.802	72	5,184	8.485	373,248	4.160
23	529	4.796	12,167	2.844	73	5,329	8.544	389,017	4.179
24	576	4.899	13,824	2.884	74	5,476	8.602	405,224	4.198
25	625	5.000	15,625	2.924	75	5,625	8.660	421,875	4.217
26	676	5.099	17,576	2.962	76	5,776	8.718	438,976	4.236
27	729	5.196	19,683	3.000	77	5,929	8.775	456,533	4.254
28	784	5.292	21,952	3.037	78	6,084	8.832	474,552	4.273
29	841	5.385	24,389	3.072	79	6,241	8.888	493,039	4.291
30	900	5.477	27,000	3.107	80	6,400	8.944	512,000	4.309
31	961	5.568	29,791	3.141	81	6,561	9.000	531,441	4.327
32	1,024	5.657	32,768	3.175	82	6,724	9.055	551,368	4.344
33	1,089	5.745	35,937	3.208	83	6,889	9.110	571,787	4.362
34	1,156	5.831	39,304	3.240	84	7,056	9.165	592,704	4.380
35	1,225	5.916	42,875	3.271	85	7,225	9.220	614,125	4.397
36	1,296	6.000	46,656	3.302	86	7,396	9.274	636,056	4.414
37	1,369	6.083	50,653	3.332	87	7,569	9.327	658,503	4.431
38	1,444	6.164	54,872	3.362	88	7,744	9.381	681,472	4.448
39	1,521	6.245	59,319	3.391	89	7,921	9.434	704,969	4.465
40	1,600	6.325	64,000	3.420	90	8,100	9.487	729,000	4.481
41	1,681	6.403	68,921	3.448	91	8,281	9.539	753,571	4.498
42	1,764	6.481	74,088	3.476	92	8,464	9.592	778,688	4.514
43	1,849	6.557	79,507	3.503	93	8,649	9.644	804,357	4.531
44	1,936	6.633	85,184	3.530	94	8,836	9.695	830,584	4.547
45	2,025	6.708	91,125	3.557	95	9,025	9.747	857,375	4.563
46	2,116	6.782	97,336	3.583	96	9,216	9.798	884,736	4.579
47	2,209	6.856	103,823	3.609	97	9,409	9.849	912,673	4.595
48	2,304	6.928	110,592	3.634	98	9,604	9.899	941,192	4.610
49	2,401	7.000	117,649	3.659	99	9,801	9.950	970,299	4.626
50	2,500	7.071	125,000	3.684	100	10,000	10.000	1,000,000	4.642

TRIGONOMETRIC RATIOS

Angle Measure	Sin	Cos	Tan	Angle Measure	Sin	Cos	Tan
0°	0.0000	1.0000	0.0000	46°	.7193	.6947	1.0355
1°	.0175	.9998	.0175	47°	.7314	.6820	1.0724
2°	.0349	.9994	.0349	48°	.7431	.6691	1.1106
3°	.0523	.9986	.0524	49°	.7547	.6561	1.1504
4°	.0698	.9976	.0699	50°	.7660	.6428	1.1918
5°	.0872	.9962	.0875	51°	.7771	.6293	1.2349
6°	.1045	.9945	.1051	52°	.7880	.6157	1.2799
7°	.1219	.9925	.1228	53°	.7986	.6018	1.3270
8°	.1392	.9903	.1405	54°	.8090	.5878	1.3764
9°	.1564	.9877	.1584	55°	.8192	.5736	1.4281
10°	.1736	.9848	.1763	56°	.8290	.5592	1.4826
11°	.1908	.9816	.1944	57°	.8387	.5446	1.5399
12°	.2079	.9781	.2126	58°	.8480	.5299	1.6003
13°	.2250	.9744	.2309	59°	.8572	.5150	1.6643
14°	.2419	.9703	.2493	60°	.8660	.5000	1.7321
15°	.2588	.9659	.2679	61°	.8746	.4848	1.8040
16°	.2756	.9613	.2867	62°	.8829	.4695	1.8807
17°	.2924	.9563	.3057	63°	.8910	.4540	1.9626
18°	.3090	.9511	.3249	64°	.8988	.4384	2.0503
19°	.3256	.9455	.3443	65°	.9063	.4226	2.1445
20°	.3420	.9397	.3640	66°	.9135	.4067	2.2460
21°	.3584	.9336	.3839	67°	.9205	.3907	2.3559
22°	.3746	.9272	.4040	68°	.9272	.3746	2.4751
23°	.3907	.9205	.4245	69°	.9336	.3584	2.6051
24°	.4067	.9135	.4452	70°	.9397	.3420	2.7475
25°	.4226	.9063	.4663	71°	.9455	.3256	2.9042
26°	.4384	.8988	.4877	72°	.9511	.3090	3.0777
27°	.4540	.8910	.5095	73°	.9563	.2924	3.2709
28°	.4695	.8829	.5317	74°	.9613	.2756	3.4874
29°	.4848	.8746	.5543	75°	.9659	.2588	3.7321
30°	.5000	.8660	.5774	76°	.9703	.2419	4.0108
31°	.5150	.8572	.6009	77°	.9744	.2250	4.3315
32°	.5299	.8480	.6249	78°	.9781	.2079	4.7046
33°	.5446	.8387	.6494	79°	.9816	.1908	5.1446
34°	.5592	.8290	.6745	80°	.9848	.1736	5.6713
35°	.5736	.8192	.7002	81°	.9877	.1564	6.3138
36°	.5878	.8090	.7265	82°	.9903	.1392	7.1154
37°	.6018	.7986	.7536	83°	.9925	.1219	8.1443
38°	.6157	.7880	.7813	84°	.9945	.1045	9.5144
39°	.6293	.7771	.8098	85°	.9962	.0872	11.4301
40°	.6428	.7660	.8391	86°	.9976	.0698	14.3007
41°	.6561	.7547	.8693	87°	.9986	.0523	19.0811
42°	.6691	.7431	.9004	88°	.9994	.0349	28.6363
43°	.6820	.7314	.9325	89°	.9998	.0175	57.2900
44°	.6947	.7193	.9657	90°	1.0000	.0000	∞
45°	.7071	.7071	1.0000				

FORMULAS

Perimeter
of a rectangle	$P = 2(l + w)$
of a square	$P = 4s$
of a regular polygon	$P = ns$
	n = number of sides

Area
of a rectangle	$A = lw$
of a square	$A = s^2$
of a parallelogram	$A = bh$
of a triangle	$A = \frac{1}{2}bh$
of a trapezoid	$A = \frac{1}{2}h(b_1 + b_2)$
of a circle	$A = \pi r^2$

Interest
Simple interest $\qquad I = prt$

Compound interest $\qquad f = P(1 + i)^n$

f = amount of money at end of compounding period

P = original amount of money

i = interest rate as a decimal

n = number of compounding periods

Temperature
Fahrenheit	$F = \frac{9}{5}C + 32$
Celsius	$C = \frac{5}{9}(F - 32)$

Relative Error
$$\frac{\text{Greatest Possible Error}}{\text{Actual Measure}}$$

Arithmetic mean
$$\frac{\text{Sum of the numbers}}{\text{Number of numbers}}$$

Circumference
of a circle	$C = \pi d$, or $2\pi r$

Volume
of a rectangular prism	$V = lwh$
of any prism	$V = Bh$

where B is the area of the base

of a cylinder	$V = \pi r^2 h$
of a cone	$V = \frac{1}{3}\pi r^2 h$
of a pyramid	$V = \frac{1}{3}Bh$
of a sphere	$V = \frac{4}{3}\pi r^3$

Surface area
of a cylinder	$SA = 2\pi r^2 + \pi dh$
of a cone	$SA = \pi r(l + r)$
of a cube	$SA = 6e^2$
of a pyramid	$SA = B + \frac{1}{2}lp$

B is the area of the base.

p is the perimeter of the base

of a rectangular prism

$$SA = 2(lw + wh + lh)$$

of a sphere	$SA = 4\pi r^2$

Permutations
(n items taken n at a time)
$$_nP_n = n!$$
(n items taken r at a time)
$$_nP_r = \frac{n!}{(n - r)!}$$

Combinations
(n items taken r at a time)
$$_nC_r = \frac{_nP_r}{r!}$$

Distance
$d = rt$

Pythagorean Theorem
$a^2 + b^2 = c^2$

Euler's formula
$V + F - E = 2$ vertices(V),faces(F), edges(E)

Sum of the measures of angles	
of a triangle	**of a polygon with n sides**
$m \angle A + m \angle B + m \angle C = 180$	$\text{Sum} = (n - 2) \times 180$

Measure of an angle of a regular polygon with n sides
$m \angle A = \dfrac{(n - 2) \times 180}{n}$

COORDINATE GEOMETRY FORMULAS

Note: (x_1, y_1) are coordinates of point A;
(x_2, y_2) are coordinates of point B.

Distance formula

$$d = \sqrt{(x_2 - x_1)^2 + (y_2 - y_1)^2}$$

Slope of a line through points A and B

$$m = \frac{\Delta y}{\Delta x} \text{ or } \frac{y_2 - y_1}{x_2 - x_1}$$
m is the slope
Δ is "the change in"

Two-point form for a line through points A and B

$$y - y_1 = \frac{y_2 - y_1}{x_2 - x_1} (x - x_1)$$

Point-slope form for a line through points A and B

$$y - y_1 = m(x - x_1) \quad m \text{ is the slope}$$

Slope-intercept form for a line through points A and B

$$y = mx + b \quad b \text{ is the } y\text{-intercept}$$

Intercept form for a line through points A and B

$$\frac{x}{a} + \frac{y}{b} = 1 \quad a \text{ is the } x\text{-intercept} \quad b \text{ is the } y\text{-intercept}$$

Horizontal line	**Vertical line**
where c is a constant	where c is a constant
$y = c$	$x = c$

General linear equation

$Ax + By + C = 0.$ A and B not both 0.

FORMULAS

SYMBOLS

+ plus or add, as in $a + b$	°F degree Fahrenheit	▭ rectangle
− minus or subtract, as in $a - b$	... continues without end	▱ parallelogram
± plus or minus	$1.\overline{3}$ repeating decimal $1.333\ldots$	△ trapezoid
× times or multiply	a^b a to the power b	$\overarc{AB}$ arc AB
÷ divide	$\sqrt{\ }$ square root	‖ is parallel to
= is equal to	$\sqrt[n]{24}$ nth root	⊥ is perpendicular to
≠ is not equal to	: is to, as in proportions, $a{:}b$ as $c{:}d$, which means $\dfrac{a}{b} = \dfrac{c}{d}$	$(3, {}^-4)$ ordered pair 3, ⁻4
> is greater than		(x,y) coordinates of a point on a plane
< is less than	2:5 ratio of 2 to 5	(x,y,z) coordinates of a point in space
≥ is greater than or equal to	$^+4$ positive 4	∴ therefore
≤ is less than or equal to	$^-4$ negative 4	⊆ is a subset of
≈ is approximately equal to	P(E) probability of event E	⊇ contains as a subset
$\overset{?}{=}$ is it equal to? (asks question, does not state fact)	a_b subscript, for descriptive discrimination	∈ is an element of
	$\overset{\leftrightarrow}{AB}$ line AB	( ) parentheses, shows order of operations
≅ is congruent to	$\overline{AB}$ line segment AB	[ ] brackets, shows order of operations
~ is similar to	$\overset{\rightarrow}{AB}$ ray AB	{ } braces, shows order of operations; also shows members of a set, when empty shows empty set
$ dollar sign	∠ABC angle ABC	
¢ cent sign	m∠ABC measure of angle ABC	
% percent	△ABC triangle ABC	sin 45° sine of 45°
π pi (approximately 3.14)	∟ right angle	cos 45° cosine of 45°
! factorial	⊙ circle	tan 45° tangent of 45°
| | absolute value	△ triangle	
° degree	▢ square	
°C degree Celsius		